Corporations, Accounting, Securities Laws, and the Extinction of Capitalism

AF757886

Ever since Marx, the future of capitalism has been fiercely debated. Marx and his followers predicted capitalism will end by violent overthrow, while others prophesied its demise will be the result of collapsing under its own weight. Still others argue that capitalism will not only continue to exist but continue to expand globally. This book takes a distinctively different approach by presenting solid evidence that capitalism has already ended.

The author argues that corporate statutory law, securities laws, and generally accepted accounting principles have combined to cause the extinction of capitalists. Without capitalists as owners of capital, there can be no capitalism. The book examines the factors that converged to contribute to and hasten the extinction of capitalists, and thus of capitalism as an economic system, in an ironic case of the law of unintended consequences. The very things that were intended to promote, protect, and sustain capitalism are the things that caused its death. It exposes the fallacy that capitalism as an economic system not only continues to exist but is expanding globally. Capitalism is extinct and the social system constructed on capitalism as an economic system cannot be sustained.

This book will appeal to economists, accountants, historians, political scientists, lawyers and sociologists, as well as students of those disciplines.

Wm. Dennis Huber received a DBA in international business, accounting, finance, and economics from the University of Sarasota, Florida; a JD, an MBA in accounting and finance, an MA in economics, an Ed.M. in educational psychology, an MS in public policy, and a BA in sociology and psychology from the State University of New York at Buffalo. He also has an LL.M. in homeland and national security law from the Western Michigan University Thomas M. Cooley School of Law. He is a certified public accountant and admitted to the New York Bar. He has taught at universities in the U.S., Canada, Mexico, and the Middle East.

Routledge Frontiers of Political Economy

The Political Economy of Transnational Governance
China and Southeast Asia in the 21st Century
Hong Liu

Economics, Science and Capitalism
Richard Westra

Production, Value and Income Distribution
A Classical-Keynesian Approach
Enrico Bellino

The Failure of Markets
Energy, Housing and Health
Craig Allan Medlen

Marx's Capital, Capitalism and Limits to the State
Theoretical Considerations
Raju J Das

Behavioral Political Economy and Democratic Theory
Fortifying Democracy for the Digital Age
Petr Špecián

Economics, Social Science and Pluralism
A Real-World Approach
Victor A. Beker

Corporations, Accounting, Securities Laws, and the Extinction of Capitalism
Wm. Dennis Huber

Moral Discourse in the History of Economic Thought
Laurent Dobuzinskis

For more information about this series, please visit: www.routledge.com/Routledge-Frontiers-of-Political-Economy/book-series/SE0345

Corporations, Accounting, Securities Laws, and the Extinction of Capitalism

Wm. Dennis Huber

Routledge
Taylor & Francis Group
LONDON AND NEW YORK

First published 2022
by Routledge
4 Park Square, Milton Park, Abingdon, Oxon OX14 4RN

and by Routledge
605 Third Avenue, New York, NY 10158

Routledge is an imprint of the Taylor & Francis Group, an informa business

© 2022 Wm. Dennis Huber

The right of Wm. Dennis Huber to be identified as author of this work has been asserted in accordance with sections 77 and 78 of the Copyright, Designs and Patents Act 1988.

All rights reserved. No part of this book may be reprinted or reproduced or utilised in any form or by any electronic, mechanical, or other means, now known or hereafter invented, including photocopying and recording, or in any information storage or retrieval system, without permission in writing from the publishers.

Trademark notice: Product or corporate names may be trademarks or registered trademarks, and are used only for identification and explanation without intent to infringe.

British Library Cataloguing-in-Publication Data
A catalogue record for this book is available from the British Library

Library of Congress Cataloging-in-Publication Data
Names: Huber, Wm. Dennis (William Dennis), 1951- author.
Title: Corporations, accounting, securities laws, and the extinction of capitalism / Wm. Dennis Huber.
Description: Abingdon, Oxon ; New York, NY : Routledge, 2022. | Includes bibliographical references and index.
Identifiers: LCCN 2021061305 (print) | LCCN 2021061306 (ebook) | ISBN 9781032147611 (hbk) | ISBN 9781032147628 (pbk) | ISBN 9781003240969 (ebk)
Subjects: LCSH: Capitalism. | Securities. | Corporation law.
Classification: LCC HB501 .H782 2022 (print) | LCC HB501 (ebook) | DDC 330.12/2--dc23/eng/20220209
LC record available at https://lccn.loc.gov/2021061305
LC ebook record available at https://lccn.loc.gov/2021061306

ISBN: 978-1-032-14761-1 (hbk)
ISBN: 978-1-032-14762-8 (pbk)
ISBN: 978-1-003-24096-9 (ebk)

DOI: 10.4324/9781003240969

Typeset in Times
by KnowledgeWorks Global Ltd.

This book is dedicated to Vivian, Jennifer, and Justin.

Contents

Other Publications by This Author

PCAOB sanctions, sanction risk, sanction risk premiums, and public policy: Theoretical framework and a call for research. *Journal of Accounting, Ethics and Public Policy*, 14(3), 647–663. (2013). https://papers.ssrn.com/sol3/papers.cfm?abstract_id=2307559.

The history of the decline and fall of the American accounting profession. *International Journal of Economics and Accounting*, 4(4), 365–388. (2014). https://papers.ssrn.com/sol3/papers.cfm?abstract_id=2260594.

The structure of the public accounting industry—Why existing market models fail. *Journal of Theoretical Accounting Research*, 10(2), 43–67. (2015). https://papers.ssrn.com/sol3/papers.cfm?abstract_id=2326297.

The research-publication complex and the construct shift in accounting research. *International Journal of Critical Accounting*, 7(1), 1–48. (2016). https://papers.ssrn.com/sol3/papers.cfm?abstract_id=2360378.

On the hegemony of financial accounting research: A survey of accounting research seen from a global perspective. *Journal of Theoretical Accounting Research*, 11(1), 14–29. (2016). https://papers.ssrn.com/sol3/papers.cfm?abstract_id=2444245.

Public accounting and the myth of the public interest. *Journal of Accounting, Ethics and Public Policy*, 16(2), 251–272. (2014). https://papers.ssrn.com/sol3/papers.cfm?abstract_id=2640375.

Guardians of the galaxy: Public accounting and the public interest. *International Journal of Critical Accounting: Special Issue on the Research Endeavours of Tony Lowe*, 7(5/6), 466–476. (2017). https://papers.ssrn.com/sol3/papers.cfm?abstract_id=2596373.

The SEC's *ultra vires* recognition of the FASB as a standard-setting body. *Richmond Journal of Law & the Public Interest*, 19(2), 120–152. (2016). https://papers.ssrn.com/sol3/papers.cfm?abstract_id=2662634.

Deep impact: Impact factors and accounting research. *International Journal of Critical Accounting*, 8(1), 56–67. (2016). https://papers.ssrn.com/sol3/papers.cfm?abstract_id=2441340.

Accounting research productivity: More heat than light? *Journal of Theoretical Accounting Research*, 11(2), 28–62. (2016). https://papers.ssrn.com/sol3/papers.cfm?abstract_id=2444543.

The myth of protecting the public interest: The case of the missing mandate in federal securities laws. *Journal of Business & Securities Law*, 16(2), 401–423. (2016). https://papers.ssrn.com/sol3/papers.cfm?abstract_id=2605301.

Can a not-for-profit membership corporation be created as a "shell" corporation? *Liberty University Law Review*, 11(1), 1–32. (2017). https://papers.ssrn.com/sol3/papers.cfm?abstract_id=2361909.

On neo-colonialism and the colonization of accounting research. *International Journal of Critical Accounting*, 9(1), 18–41. (2017). https://papers.ssrn.com/sol3/papers.cfm?abstract_id=2548742.

Law, language, and corporatehood: Corporations and the U.S. Constitution. *International Journal for the Rule of Law, Courtroom Procedures, Judicial Linguistics & Legal English*, 1(2), 78–110. (2018). https://papers.ssrn.com/sol3/papers.cfm?abstract_id=2835563.

Irreconcilable differences? The FASB's Conceptual Framework and the public interest. *International Journal of Critical Accounting*, 9(5/6), 514–523. (2018). https://papers.ssrn.com/sol3/papers.cfm?abstract_id=2789907.

The Supreme Court's subversion of the constitutional process and the creation of persons *ex nihilo*. *International Journal for the Rule of Law, Courtroom Procedures, Judicial Linguistics & Legal English*, 2(1), 53–72. (2018). https://papers.ssrn.com/sol3/papers.cfm?abstract_id=2841825.

The FASB's sabotage of Congressional policy and federal securities laws. *Journal of Accounting, Ethics, and Public Policy*, 20(1), 31–75. (2019). https://papers.ssrn.com/sol3/papers.cfm?abstract_id=2841825.

The FASB's Conceptual Framework—A case of the Emperor's New Clothes. *Journal of Accounting, Ethics & Public Policy*, 21(1), 77–114. (2020). https://papers.ssrn.com/sol3/papers.cfm?abstract_id=3400769.

Social/Critical/Emancipatory accounting research: Its failure and prospects for redemption. In *Accounting, Accountability and Society*, Del Baldo, Baldarelli, Dillard, Ciambotti (Eds.), London: Springer. (2020).

Corporate law and the theory of the firm: Reconstructing corporations, shareholders, directors, owners, and investors (The Economics of Legal Relationships). New York: Routledge. (2020).

Economics, capitalism, and corporations: Contradictions of corporate law, economics, and the theory of the firm (The Economics of Legal Relationships). New York: Routledge. (2021).

Corporate governance and disclosure—purpose, scope, and limitations (with James A. DiGabriele). *International Journal of Disclosure and Governance*, 18(2), 153–160. (2021).

Acknowledgments

Thanks to Dr. Dina Rady and Dr. Stephen Errol Blythe.

Thanks to Kristina Abbots and the production staff at Routledge.

Thanks to Vivian for proofreading portions and making helpful suggestions.

Prologue

This is the third in a series examining the relationship of corporate law, property law, economics, accounting, finance, and capitalism. In the first book, *Corporate Law and the Theory of the Firm: Reconstructing Corporations, Shareholders, Directors, Owners, and Investors*, I exposed the contradictions between property law, agency law, corporate law, and the theory of the firm. In the second, *Economics, Capitalism, and Corporations: Contradictions of Corporate Law, Economics, and the Theory of the Firm*, I revealed the contradictions between corporate law and economics with an emphasis on capitalism. In this book, I explore the concept of capital and its ownership, and the relationships between capital, capitalists, and capitalism, and determine that capitalists and capitalism are extinct.

Capitalism is more than an economic system. It is also a social system. An entire social system has been constructed on the concept of capital and its ownership, and the relationships between capital, capitalist, and capitalism. Of course, non-capitalist economic and social systems have also been constructed on the concept of capital and its ownership, but in such systems there are no relationships between capital, capitalist, and capitalism.

Social systems are a function of legal and economic systems. Capitalism is dependent on a legal system that supports and enforces private property laws. But capitalism is itself not a legal system. And, while the system that is erroneously called capitalism is related to political systems, in particular democracy,[1] capitalism is not itself a political system.

There were many factors that contributed to the advent of capitalism and that sustained the development and expansion of capitalism over centuries, which are reviewed in Chapter 3. There are several conditions necessary in order for capitalism to exist. One of the foundations of capitalism is that of private property. Capitalism as a social and economic system is built on a legal system that recognizes and enforces private property laws. In capitalism, privately owned firms—sole proprietorships, partnerships, privately owned corporations, and corporations whose shares are not traded in the public—own capital, the means of production, rather than the government. Yet, private property law and corporate law are completely ignored by those who argue capitalism still exists. Refusing to interpret capital, capitalist, and capitalism within the parameters of corporate law and property law corrupts the meaning of capital, capitalist, and capitalism.

Cambridge University Press publishes a series *Studies in Modern Capitalism*, "devoted to an attempt to comprehend capitalism as a world-system."[2] In 2004 Oxford University Press published Bruno Amable's *The Diversity of Modern Capitalism* that argues capitalism exists today across the globe but in different forms. Immanuel Wallerstein is a staunch advocate of capitalism as a world economy with such works as *The Capitalist World-Economy*[3] and *A Theory of Global Capitalism*.[4] None of these have presented, nor have any others presented, any proof, argument, or evidence that capitalism still exists.

Then, there are those who attempt to separate capitalism from capitalists with titles such as Hartmut Elsenhans' 2015 *Saving Capitalism from the Capitalists: World Capitalism and Global History*,[5] a refusal to accept that it is capitalists that make capitalism. Others, such as Jonathan Haskel and Stian Westlake's 2018 *Capitalism Without Capital: The Rise of the Intangible Economy*, would separate capitalism from capital, a failure to recognize that capitalism only exists because of capital. Taken together, capitalism would exist with neither capital nor capitalists. (Curiously, none have attempted to separate labor from capitalism.)

Every time there is a financial crisis—1929, 1987, 2008 to name a few—those who condemn capitalism and call for an end to capitalism blame capitalism for the crisis. Those who promote the virtues of capitalism argue that while it may be a crisis, it is not a crisis that requires an end of the system of capitalism. The crisis is merely a blip, a glitch; it is self-correcting or merely needs to be reformed in some way such as by enacting stronger securities or stricter banking laws. But both those who condemn capitalism and those who endeavor to reform it are blinded to the fact that capitalism has been extinct for decades. Both are guilty of trying to regress and impose onto the present an economic system that no longer exists and cannot exist, having been rendered extinct by corporate law, accounting, and securities laws.

Ever since Marx's *Capital, A Critique of Political Economy*,[6] critics of capitalism have called for its end. Others, such as Samir Amin (2013), have predicted its imminent demise. But both those who call for its end and those who predict its demise, as well as those who claim it is a global system, make the same fatal error. They assume that capitalism exists. That capitalism exists is taken for granted. Literally all accept the existence of capitalism as a valid premise. Everyone knows it exists. That capitalism exists is an axiom that needs no proof and therefore that capitalism exists has never been proven.

An example of the extent of the assumptions concerning the present existence and extent of capitalism can be found in Columbia University's *Center on Capitalism & Society*. The purpose of Columbia's *Center on Capitalism and Society* is to "advance our scholarly understanding of capitalism's workings, its social benefits and costs, and its place in a democracy."[7] The

Center professes "Capitalism is a system of largely private ownership that is open to new ideas, new firms and new owners—in short, to new capital." Conspicuously absent is an explanation of private ownership of what (Capital? What kind of capital?), what kind of new firms (New corporations?), new owners of what (New partnerships?), what kind of new capital (New machines?). The *Center* is equating private ownership, new firms, and new owners, all of which are undefined, to new capital, which is also undefined.

More revealing is their series of questions: "What economic and social institutions engender innovation in the more capitalist of today's advanced economies ...? How large are the benefits of this system...? How much worse (if at all) is this system with respect to stability and inclusion ...?"[8] Equally revealing is the statement that "It is no longer disputed, however, that capitalist systems, where they have been well-functioning in some key respects, have set records for dynamism."[9] What is revealed in these questions is again an assumption that capitalism exists.

Branko Milanovic's apologetic for capitalism, *Capitalism, Alone: The Future of the System That Rules the World,* posits that the capitalist mode of production is the uncontested dominion in the global economy. Furthermore, the global economic base and political and judicial institutions are aligned which helps global capitalism not only maintain its uncontested dominion in the global economy, but also makes people from all classes understand the same language of profit-making. Milanovic further defends capitalism because "Capitalism has been remarkably successful in imparting its objectives to people, prompting or persuading them to adopt its goals and thus achieving an extraordinary concordance between what capitalism requires for its expansion and people's ideas, desires, and values" (p. 4). Of course, capitalism can have no objectives.

But capitalists are extinct, as I prove in this book. Capitalism as an economic system is extinct, which I also prove in this book. Both capitalists and capitalism have been extinct for nearly a century, their extinction caused by politicians, lawyers, and economists through corporate law, accounting, and securities laws which, when combined with the trading of securities on exchanges, removed any ownership interest by shareowners in productive capital. Unfortunately, capitalism has never been given a decent burial. In fact, no burial at all. Not even a funeral. Its decayed carcass continues to be displayed in public as if it were still viable much like the movie *Weekend at Bernies*, propped up by rhetoric that has long since lost any real meaning or relevance, but which nevertheless continues to shape economic, political, and social relations.

The purposes of this book are to reveal the assumptions that are not legally, historically, economically, or sociologically valid. This book examines the factors that converged to contribute to the extinction of capitalists, and thus of capitalism as an economic system. In an ironic case of the law of unintended consequences the very things that were intended to promote, protect, and sustain capitalists and capitalism—corporate law, generally accepted accounting principles, and securities laws—are the very things that caused their extinction. Although unintended, it is as much an execution as if it were intended.

Excluded from consideration here are merchandising concerns, service organizations, and financial intermediaries. While all are necessary to support capitalism in an historic sense, none are producers of commodities, an essential component of capitalism. None appropriate labor's surplus value or accumulate capital.

In order to understand how corporate law, accounting, and securities laws contributed to the extinction of capitalism, it is necessary to investigate separately the role of capital and capitalists in the development of capitalism, corporate and securities laws, and accounting (both double-entry bookkeeping and principles of financial reporting). There is of necessity overlap between and among the various topics as they are presented in different contexts and from different perspectives. They will then be brought together to show how the law of unintended consequences resulted in the extinction of capitalists and capitalism.

Before the critics say I neglected to include this work or omitted that author, I plead guilty. There are literally multiple dozens of books and research papers in law reviews, economic journals, sociology journals, and accounting journals that could have been included here but are not. There are, obviously, space limitations to contend with, but more important, it is not necessary to include all of them, or even more of them. The arguments I make herein are sufficiently supported by a representative sample. Citing additional authors, books, or articles would not make the arguments presented herein more accurate or more persuasive. To those whose works I have omitted, living or deceased, I offer my apologies.

Notes on Limitations and Usage of Terms

The "firm" and the "corporation" are sometimes considered identical in the literature, but most times they are considered different. Robé (2011), for example, explains that "the corporation is a legal entity entitled to … own assets … The firm is the economic activity developed as a consequence of the cluster of contracts connecting the corporation owning these assets to various holders of resources" (p. 1). Similarly, Ellerman (1975) differentiates a corporation from a firm. The corporation, as correctly noted by Ellerman, is that which is created, exists, and operates according to corporate statutory law. The firm, on the other hand, makes the decisions about allocating resources of production and owns the net production proceeds. The firm may or may not be the same as the corporation depending on whether the capital is hired out or labor is hired in.

Such a distinction serves no purpose. To distinguish the corporation from the firm implies that each may have separate goals or may make separate decisions. If the firm and the corporation are not the same, it implies those who make decisions for the corporation are not the ones who make decisions for the firm. If those who make decisions for the corporation are the same as the ones who make decisions for the firm, then a distinction is pointless.

In this book, I use firm and corporation interchangeably. Furthermore, only corporations whose shares are traded in the public are considered here. The corporation as an alter-ego of an individual, or small group of individuals, is created mainly as a means to reduce risk for the owner who, unlike shareowners of corporations whose shares are traded in the public, actually does own the corporation.

> It has long been possible for an individual to incorporate his business even though it still represents his own investment, his own activities and his own business transactions; he has in fact merely created a legal alter ego by setting up a corporation as the nominal vehicle ...[10]
>
> (Berle & Means, 1992, p. 5)

Regarding corporations, I use the more lengthy, but more accurate, term "corporation whose shares are traded in the market" or "in the public" rather than "publicly traded corporation" because it is not the corporation that is publicly traded, but the shares of the corporation that are publicly traded in the market (e.g., the New York Stock Exchange) and the reader should bear this in mind when seeing that term. Furthermore, I use the term "shareowner" rather than "shareholder" because "shareholder" has a connotation that the shareholder holds a share of the corporation. They do not. Shareowners own shares of stock; they do not own any part of the corporation.

Notes on Style

As with the first two volumes, *Corporate Law and the Theory of the Firm: Reconstructing Corporations, Shareholders, Directors, Owners, and Investors*, and *Economics, Capitalism, and Corporations: Contradictions of Corporate Law, Economics, and the Theory of the Firm*, I endeavor to maintain a "Goldilocks" approach. That is, while there is a small core of lawyers, judges, and legal scholars who have training in economics, and likewise a small cadre of economists and economics researchers who have training in law, there are many lawyers, judges, and legal scholars who have insufficient training in economics, and many economists and economics researchers who have no training in law. My goal is to present a work that is sufficiently technical and accurate from a legal perspective to be meaningful to law students, lawyers, and judges but not so technical as to be irrelevant to economists and economics researchers. At the same time, although there are no charts, graphs, statistics, or econometrics (or even any equations other than assets = liabilities + equity, a production function, or the financial asset pricing model) which are the mainstay of economists, my aim is to make this work sufficiently technical and accurate from an economics perspective to be meaningful to economists and economics researchers, but not so technical as to make it irrelevant to law students, lawyers, and judges. A challenge at the very least, and I apologize in advance if I fall short in achieving that goal.

There is obviously overlap between and among the fields and disciplines of corporate law, economics, accounting, history, and sociology. There is, therefore, a cross-referencing within and between the chapters in this book. What may appear as repetition, however, is not actually repetition. It is an examination of theories and principles from different perspectives and in different contexts which is necessary since I am examining each factor not only in isolation, but in relation to all the others, much like a polygon.

Finally, portions of this book are adopted and summarized from *Corporate Law and the Theory of the Firm: Reconstructing Corporations, Shareholders, Directors, Owners, and Investors*, and *Economics, Capitalism, and Corporations: Contradictions of Corporate Law, Economics, and the Theory of the Firm*, both part of the Routledge Economics of Legal Relationships series, with permission.

Notes

1 See, for example, Milton Friedman's *Capitalism and Freedom* and Michael Novak's *The Spirit of Democratic Capitalism*.
2 *Studies in Modern Capitalism*, Cambridge University Press. https://www.cambridge.org/core/series/studies-in-modern-capitalism/E0B66EFA72466D596A237F11DCBCC551.
3 Wallerstein, I. (1979). *The capitalist world-economy*. Cambridge University Press.
4 Wallerstein, I. (2004). *A theory of global capitalism*. The Johns Hopkins University Press.
5 Elsenhans, H. (2015). *Saving capitalism from the capitalists: World capitalism and global history*. SAGE Publications.
6 Marx, K. (1990). *Capital, A critique of political economy* (3 volumes). Penguin Classics.
7 The Center on Capitalism and Society. https://capitalism.columbia.edu/theory-capitalism.
8 The Center on Capitalism and Society. https://capitalism.columbia.edu/theory-capitalism.
9 The Center on Capitalism and Society. https://capitalism.columbia.edu/theory-capitalism.
10 Berle and Means' *The Modern Corporation and Private Property* was first published in 1932 when sexist language was the norm.

Bibliography

Amable, B. (2004). *The diversity of modern capitalism*. Oxford University Press.
Amin, S. (2013). *The implosion of contemporary capitalism*. Monthly Review Press.
Berle, A. A., & Means, G. C. (1992). *The modern corporation and private property* (2nd ed.). Routledge.

Ellerman, D. (1975). The 'ownership of the firm' is a myth. *Administration & Society*, *7*(1), 27–42. Retrieved from https://ellerman.org/wp-content/uploads/2020/11/Ownership-Firm-Myth.pdf

Elsenhans, H. (2015). *Saving capitalism from the capitalists: World capitalism and global history*. SAGE Publications.

Friedman, M. (1962). *Capitalism and freedom*. University of Chicago Press.

Haskel, J., & Westlake, S. (2018). *Capitalism without capital: The rise of the intangible economy*. Princeton University Press.

Marx, K. (1990). *Capital, A critique of political economy* (Vol. 3). Penguin Classics.

Milanovic, B. (2019). *Capitalism, alone: The future of the system that rules the world.* Belknap Press.

Novak, M. (1990). *The spirit of democratic capitalism*. Madison Books.

Robé, J.-P. (2011). The legal structure of the firm. *Accounting, Economics, and Law—A Convivium*, *1*(1), 1–85. https://doi.org/10.2202/2152-2820.1001

Wallerstein, I. (1979). *The capitalist world-economy*. Cambridge University Press.

Wallerstein, I. (2004). *A theory of global capitalism*. The Johns Hopkins University Press.

Part I

Capital, Capitalists, and Capitalism

Chapters 1, 2, and 3 examine the various concepts, theories, and definitions of capital, capitalists, and capitalism in order to establish the foundation for understanding why capitalists and capitalism were rendered extinct by corporate law, accounting, and securities laws. Relevant aspects of corporations and corporate law are dealt with in Chapters 4 and 5, accounting in Chapter 6, and securities laws in Chapter 7. This part encompasses an examination of capital, capitalists, and capitalism separately and collectively in order to properly place them in the contexts of corporate law, accounting, and securities laws.

That capitalism exists is an assumption that has never been questioned. But capitalism has never been proven to exist in the present. No one has ever attempted to demonstrate by legal, sociological, or economic argument that capitalism exists. While the development, origin, evolution, and expansion of capitalism has been studied multiple dozens, if not hundreds, of times historically, sociologically, and economically, an examination of the relationships between and among capital, capitalists, and capitalism has been ignored. Incredulously, whether the necessary conditions for the existence of capitalists and capitalism continue to exist has never been challenged, or even questioned. Curiously, no one has examined capital, capitalists, and capitalism separately and collectively in the context of property law and corporate law.

Capital and capitalist have only one meaning applicable to capitalism. As a result of capital and capitalist having only one meaning, capitalism itself has only one meaning, contrary to those who assert otherwise. Capitalism is not about the efficient allocation of scarce resources of production, innovations, or free-markets. Capitalism is about the ownership of the means of production.

Note that there is a natural overlap between and among capital, capitalists, and capitalists. They are intertwined, inseparable, but distinct. Thus, the reader may detect some repetition between and within the three chapters of this section. However, the repetition is necessary in order to situate capital, capitalists, and capitalists in different contexts and from perspective, and to understand how they are inextricably related.

DOI: 10.4324/9781003240969-1

Contrary to Berle (1954) who said, "The capital is there; and so is capitalism. The waning factor is the capitalist. He has somehow vanished …" (p. 39), since there is capital, but no capitalist, there is no capitalism either. And while capitalists did vanish, they vanished long before 1954.

But both those who condemn capitalism and those who endeavor to reform it are blinded to the fact that capitalism has been extinct for decades. Both are guilty of trying to regress and impose onto the present an economic system that does not and cannot exist. While something that is broken can be fixed, something that does not exist is not broken and therefore cannot be fixed.

1 Capital

Introduction

I begin with an examination of "capital" since understanding the concept of "capital" is necessary in order to understand the meaning of "capitalist" and "capitalism," and thus to understand why both capitalists and capitalism are extinct.

"Capital" is the root and the source of both the terms and the meanings of "capitalist" and "capitalism." "Capital" is a concept, or notion (Chiapello, 2007). "Capital" is also "a unique web of social and legal relationships" (Žmolek, 2013). It is thus important to understand "capital" and the relation of "capital" to "capitalist" and "capitalism."[1] While it may appear obvious, it is not as obvious as it may appear because "capital" has multiple meanings.

Levy (2014) cites Justice Edwards' opinion in *United Steel Workers of America v. United States Steel Corporation*: "with a different definition of profit," the "outcome of an accounting analysis could be made to be non-profitability" (p. 175).[2] The same reasoning applies to capital. With a definition of capital other than the resource of production created by humans to be used in production, a different outcome would result. For example, referring to slaves as a "type of capital" is a prime example of a different definition of capital resulting in a different definition of capitalism. But if you transform labor (slaves) into a form of capital, then you can just as easily transform capital (slaves) back into labor. You can also just as easily define capital (machines) as a form of labor.[3]

In 1906, Fisher wrote "Capital has been so variously defined, that it may be doubtful whether it have any generally received meaning. In consequence, almost every year there appears some new attempt to settle the disputed conception, but, unfortunately, no authoritative result has as yet followed these attempts." Von Mises (2009) adds, "The views of scholars on the definition of capital are more divergent than their views on any other point in economics." Žmolek (2013) comments that "capital" is a term that is used "fast and loose."

DOI: 10.4324/9781003240969-2

Milios (2018) states that the word "capital" appeared during the reign of Emperor Leo III in the late eighth century and in Muslim writings in the early ninth century. Sée (1928), on the other hand, indicates that "use of the word *capital* originated fairly late and the word was first employed to designate a sum designed to be invested to bring in an interest" (p. 2, emphasis in original). However, a sum designed to be invested to earn interest has no relationship to means of production or the production of commodities. A sum invested to earn interest is fictitious capital as explained below. Regardless, the meaning of "capital" has been contorted by confusing either the value of capital with capital itself thereby erroneously equating the value of capital as the means of production with capital itself, or by confusing capital as a means of production with both financial and fictitious capital.

In this chapter, I briefly review various definitions and concepts of "capital," meaning the different ways in which the term "capital" is used, misused, confused, and abused. It is perhaps strange to think of a word being misused or abused, but that is exactly what frequently occurs in economics, sociology, history, legal, and accounting research. Researchers in accounting, sociology, history, and economics, including Nobel Prize winners in economics, talk past each other, frequently using the term "capital" carelessly to mean one thing, when they actually mean something else, and Marx is no exception. This in turn leads to confusion in what is meant not only by "capital," but consequently by "capitalist" and "capitalism."

In this chapter, indeed in the entire book, unless otherwise stated "capital" without a preceding adjective or following noun refers to capital as the resource of production, i.e., productive capital or industrial capital (e.g., tools, machines, equipment, computer programs), which, along with land and labor, is one of the three scarce resources of production.

I first present an overview of the concept of capital as characterized by Karl Marx, Max Weber, and Irving Fisher. While it must be noted that there are many others who set forth concepts of capital, Marx, Weber, and Fisher are among the three most important.

Next, I discuss various types and definitions of capital as found in the literature including financial capital, productive capital, mercantile capital, and commercial capital. Third, I review the relationship between capital and labor, and fourth, the relationship between capital, accounting, and profit. Fifth, I summarize the relationship between capital and the capital account.

Capital—Concepts

I begin with a discussion of the concept of capital in order to establish a basic understanding of the relationship of capital to other resources of production, to capitalists, and to capitalism.

Capital is a universal concept present in all societies where there is trade (Žmolek, 2013). However, trade is not required in order for capital to exist.

While capital existed for thousands of years, the concept of capital did not. The concept of capital only became possible with the invention of double-entry bookkeeping and the capital account.

While Sée (1928) indicates that capital was first used to designate "a sum designed to be invested to bring in an interest" (p. 2). Yet, a sum designed to be invested to bring in an interest has no actual relationship to capitalism. Marx, in fact, referred to a sum designed to be invested to bring in an interest as "fictitious capital."

Without question, capital is a resource of production, along with land and labor. Each resource of production is governed by the laws applicable to that resource according to particular legal regimes. Labor, regardless of how classified, is governed by labor laws, although different laws apply to different types of labor. Similarly, different laws apply to different types of capital and different laws apply to different types of land. Labor laws do not apply to capital or land, just as laws of capital and land do not apply to labor. The laws that apply to land, labor, and capital are beyond the scope of this book except some laws that apply to capital are discussed in later chapters.

There are those who insert other types of resources into resources of production, in particular entrepreneurship (or managerial skills), and even money. But entrepreneurship (or managerial skills) is human and therefore labor, regardless of whether they coordinate production, supervise other labor, engage in actual production, or any other activity concerning production. Nor does it matter whether there are divisions of labor within labor (e.g., Durkheim, 1997), or whether labor is free and paid or forced and not paid (slaves).

To see that labor is an all-inclusive, singular concept encompassing human effort in the production of commodities, one need only consider the production function $Q = f(L, K)$ where Q is the Quantity of output, and inputs are the quantities (costs) of L (labor) and the quantities (costs) of K (capital).[4] Money is not a resource of production. The production function shows, usually graphically, how one resource of production, K, can be substituted for another resource of production, L (or vice versa), holding land constant. Production functions do not incorporate quantities (costs) of entrepreneurship (or managerial skills), nor the cost of money (interest).

Granted there are both theoretical and empirical problems with the production function, some of which are obvious and others not so obvious, but beyond the scope of this book. Nevertheless, it is useful to show the relationship between output produced and resources used to produce the output. The point is that both outputs and cost of inputs must be quantifiable. Not only is entrepreneurship (or managerial skills) not quantifiable, it cannot be substituted for either labor or capital. (Money, of course, cannot be substituted for either labor or capital.)

Capital is physical (although today it can also be intangible). It is therefore property, and property is governed by property laws. Capital is owned by someone, or something, according to the laws of property of a particular legal regime whether it is owned by a *bourgeois* capitalist, the state, or a corporation. Thus, ownership of capital is the social and legal relationship between the capital and its owner. Ownership of capital does not make capital, capital. Capital is capital regardless of who owns it. The legal ownership of capital, however, determines whether capitalism exists, assuming all other requirements are met (see Chapter 3).[5]

Capital as a resource of production is anything made, created, manufactured, or produced by humans to be used in producing commodities such as food (planting and harvesting, for example) and clothing and is therefore thousands of years old. A wrench used to repair an automobile, a table saw used to make a cabinet, or a computer to surf the Internet in the hands of a household are not capital because they are not used to produce commodities for the market. Those same items in the hands of a business firm are capital since they are used by labor to produce commodities for the market. The former are examples of consumer goods (C), the latter are long-term assets (property, plant, and equipment) on a balance sheet (I), the C + I in the GDP equation.

Land and labor cannot be produced by humans; only capital can be produced by humans. Granted labor can reproduce biologically, and unproductive land can be transformed by humans into productive land, they are not produced by humans.

While capital is without question a resource of production, when the term "capital" is transported out of the context of production its meaning becomes distorted, vague, and questionable, as discussed below.

Marx's three volume *Capital, A Critique of Political Economy*, consisting of more than 1,800 pages, obviously has much to say about capital, capitalists, and the capitalist mode of production, otherwise known as capitalism.

Marx describes several types of capital—financial, productive, and fictitious. Each are examined below. Unfortunately, Marx is not always consistent in his use of the term "capital," which renders his critique of political economy problematic. The capital that Marx envisions in his polemic against the capital mode of production is the capital consisting of machines and factories.

A cornerstone of Marx's *Critique of Political Economy* is found in his concept of the accumulation of capital. But capital cannot be accumulated just for the sake of accumulating it. It must actually be used in production or it has no value.

Marx considered that a certain amount of accumulation of capital in the hands of individual producers of commodities forms the necessary preliminary of the capitalistic mode of production that occurs during a period of transition from the handicraft to capitalistic industry. He considered the role played by primitive accumulation as original sin plays in theology. Primitive accumulation is the historical process of separating the producer (labor) from the means of production (capital) (*Capital*, Vol. I).

Capital accumulation, on the other hand,

> becomes the means of new accumulation. With the increasing mass of wealth which functions as capital, accumulation increases the concentration of that wealth in the hands of individual capitalists, and thereby widens the basis of production on a large scale and of the specific methods of capitalist production.
>
> (p. 440)

The problems presented here are enormous. For one thing, wealth is not capital and thus capital is not wealth. Second, wealth does not and cannot function as capital. Commodities cannot be produced with wealth. Commodities are produced with capital. A capitalist, as the owner of capital, may accumulate wealth entirely separate from capital. Indeed, non-capitalists can accumulate wealth. Hicks (1975) recognized that, "The enterprise is where resources of production are transformed into commodities. The enterprise is a separate economic unit detached from the private account of the entrepreneur" (p. 79).

Fisher (1906) defines capital as "a fund, or a stock of wealth." Problems are again immediately apparent. First and foremost, a fund or stock of wealth is not a resource of production. Thus, capital in Fisher's context cannot refer to productive capital and therefore has no relationship to capitalism. Nor does a fund or stock of wealth apply to financial capital. Financial capital is money that is used to acquire and pay for resources of production.

The second problem with Fisher's definition is that capital is not wealth. Wealth pertains to individuals in their private lives while capital applies only to enterprises that produce commodities.

Types of Capital

Definitions of capital are related to types of capital, only one of which has any relationship to capitalism. However, types of capital must be examined in order to understand why none has any relationship to capitalism.

There are various "types" of capital found in the literature so the term "capital" without a preceding adjective or following noun causes confusion. For example, as a noun there is social capital, cultural capital, financial capital (money), and physical capital (a resource of production). There is constant capital, permanent capital, variable capital, working capital, venture capital, human capital, intellectual capital, imaginary capital, financial capital, productive capital, industrial capital, paid in capital, and fictitious capital. Marx referred to labor as "variable capital," and physical capital, productive capital, and industrial capital as "constant capital." Fisher used "permanent capital" to mean physical capital. Thus, physical capital, productive capital, constant capital, industrial capital, and permanent capital are merely synonyms for the same thing—the resource of production. But, it is not uncommon for Marx, and many others, to use "capital" sometimes referring to productive capital and sometimes to financial capital without clarifying which he is referring to.

As an adjective, there are capital assets and capital equipment (physical assets such as machines), as well as that which is erroneously referred to as capital assets (meaning shares of stock traded in the market as in the erroneously named "Capital Asset Pricing Model"),[6] capital markets (for trading shares of stock), capital stock (the shares of a corporation), capital structure (referring to the right side of the balance sheet, another misnomer[7]), and capital expenditures (cash used for acquiring physical assets). There is also mercantile capital and commercial capital.

There are two definitions or types of capital that are relevant for understanding capitalists and capitalism—financial capital and physical capital—but only one that is related to both capitalist and capitalism. In the following sections, I examine the distinction between financial capital and physical capital in order to relate them to *bourgeois* capitalists and capitalism discussed in the next two chapters.

Financial Capital

Importantly, omitted from being classified as a resource of production is money or financial capital (although Sée [1928] does erroneously classify money as a resource of production with land and labor). But what, exactly, is financial capital? Money in the hands of consumers is not capital. Money is financial capital only when it is intended to be used to acquire productive capital. Financial capital "is any money thrown into the sphere of circulation for the purpose of being recovered with a surplus" through the production of commodities (Chiapello, 2007, p. 279), whether by *bourgeois* capitalists or corporations.

Money is not a scarce resource of production.[8] Money is not used in production. Money cannot be traced to goods, either directly or indirectly. Money has no production value. While some resources can be substituted for others in a $Q = f(L, K)$ production function, e.g., capital for labor, an enterprise cannot substitute money for labor, money for capital, or money for land in order to increase production. It can only be used to acquire land or capital, or to pay labor.

Financial capital is the reason for the existence of capital markets, the place where financial capital (cash) is obtained by corporations when they issue shares in an initial public offering ("IPO"). (See Chapter 7 for an explanation of the term capital markets to refer to trading of securities.)

Berle (1954) explains that "When an individual invests capital in the large corporation, he grants to the corporate management all power to use that capital to create, produce and develop, and he abandons all control over the product" (p. 30). But individuals do not invest in corporations, they invest in the shares. Also, they do not invest capital; they invest money which is their savings. Money, savings, and shares are merely forms of individual wealth. The capital that corporations use to acquire productive capital is their financial capital obtained when they issue shares to the public.[9]

Since the nineteenth century, "financial capitalism increasingly came to characterize capitalism itself, rather than referring simply to the use of capital provided by the owners of a business or borrowed from their immediate circle of family, friends, and business associates" (Michie, 2014, p. 261). Williamson (1987) concurs, "One possibility would be for entrepreneurs to supply all their equity financing directly—from their own funds or from friends and family who know and trust them...This would place a severe limit, however, on the amount of equity funding available" (p. 305). As the business expands, the capitalist entrepreneur may also borrow money from a bank.

Marx links the *bourgeois* capitalist's financial capital (money) and physical capital. The link between financial capital and physical capital forms the cycle $M \rightarrow C \rightarrow M \rightarrow C \rightarrow$ *ad infinitum*, where C represents commodities and M represents money (the financial capital).[10] Within the cycle is the accumulation of surplus value (profit, which Marx considers the result of the exploitation of wage-labor) that is added to capital. (Whether he means financial capital or productive capital is not clear, but in the context it must mean financial capital.) Money is transformed into commodities, which are productive capital, which in turn are sold for money, etc. But the two—financial capital (money) and physical capital (commodities) are not, and cannot be, identical. Thus, when just the term "capital" is used, its meaning must be inferred from the context.

Marx explains that the capitalist mode of production involves

> the *conversion of a sum of money* [financial capital] *into means of production* [productive capital] and labour-power, is the first step taken by the quantum of value that is going to function as capital. This conversion takes place in the market, within the sphere of circulation. The second step, the process of production, is complete so soon as the means of production have been converted into commodities whose value exceeds that of their component parts, and, therefore, contains the capital originally advanced, plus a surplus-value. These commodities must then be thrown into circulation. They must be sold, their value realised in money, this money afresh converted into capital, and so over and over again. This circular movement, in which the same phases are continually gone through in succession, forms the circulation of capital.
>
> (*Capital*, Vol. I, p. 400, emphasis added)

Productive/Industrial Capital: The Resource of Production

Capital, with no preceding adjective or following noun, is one of the three resources of production—land, labor, and capital. Capital as a resource of production is anything created or manufactured by humans that is used in the production of other goods—tools, machines, computers, computer programs—as opposed to goods produced for consumer use (Krugman & Wells, 2008). Capital can be as simple as a stone tool used to plow, or as complex and sophisticated such as machine and equipment in an assembly line in an auto plant. Physical capital includes

> implements of work, which include tools, apparatus, and machines. In some cases only one or another of these means of production may be used, or none. "Tools" are those aids to labor, the design of which is adapted to the physiological and psychological conditions of manual labor. "Apparatus" is something which is "tended" by the worker. "Machines" are mechanized apparatus. These rather vague distinctions have a certain significance for characterizing epochs in the development of industrial technology.
>
> (Weber, 1978, p. 121)

Tools, apparatus, and machines are not land since land exists naturally. Obviously, they are not labor since they are designed to be used by labor, or possibly even replace, labor. Thus, tools, apparatus, and machines (and computer programs) are the capital resources of production made by humans (referred to herein simply as "capital" or occasionally "physical capital," or "productive capital").

Traditionally, capital is the physical resource of production used by labor, or to replace labor, to produce commodities. As a resource of production, however, capital has acquired non-physical aspects such as computer programs created by humans to use in the production of commodities. While capital as a resource of production is referred to herein as physical capital or productive capital for convenience, it also includes non-physical capital. The distinguishing characteristic of capital is that it is created by humans to be used by humans to produce commodities.

Capital as a resource of production obviously occupies a significant part of Marx's theories of the capitalist mode of production. Whom Marx considered to be the owners of capital as the means of production is of the utmost importance and is the subject of the next chapter.

Other Types of Capital

Other "types" of capital have often been referred to in the literature, but instead of adding to our understanding of capital and capitalism, they take away from it.

Mercantile (Merchant) Capital

One is forced to confront the question: is mercantile (merchant) capital "different" from capital owned by capitalist entrepreneurs and used by labor and if so, how?

In point of fact, it is different. According to Marx,

> only merchant and usurers' capital had existed up to [the Industrial Revolution]; industrial capital was yet to be developed. Production was still predominantly in the hands of workers owning their own means of production, whose work therefore yielded no surplus-value to any capital.
>
> (*Capital*, Vol. III, p. 642)

Marx differentiates merchant capital from industrial capital: "*merchant's capital* [is] (the first form of which is always money, since the merchant as such does not create any 'product' or 'commodity')..." (*Capital*, Vol. II, p. 257, emphasis in original). Although contested, Lis and Soly (1997) generally support Marx's view: "merchants in general and wholesalers in particular did their best to avoid production until the mid-eighteenth century" (p. 217).

Polanyi (2001) suggests that it was the merchants of the eighteenth century who fostered the factory system. The merchant evolved into the industrial capitalist through the introduction of elaborate machines and factories that required specialization and continued long-term investment which in turn intensified specialization. Industrial production requires a continuous supply of factors of production, which oddly, and with no explanation, Polanyi considers to be land, labor, and money. But money is not a resource of production. Money is not even financial capital unless it is intended to be used to acquire productive capital.

Any capital that merchants may have owned was insignificant because merchants did not replace labor with the little capital they did own, as did capitalists during and following the Industrial Revolution. Merchants hired labor and the labor they hired often owned their own capital. Thus, to call the capital that merchants owned "merchant capital" has no real meaning. It was only later that merchants evolved into capitalists and replaced labor with machines.

Commercial Capital

The term "commercial capital" is also encountered in the literature. One is thus also forced to confront the question: is commercial capital "different" from capital owned by capitalist entrepreneurs and used or produced by labor and if so, how?

In point of fact, commercial capital is also different. Commercial capital, like merchant capital, is not used or produced by labor to produce commodities. However, the term is used in the literature and, therefore, must be included here as a type of capital but need not be further considered.

Fictitious Capital

Fictitious capital is an asset on a balance sheet, but obviously not labeled as such. Fictitious capital was well known to Marx, although he did not originate the term. Marx described fictitious capital as periodic income that is capitalized and the creation of fictitious capital is called capitalization. In referring to banker's capital, for example, Marx calls it purely fictitious because it consists of claims on future revenue and not on production of commodities (*Capital*, Vol. III; Chiapello, 2007). Thus, fictitious capital is nothing more than an alternative label for the net present value of an expected stream of future cash inflows (Cooper, 2015).

But fictitious capital is neither financial capital because it is not money to be used to acquire productive capital nor productive capital since it is not used to produce commodities. Furthermore, fictitious capital is neither a liability nor equity. Thus, classifying fictitious capital as a type of capital has no legitimacy. But, as Tevye says, "it's tradition."[11]

Ellerman (1975) clothes fictitious capital in terms of hiring out capital vs. hiring in labor, which both confuses capital and negates the basis of capitalism, while at the same time exposing the subconscious acceptance that capitalism (the capitalist system) continues to exist as a viable economic system. As many others, Ellerman makes a distinction between the corporation as a legal entity (discussed in Chapter 5) and the firm as an economic entity. Ellerman attempts to directly relate the distinction between the corporation and the firm, to the ownership of capital, and consequently to *bourgeois* capitalists and capitalism. In Ellerman's framework, there is "a logical distinction and separation of the legal party undertaking production (herein called the 'firm') from the capital-owning party (herein called 'Capital' and assumed to be a corporation)" (p. 38).

The corporation owns the capital, but it is the "firm" that makes the decisions concerning the production process. The firm may decide to hire labor. But if the capital is hired out in its entirety, there is no production value from the capital since all proceeds are derived solely from the rent of the capital (Ellerman, 1991).

However, renting out capital in its entirety by the firm merely transforms the manufacturing firm into a financial firm where all net earnings are a function solely of the net present value of future cash inflows (the rent from hiring out capital), which, by definition, is fictitious capital.

Ellerman (1975) refers to shareowners as "Capital." "The myth of Capital's (e.g., the corporate shareholders') ownership of the firm is at the *foundation of capitalist ideology*" (p. 31, emphasis added).

In approaching the conventional joint stock company, what he calls a "capitalist corporation," Ellerman asks, "Does *physical or financial capital* (the capital on the asset side of the corporate balance sheet) play any special role vis-à-vis the corporate ownership rights?" (p. 13, emphasis added). This question is of interest for two reasons. (But first, it must be recognized that shareowners have no ownership rights in the corporation, as explained in Chapter 5.)

One, he recognizes the two types of capital on the balance sheet—financial and productive. Coupled with his acknowledgment that it is the corporation that owns the capital resource of production, then he is also acknowledging that it is the corporation that owns both the financial capital and the productive capital. Two, he correctly places both financial capital and productive capital on the left side of the balance sheet.

But, the right side of the balance sheet is referred to as the corporation's "capital structure" (Brigham & Ehrhardt, 2016; Huber, 2021). That leaves us with nothing other than the right side of the balance sheet equals the left side of the balance sheet; i.e., the tautological equation capital equals capital, which obviously explains nothing.

The Money-Commodity/Financial Capital-Physical Capital Cycle

Marx employed the concept of the money-commodity cycle, but financial capital-physical capital is more appropriate since there is an essential difference between capital commodities and consumer commodities. In addition, there is a difference between money and financial capital. Furthermore, by itself the money-commodity cycle, or financial capital-physical capital cycle, is quite inadequate since it applies only to individual (or partnership) capitalist entrepreneurs, not to corporations, and omits important stages.

The Capitalist Entrepreneur Cycle

Marx links financial capital to physical capital, but not directly. The link between financial capital and physical capital forms the cycle M → C → M → C → … *ad infinitum*, where C is commodities and M is money. Within the cycle is the accumulation of surplus value (profit which Marx considers as the exploitation of wage-labor) which is added to capital (the accumulation of capital).

But it is here that Marx skipped an important step in the financial capital/physical capital (commodities) cycle. Money is not transformed into commodities directly. Financial capital "is any money thrown into the sphere of circulation for the purpose of being recovered with a surplus" through the production of commodities (Chiapello, 2007, p. 279). Money is transformed into commodities, which are capital, by labor through the production process which in turn are sold for money. But Marx does not recognize what commodities consist of.

The financial capital/physical capital cycle, i.e., the cycle for the individual capitalist entrepreneur, is actually as follows (implicit in profit is depreciation and interest expenses for money borrowed from friends and family or a bank, and taxes):

Capitalist:		*Resources:*		*Commodities:*		
Money (M_1) (provided by capitalist and borrowed)	→ M_1 (financial capital used to pay or acquire)	• Land/raw materials • Capital • Labor	→ (transformed into)	C_C C_G	→ (sold for)	Money (M_2) → (including profit)

The source of the capitalist's financial capital (M_1) is provided from the savings of the capitalist and obtained by the capitalist by borrowing. If the financial capital is borrowed, some of the money (M_2)[12] received from selling the commodities (C)[13] must be used to pay interest to the creditors. M_2 is then used to acquire and pay for more capital commodities to transform into other commodities, both consumer commodities (C_C) and capital goods (C_G). The capital commodities acquired must be capital commodities produced by other enterprises.

The capitalist mode of production is characterized by the circular movement of financial capital and physical capital which Marx classifies into three stages: in Stage One, the capitalist purchases commodities (raw materials and capital goods to use in production) and hires and pays labor. His money is transformed into commodities: $M \rightarrow C$. In Stage Two, the commodities are consumed by the capitalist in the production process, where commodities are capital goods, not consumer goods. In Stage Three, the capitalist re-enters the market as a seller of his capital commodities which are sold thereby transforming commodities back into money, $C \rightarrow M$, thus completing the cycle which begins again.

But Marx is inexcusably careless. First, money is not transformed into commodities directly. To transform money into commodities requires the capitalist first to acquire certain commodities in the market—capital goods and raw materials—and to pay labor to transform those commodities into other commodities to sell in the market at a profit, which he does acknowledge elsewhere but omits it from his explanation of the cycle. Furthermore, to acquire capital commodities in order to transform them into other commodities, then transforming those commodities into other capital commodities, whether to sell or merely accumulate in the factory or warehouse, would terminate the cycle. Marx seriously de-emphasizes this step. The transformed commodities must be sold in the market to complete the cycle, which he does acknowledge, but there are different types of commodities which significantly impact the cycle which he does not acknowledge in his explanation of the cycle.

Second, as a result of the first, the cycle can only function on an economy-wide basis, thus requiring capitalists to interact with each other. The reason the cycle can only function on an economy-wide basis is that commodities consist of both consumer goods sold to consumers (the "C" of C + I + G) and capital goods sold to other enterprises to become their capital factor of production (the "I" of C + I + G). Enterprises do not, for the most part, manufacture their own capital resources of production. Commodities can only be transformed back into money if they are sold in the market. Here we see the impact of different commodities on the cycle.

If the capitalist produced only consumer commodities, eventually the capital resources used in production would wear out and become useless and there would be no way to replace it. If the capitalist produced only capital commodities, then consumers would have no goods available to purchase. Thus, some capitalists produce consumer commodities and others produce capital commodities. Marx neglects to consider this. Thus, C must be broken down into two categories: C_C for consumer commodities, and C_G for capital goods. The distinction is crucial because the sale of consumer goods only terminates the cycle, and the cycle never gets started with only the production of capital goods, thus making it impossible to accumulate capital in the long run.

Since the capitalist owns all the assets, it is her financial capital to be used to acquire productive capital, and it is her productive capital to be used in production.[14] She makes all the decisions on how to allocate the resources. The capitalist uses her financial capital, some of which may have been borrowed, to acquire (or rent) land, to acquire physical capital and raw materials, and to pay labor to transform the raw materials into commodities to be sold for money, thus beginning the cycle. It is the financial capital, not her equity or the debt, which is only a legal obligation, that is used to acquire commodities to produce other commodities to sell at a profit, both consumer and capital, thus accumulating financial capital.

The Corporate Cycle

Marx also failed to differentiate the capitalist cycle from the corporate cycle although he was sufficiently acquainted with corporations. (Note that some of this discussion here draws on information presented in more depth in Chapters 5 and 6.)

When corporations whose shares are traded in the public are inserted into the financial capital-productive capital cycle, the Capitalist Cycle disappears, replaced by the Corporate Cycle.

The capitalist entrepreneur cycle must be modified to account for the fact that no individual capitalist or entrepreneur is involved. Unlike an individual capitalist or capitalist partnership, a corporation has no financial capital to invest in itself. A corporation must go outside itself to obtain financial capital in order to acquire in the market certain capital commodities to transform into other commodities to sell in the market. A corporation obtains its financial capital through an IPO by issuing stock to the public.

(Of course, financial capital may also be obtained by issuing bonds to the public or borrowing from a bank, which is ignored here.)

The Corporate Cycle is:

Shareowners: (provide financial capital to corporation in IPO)	→ M_1	M_1 (corporate financial capital)	→ M_1 (used to acquire)	*Resources:* • Land/raw materials • Capital • Labor	→ (transformed into)	*Commodities:* C_C C_G	→ (sold for)	M_2 (including corporate profit)

The savings of shareowners are transferred to the corporation in an IPO as financial capital (M_1).[15] Shareowners purchase a set of rights (e.g., dividends, voting for directors). The shares are now the chosen means of savings and a part of the wealth of the shareowners. It is now the corporation that owns the financial capital, not the shareowner. The shareowners own the shares of stock, not the corporation's financial or productive capital. The vertical line represents the fact that shareowners have no ownership interest in the corporation.

Capital, Accounting, and Profit

Marx argued that *bourgeois* capitalists accumulated capital, which is profit. But that is not quite accurate. Conceptually, the accumulation of capital, one of the fundamental principles of Marx's critique of political economy and a cornerstone of capitalism, does not make sense. Capital is not "accumulated." That is, *bourgeois* capitalists do not accumulate machines. While they may "accumulate" profit as financial capital, they purchase machines using the financial capital obtained at start up plus the money received from selling commodities at a profit. Marx rightly equated money with profit in the M → C → M cycle (explained in Chapter 3) since profit at the time, and historically, was money, and money is financial capital to be used to acquire productive capital. To be sure, a *bourgeois* capitalist may accumulate financial capital, money, obtained from selling commodities at a profit.

Profit is the difference between the cost of the resources of production used to produce commodities, and the value for which the commodity is sold. When a *bourgeois* capitalist produces a commodity and sells it at a profit, the profit becomes part of her wealth, not directly, but indirectly because she owns the enterprise. As discussed in Chapter 3, double-entry bookkeeping and the capital account allowed the business owner to separate personal wealth from business assets. Profit thus is added to business assets.

Of course, one does not have to be a capitalist to earn a profit. For example, an individual who produces a commodity without labor, i.e., with only two resources of production, land and capital, using only his own effort, can sell his commodity at a profit.[16] That, however, is not capitalism and thus not relevant to the purposes of this book.

How does the capitalist know if she has earned a profit? Accounting. While profit was extremely important to Marx, he had little to say about accounting per se. For Marx, accounting was implicit because whether discussing exchange value or surplus value, accounting was necessary to calculate value.

Profit was pursued long before it could be calculated rationally. But without accounting to quantify objectively the difference between the costs of the resources of production used to produce commodities and the price of the commodities sold in the market, profit would be a matter of subjective judgment.

There are two aspects of accounting—the bookkeeping aspect, which relates only to the actual recording of transactions, and the reporting aspect, which pertains only to corporations whose shares are traded in the public (explained in Chapter 6).

The profit of a corporation whose shares are traded in the public does not become part of the wealth of a shareowner. The wealth of the shareowner is increased not by the profit of the corporation, but by the increase in the value of the shares owned which may be the result of the profit earned by the corporation, but is also the result of the increase in the price of the stock in the market that may or may not be directly related to the profit earned by the corporation.

Sombart regarded double-entry bookkeeping as having an important role in the rational pursuit of profit and had a transformative effect in the medieval attitude toward economic life (Yamey, 1949). Sombart proposed that double-entry bookkeeping allowed the goals of the enterprise to be placed in a specific form that made the concept of capital possible which in turn made it possible for entrepreneur to pursue profits rationally (Winjum, 335).

The value of capital obviously must be accounted for. Weber (1978) describes capital accounting as

> the valuation and verification of opportunities for profit ... by means of a valuation of the total assets (goods and money) of the enterprise at the beginning of a profitmaking venture, and the comparison of this with a similar valuation of the assets still present and newly acquired at the end of the process ...
>
> (p. 91)

and "the means of profit-making...are those goods and other economic advantages which are used in the interests of economic profit-making" (p. 91). It must be understood that there is an implicit assumption that the difference in the value between beginning balance and ending balance is the result of transactions. The difference could, for example, be the result of inflation, which is not profit by any definition.

Weber (1978) explains the necessity of separating the business from the individual owner of the business which is only possible with the invention of double-entry bookkeeping, in particular, the capital account (discussed below). The pursuit of profit is rational, but it is necessary to separate private affairs from the business because the interest in maintaining the private wealth of the owner [of the business] is often irrational.

Fisher (1912) defines income as a flow which is the difference between beginning and ending balances. But income is not profit. While income may be a flow from the beginning of a specified period of time to the end of that period of time, it is not the difference between the beginning and ending balances unless there were transactions.

Fisher, unlike Sombart and Weber, defines the "capital account" as "synonymous with the balance sheet," which is "a *person's* assets and liabilities" (emphasis added), while he defines the "capital balance" as the "difference between assets and liabilities" on a balance sheet which is nothing other than the net assets, or equity. These are, of course, contradictions. A capital account cannot be a balance sheet. A capital account is the equity account, even if equity is itself not capital, which records the monetary value of the net capital assets, both financial and productive. Defining the capital account as a person's assets and liabilities negates the purpose for which the capital account was created—to separate personal wealth from enterprise assets.

Fisher does not distinguish individual wealth from enterprise assets as do Sombart and Weber, an unfortunate omission since, while money is a part of wealth it is not financial capital if it is not intended to be used to acquire physical capital resources of production by an enterprise. More important, however, is that by not distinguishing individual wealth from enterprise capital he annihilates another key component of capitalism and thus capitalism itself. While both businesses, regardless of the form, and individuals have balance sheets, the balance sheet of individuals has nothing to do with capital which is only relevant to production.

Third, a balance sheet is not a capital account. The capital account is the equity, the monetary value of capital (i.e., the net assets, the value of the financial capital plus productive capital less liabilities), which is not itself capital, although it has been called that for centuries. It is merely a measurement of the net value of the capital; i.e., the balance on the credit side in double-entry accounting which gave rise to the concept of capital and the separation of the owner from the business (see Chapter 6).

Consider that it is virtually impossible for any business in the long run to produce something merely to sell it for something of the same value. Selling something produced for something of the same value would not provide the producer with the future resources to replenish the materials necessary for the production of future commodities. Profit is simply the difference between the value of something sold, and the value of something received in exchange, surplus value or exchange value in Marx's terms. Marx, Weber, Fisher—all recognize this. What is done with the profit—accumulated or distributed—is a distinction between capitalism and Marxism. However, it cannot be overemphasized that profit simply cannot be distributed unless the profit is money because profit is merely an equation, a definition.

The pursuit of profit is a bedrock of capitalism but has existed since production of commodities has existed—thousands of years. Yet, until the Protestant Reformation and the Enlightenment (the Age of Reason, rationalist philosophy), and Industrial Revolution, the pursuit of profit was often constrained by religious or spiritual prohibitions. The Protestant Reformation freed businesses from many of the constraints placed on profit seeking by the Catholic Church. There were still limitations placed on the pursuit of profit, just different limitations and less strict. The Enlightenment and Industrial Revolution removed any religious or spiritual principals guiding the pursuit of profit and the floodgates were opened for essentially what amounted to the pursuit of profit unlimited except by the market forces.

In practice, double-entry accounting may not have been taken advantage of in its entirety. Furthermore, in spite of what appeared as meticulous entries, there is evidence that accounts were infrequently balanced (Carruthers & Espeland, 1991). Critics of Weber and Sombart point to this as evidence that there was no connection between the development of capitalism and accounting (Carruthers & Espeland, 1991). However, that misses the point. One of the consequences of rationality is that symbols of rationality become tools of legitimation even if decoupled from practice. Double-entry bookkeeping is a symbol of rationality. Double-entry bookkeeping and the capital account legitimized business activities, even if the actual accounts did not conform exactly to the requirements of double-entry bookkeeping and the capital account[17] (Carruthers & Espeland, 1991).

The role of double-entry accounting is important for more than just calculating profit. "There is a causal efficacy of accounting that helped to transform the ways in which business was interpreted and understood" (Carruthers & Espeland, 1991, p. 55; Meyer, 1986, pp. 348, 35). In other words, "To provide an account is to provide a classificatory scheme. It is a cognitive device that sorts, orders, and names. Accounts frame an economic reality in a particular way" (Carruthers & Espeland, 1991, p. 54). Thus, it is the classification and not the numbers or the balances that is important. It is the concept, or the notion, not the actual numbers recorded.

Levy (2014) further contends that double-entry bookkeeping failed to realize its logic of separation of the profit and loss statement from the capital until the nineteenth century. But that is not quite accurate. First, in the Sombart/Weber thesis it was not the primary purpose of the capital account to separate profit from capital, but to separate the capital of the business (including profit) from the personal wealth of the owner(s), which allowed profit to be calculated separately from individual wealth. Second, even if the capital account was not widely used to separate profit from capital, it did make such a separation possible.

Levy further contends that, "double-entry bookkeeping ... emerged from the complex forms of partnership and debt that constituted merchant capital in late medieval Italian city-states—which created the need for new forms of accountability" (p. 178). Accountability naturally pertains to profit. But, while it is indisputable that Italian merchants used double-entry bookkeeping in order to distribute profits to the partners, Sangster et al. (2018) established that double-entry bookkeeping actually originated with Italian banks, which was then subsequently incorporated into merchant bookkeeping. (It should be noted that banks are not capitalists since they produce nothing although they facilitate merchants obtaining financial capital via loans.)

Capital and Labor

Labor exists without capital, but capital does not exist without labor. Indeed, capital exists without capitalists, but capitalists do not exist without capital. Labor is extremely important in the discourse of capitalism. Capitalism cannot be discussed in any meaningful way without considering the relationship of labor and capital.

It was not capital that played a central role in Marx's *Critique*, but labor and the owners of capital. It is labor that is exploited by the owners of capital, in Marx's view, not the owners of land. It is only labor that creates value. Neither capital nor land create value.

Capital and labor cannot be separated. That is, labor creates the capital and it is labor that uses the capital. There has been labor since the dawn of civilization. It is labor that hunted animals with spears to produce meat, invented tools to kill animals, and invented metallurgy that improved hunting (as well as weapons). Capital can do nothing. Capital remains at rest until acted upon by an outside force—labor.[18]

Capital is the resource of production created or manufactured by humans to be used by humans to produce commodities. Yet, there are those who pervert the meaning of capital by egregiously defining labor as capital. Ransom and Sutch (1988), for example, substitute human capital (slaves) for capital thus transforming labor into capital.

> The slave system was able to flourish in the midst of a capitalist market economy because it was itself *a form of capitalism*. The southern plantation system, though, was an unusual species of capitalism in which the *capital assets were land and slaves rather than physical or financial capital.*
>
> (p. 134, emphasis added)

The error is, of course, readily apparent. Merely calling slaves "capital" does not in fact make them capital any more than calling land capital makes land capital. Slaves are labor where the wage rate is zero.

Their error reveals how extensive is the confusion and perversion of "capital" that in turn leads to confusion and perversion of "capitalism."

Chapter Summary

This chapter examined various definitions, concepts, and types of capital found in the literature that revealed how the different definitions, concepts, and types of capital has resulted in great confusion of what capital is and what it means. We understand from this chapter that the meaning of capital has been so twisted that anything can be defined as capital.

Recall Fisher's (1906) observation more than a century ago that,

> Capital has been so variously defined, that it may be doubtful whether it have any generally received meaning. In consequence, almost every year there appears some new attempt to settle the disputed conception, but, unfortunately, no authoritative result has as yet followed these attempts.

Von Mises (2009) adds, "The views of scholars on the definition of capital are more divergent than their views on any other point in economics." Žmolek (2013) comments that "capital" is a term that is used "fast and loose."

Capital is one of the three resources of production. Nothing more. Nothing less. The owners of financial capital cannot exploit labor because labor does not use financial capital to create more value or to create more capital.

Notes

1 "Capitalist" is dealt with in chapter 2. "Capitalism" is addressed in chapter 3.
2 631 F.2d 1264 (6th Cir. 1980).
3 With advances in robotics and artificial intelligence, the possibility is more than imaginary.
4 The inputs K and L are in terms of quantities, but quantities of inputs naturally have costs.
5 Land is also property and is owned by someone or something and governed by the laws of property of the particular legal regime. Land and laws governing its ownership are not considered in this book.
6 See *Economics, Capitalism, and Corporations: Contradictions of Corporate Law, Economics, and the Theory of the Firm.*
7 See *Economics, Capitalism, and Corporations: Contradictions of Corporate Law, Economics, and the Theory of the Firm.*
8 While money may be scarce, as the author of this article can personally attest to, it is not a "scarce resource" of production.
9 Purchasers of shares in an IPO do not actually invest in the corporation because they have no ownership rights in the corporation. They invest in the shares.
10 Commodities are both consumer goods and capital goods, but Marx emphasizes capital commodities since capitalists accumulate capital commodities.
11 Tevye is a character in *Fiddler on the Roof* who says, "You may ask, how did this tradition start? I'll tell you—I don't know. But it's a tradition."

12 M_1 and M_2 should not be confused with the money supply M1, which is cash plus demand deposits, and M2, which is M1 plus time deposits. M_1 and M_2 merely designate the source of the money.
13 Note that Marx sometimes uses C to represent "commodities" and at other times to represent "capital." For example, "The surplus-value generated in the process of production by C, the capital advanced, or in other words, the self-expansion of the value of the capital C, presents itself for our consideration, in the first place, as a surplus, as the amount by which the value of the product exceeds the value of its constituent elements," (*Capital*, Vol. I, p. 150) and "The result of the whole process is, so far as concerns the objects themselves, C – C, the exchange of one commodity" (*Capital*, Vol. I, p. 72).
14 An individual may incorporate his business, or a small group of people may incorporate. As a corporation whose shares are not publicly traded, the corporation is merely an "alter ego" of the incorporators.
15 Money not spent on consumer goods by individuals is by definition saved, regardless of how it is saved—savings accounts, owning bonds, or owning shares of stock.
16 It is unimaginable, although theoretically possible, to produce something much above a level of subsistence without using some capital.
17 Even today, there is much fraud in corporate financial statements.
18 To be more precise, labor cannot be owned. Humans can be owned as slaves, but labor is not the actual human although it is commonly used as a label, a noun, for the humans who perform the work. But labor is actually a force, i.e., the effort, the work, the energy expended by humans that results in the production of a commodity.

Bibliography

Berle, A. A., Jr. (1954). *The 20th century capitalist revolution*. Harcourt Brace & World, Inc.

Brigham, E. F., & Ehrhardt, M. C. (2016). *Financial management: Theory & practice* (15th ed.). Cengage.

Carruthers, B. G., & Espeland, W. N. (1991). Accounting for rationality: Double-entry bookkeeping and the rhetoric of economic rationality. *American Journal of Sociology*, *97*(1), 31–69. Retrieved from https://www.jstor.org/stable/2781637

Chiapello, E. (2007). Accounting and the birth of the notion of capitalism. *Critical Perspectives on Accounting*, *18*(3), 263–296. https://doi.org/10.1016/j.cpa.2005.11.012

Cooper, C. (2015). Accounting for the fictitious: A Marxist contribution to understanding accounting's roles in the financial crisis. *Critical Perspectives on Accounting*, *30*, 63–82. https://doi.org/10.1016/j.cpa.2014.08.002

Cooper, W. W. (1949). Theory of the firm: Some suggestions for revision. *The American Economic Review*, *39*(6), 1204–1222. Retrieved from https://www.jstor.org/stable/1816597

Durkheim, E. (1997). *The division of labour in society (W. D. Halls, Trans.)*. Free Press.

Ellerman, D. (1975). The 'ownership of the firm' is a myth. *Administration & Society*, *7*(1), 27–42. Retrieved from https://ellerman.org/wp-content/uploads/2020/11/Ownership-Firm-Myth.pdf

Ellerman, D. (1991). Myth and metaphor in orthodox economics. *Journal of Post-Keynesian Economics*, *13*(4), 545–564. Retrieved from https://www.jstor.org/stable/4538263

Federal Reserve Bank of St. Louis. (n.d.). Retrieved from https://www.stlouisfed.org/education/economic-lowdown-podcast-series/episode-2-factors-of-production

Financial Accounting Standards Board. (1978). *Statement of financial accounting concepts no. 1, objectives of financial reporting by business enterprises*. FASB.

Financial Accounting Standards Board (FASB). (2018). *Statement of financial accounting concepts no. 8, conceptual framework for financial reporting*.

Fisher, I. (1906). *The nature of capital and income*. Macmillan.

Hicks, J. R. (1975). *Value and capital* (2nd ed.). Oxford University Press.

Huber, W. D. (2020). *Corporate law and the theory of the firm: Reconstructing corporations, shareholders, directors, owners, and investors*. Routledge.

Huber, W. D. (2021). *Economics, capitalism, and corporations: Contradictions of corporate law, economics, and the theory of the firm*. Routledge.

Krugman, P., & Wells, R. (2008). *Microeconomics* (2nd ed.). Worth Publishers.

Levy, J. (2014). Accounting for profit and the history of capital. *Critical Historical Studies, 1*(2), 171–214. Retrieved from http://www.jstor.org/stable/10.1086/677977

Lis, C., & Soly, H. (1997). Different paths of development capitalism in the Northern and Southern Netherlands during the Late Middle Ages and the Early Modern Period. *Review, XX*(2), 211–242. Retrieved from https://www.jstor.org/stable/40241399

Marx, K. (1990). *Capital, A critique of political economy* (Vol. 3). Penguin Classics.

Michie, R. (2014). The rise of capitalism from ancient origins to 1948. In L. Neal & J. G. Williamson (Eds.), *The Cambridge history of capitalism* (Vol. 2, pp. 230–263). Cambridge University Press.

Milios, J. (2018). *The origins of capitalism as a social system: The prevalence of an aleatory encounter*. Routledge.

Neal, L. (2016). Introduction. In L. Neal & J. G. Williamson (Eds.), *The Cambridge history of capitalism* (Vol. 1, pp. 1–23). Cambridge University Press.

Polanyi, K. (2001). *The great transformation: The political and economic origins of our time*. Beacon Press.

Ransom, R., & Sutch, R. (1988). Capitalists without capital: The burden of slavery and the impact of emancipation. *Quantitative Studies in Agrarian History, 62*(3), 133–160. Retrieved from www.jstor.org/stable/3743211

Robé, J.-P. (2011). The legal structure of the firm. *Accounting, Economics, and Law—A Convivium, 1*(1), 1–85. https://doi.org/10.2202/2152-2820.1001

Sangster, A., Kuter, M., Gurskaya, M., & Andreenkova, A. (2018). The determination of profit in medieval times. In T. Antipova & A. Rocha (Eds.), *Information technology science*. Springer.

Sée, H. (1928). *Modern capitalism: Its origin and evolution*. Adelphi Co.

Sharpe, W. F. (1964). Capital asset prices: A theory of market equilibrium under conditions of risk. *Journal of Finance, 19*(3), 425–442. https://doi.org/10.1111/j.1540-626.1964.tb02865.x

von Mises, L. (2009). *The theory of money & credit* (J. E. Batson, Trans.). Ludwig von Mises Institute.

Weber, M. (1978). *Economy and society: An outline of interpretive sociology* (E. Fischoff & H. Gerth, et al., Trans.). In G. Roth & C. Wittich (Eds.). University of California Press.

Weber, M. (1992). *The protestant ethic and the spirit of capitalism* (T. Parsons, Trans.). Routledge.

Williamson, O. E. (1985). *The economic institutions of capitalism*. Simon and Schuster.

Winjum, J. O. (1971). Accounting and the rise of capitalism: An accountant's view. *Journal of Accounting Research*, *9*(2), 333–350. Retrieved from https://www.jstor.org/stable/2489937.

Yamey, B. S. (1949). Scientific bookkeeping and the rise of capitalism. *The Economic History Review*, *1*(2–3), 99–113. https://doi.org/10.2307/2589824.

Žmolek, M. A. (2013). *Rethinking the industrial revolution: Five centuries of transition from agrarian to industrial capitalism in England*. Haymarket Books.

2 Capitalists

Introduction

In 1954, Berle exclaimed, "The capital is there; and so is capitalism. The waning factor is the capitalist. He has somehow vanished …" (p. 39). Berle was wrong. While there can be, and obviously has been, capital for thousands of years, there can be no capitalism without capitalists.

Heilbroner (1974) defined capitalism first as an "economic order marked by the private ownership of means of production vested in a minority class called 'capitalists'" (p. 63) and second as a market system that determines the income and distributes the output arising from its productive activities. But he also defined capitalism as "a social order characterized by a 'bourgeois' culture among whose manifold aspects the drive for wealth is the most important" (p. 63).

Capitalists are an indispensable ingredient of capitalism. Capitalists are persons who own capital (the resource of production), who Marx referred to as *bourgeois* capitalists, and who employ wage-labor that use the capital owned by the capitalist to transform raw materials into commodities. It is the *bourgeois* capitalists who embody what Weber (1992) referred to the "capitalist spirit."

It is essential, therefore, to understand capitalists and their relation to capital and labor and therefore to capitalism. This chapter focuses on capitalists and explains their role in the development of capitalism as both an economic system and a social system. It provides the background for understanding why capitalists and capitalism are extinct.

As noted, there was capital before there were capitalists. As discussed in Chapters 4 and 5, there were also corporations before there was either capitalists or capitalism. Capitalists and capitalism arose concurrently. One cannot study the origin, history, and development of capitalism (see Chapter 3) without simultaneously studying capitalists. Just as there is no capitalism without capitalists, there are no capitalists without capitalism. They cannot be separated.

DOI: 10.4324/9781003240969-3

I begin with a review of who are capitalists, then proceed to a discussion of capitalists and primitive accumulation, and finally capitalists and capital accumulation.

Capitalists

Marx obviously has much to say about capitalists. A capitalist is a person, an individual. "To be a capitalist, is to have not only a purely personal, but a social status in production" (*Manifesto*, p. 23). It is the "*bourgeois* capitalists" who own the capital resources of production (*Capital*, Vol. I); "the means of production are the property of private persons …" (*Capital*, Vol. I, p. 439); and one of the "Three cardinal facts of capitalist production [is] Concentration of means of production in few hands" (*Capital*, Vol. III, p. 185).

Engels explains Marx's linking *bourgeois* capitalists to capital. "By *bourgeoisie* is meant the class of modern capitalists, owners of the means of social production and employers of wage labour" (*Manifesto*, p. 14). A person who owns financial capital is not a *bourgeois* capitalist just by the fact that she owns financial capital. Nor is a person who owns mercantile capital or commercial capital, or any other "type" of capital. A person who owns the productive capital, the means of production, is a *bourgeois* capitalist. Owners of financial capital are not capitalists by virtue of their owning financial capital. *Bourgeois* capitalists also own financial capital, but it is the ownership of productive capital, the means of production, that makes them *bourgeois* capitalists.

A capitalist entrepreneur owns the enterprise. In other words, a capitalist is an individual[1] who, according to the laws of private property (see Chapter 5), has ownership rights in the firm. Hicks (1975) recognized that, "The enterprise is where resources of production are transformed into commodities. The enterprise is a separate economic unit detached from the private account of the entrepreneur" (p. 79). The *bourgeois* capitalist invests her money in the enterprise which comes from her savings, supplemented by borrowing from family and friends (Michie, 2014; OECD, 2016) to obtain the financial capital used to acquire productive capital, and to operate and produce commodities. The money she invests becomes the financial capital of the enterprise. Thus, for a *bourgeois* capitalist the balance sheet is assets equals liabilities plus equity (see Chapter 6) where the capitalist owns the assets and owes the liabilities. She does not issue stock to the public.

Since the *bourgeois* capitalist owns all the assets, it is also her productive capital to be used in production. She makes all the decisions on how to allocate the productive capital and wage-labor to hire. The *bourgeois* capitalist uses her financial capital to acquire (or rent) land, to acquire raw materials and physical capital, and to pay labor to transform the raw materials into commodities to be sold for money thus beginning the cycle. It is money, i.e., the financial capital, not the debt or equity that is used to acquire productive capital to produce commodities.

Capitalists and Primitive Accumulation

As noted in Chapter 1, capitalists do not actually accumulate capital, i.e., machines. They accumulate wealth and financial capital. Wealth is personal. Financial capital is money that is intended to be used to acquire productive capital.

Although it appeared relatively quickly, the capitalist mode of production did not appear suddenly. It took a period of approximately 200 years to fully develop, along with *bourgeois* capitalists who own the capital and hire free wage-labor.

Marx begins his analysis of the development of the capitalist mode of production and the *bourgeois* capitalist by considering the influence of the growth of capital on labor. He considered the most important factor of this inquiry to be "the composition of capital and the changes it undergoes in the course of the process of accumulation" (*Capital*, Vol. I, p. 434).

The change in the technical composition of capital, meaning the growth of productive capital as the means of production, compared to labor is reflected in the increase of capital (which Marx referred to as "constant capital") at the expense of labor (which he referred to as "variable capital"). He gives an example where the capital:labor ratio is 50:50 but later becomes 80:20 as the use of capital increases. Thus, capital replaces labor.

Where the means of production are the property of private persons, an artisan either produces commodities in isolation and independent of others, or sells his labor because he lacks the means for independent industry. But large-scale production of commodities can only exist in the capitalistic form, and "A certain accumulation of capital, in the hands of individual producers of commodities, forms therefore the necessary preliminary of the specifically capitalistic mode of production" (*Capital*, Vol. I, p. 440). Marx refers to this as accumulation of capital as "primitive accumulation, because it is the historic basis, instead of the historic result of specifically capitalist production" (*Capital*, Vol. I, p. 440). Primitive accumulation is the process of separating labor from the means of production. It is primitive because "it forms the prehistoric stage of capital and of the mode of production corresponding with it" (*Capital*, Vol. I, p. 508). Those who accumulate capital are *bourgeois* capitalists.

> If, therefore, a certain degree of accumulation of capital appears as a condition of the specifically capitalist mode of production, the latter causes conversely an accelerated accumulation of capital. With the accumulation of capital, therefore, the specifically capitalistic mode of production develops, and with the capitalist mode of production the accumulation of capital. Both these economic factors bring about, in

> the compound ratio of the impulses they reciprocally give one another, that change in the technical composition of capital by which the variable constituent becomes always smaller and smaller as compared with the constant.
>
> (*Capital*, Vol. I, p. 440)

> The development of the capitalist mode of production and of the productive power of labour—at once the cause and effect of accumulation—enables the capitalist, with the same outlay of variable capital ... the capitalist buys with the same [financial] capital a greater mass of labour power, as he progressively replaces skilled labourers by less skilled, mature labour power by immature, male by female, that of adults by that of young persons or children."[2]
>
> (*Capital*, Vol. I, p. 446)

Capitalists and Capital Accumulation

The basis of the production of commodities on a large scale can only be accomplished in the capitalistic form of production. "A certain accumulation of capital, *in the hands of individual producers of commodities*, forms therefore the necessary preliminary of the specifically capitalistic mode of production" (*Capital*, Vol. I, p. 440, emphasis added). It is important to note first, that Marx explicitly identifies the accumulation of capital and the capitalist mode of production with individual producers, and second, he does not explain what he means by "capital," that is, the type of capital that is being accumulated leaving it to the reader to infer from the context what he means in any particular passage.

As soon as the capitalist production is "on its own legs," it not only maintains the separation of labor from the means of production, but continually reproduces it, clearing the way for the capitalist system. With primitive accumulation complete, capitalist accumulation can now begin since the capitalist mode of production "presupposes the pre-existence of considerable masses of capital and of labour power in the hands of producers of commodities" (*Capital*, Vol. I, p. 507); i.e., the capitalist. In other words, "The economic structure of capitalist society has grown out of the economic structure of feudal society. The dissolution of the latter set free the elements of the former" (*Capital*, Vol. I, p. 508). The industrial capitalists displaced the guild masters of handicrafts and the feudal lords who were the possessors of the sources of wealth.

Marx further explains the relation and evolution of the capitalist mode of production, capitalists, labor, and private property. "The capitalist mode of appropriation, the result of the capitalist mode of production, produces capitalist private property. This is the first negation of individual private property, as founded on the labour of the proprietor" (*Capital*, Vol. I, p. 542). Moreover, "The transformation of scattered private property, arising from individual labour, into capitalist private property is, naturally, a process" (*Capital*, Vol. I, p. 542).

Marx sees that process as violent, and as soon as the capitalist mode of production stands on its own feet, and the process has sufficiently decomposed the old society and laborers are turned into proletarians, the further expropriation of private proprietors takes a new form. The expropriation is accomplished "by the action of the immanent laws of capitalistic production itself, by the centralisation of capital" (*Capital*, Vol. I, p. 417).

Writing in the mid-nineteenth century, Marx uses England from 1846 to 1866 to illustrate "the General Law of Capitalist Accumulation" because "No period of modern society is so favourable for the study of capitalist accumulation as the period of the last 20 years ... because it holds the foremost place in the world-market, because capitalist production is here alone completely developed" (*Capital*, Vol. I, p. 453).

The capitalist mode of production is a function of first the greater ratio of capital to labor as the mode of production, and second, and more important, who owns the capital as a means of production.

Chapter Summary

This chapter examined who *bourgeois* capitalists are and what they do. *Bourgeois* capitalists are individuals (or partnerships) who own the capital resources of production and who hire wage-labor to use the capital to produce commodities to sell in the market. This chapter considered what Marx called the primitive accumulation of capital leading to what he called the accumulation of capital by capitalists.

Bourgeois capitalists are necessary for capitalism. That is, there is no capitalism without *bourgeois* capitalists.

In 1954, Berle exclaimed, "The capital is there; and so is capitalism. The waning factor is the capitalist. He has somehow vanished ..." (p. 39). Berle was wrong. Capitalists became extinct along with capitalism.

While there can be, and obviously has been, capital for thousands of years, there can be no capitalism without capitalists.

Notes

1 An enterprise may be owned by a *bourgeois* capitalist, or a *bourgeois* partnership. It may also be incorporated where the corporation is merely an "alter ego" of the owners of the shares.
2 Marx is implying that female workers are less skilled than male workers; a product of his times.

Bibliography

Berle, A. A. Jr. (1954). *The 20th century capitalist revolution*. Harcourt Brace & World, Inc.

Heilbroner, R. (1974). *An inquiry into the human prospect*. W. W. Norton.
Hicks, J. R. (1975). *Value and capital* (2nd ed.). Oxford University Press.
Huber, W. D. (2020). *Corporate law and the theory of the firm: Reconstructing shareholders, directors, owners, and investors*. Routledge.
Huber, W. D. (2021). *Economics, capitalism, and corporations: Contradictions of corporate law, economics, and the theory of the firm*. Routledge.
Marx, K. (1990). *Capital, a critique of political economy* (Vol. 3). Penguin Classics.
Marx, K., & Engels, F. (1848). *Manifesto of the Communist Party*. Retrieved from https://activistmanifesto.org/assets/original-communist-manifesto.pdf
Michie, R. (2014). The rise of capitalism from ancient origins to 1948. In L. Neal & J. G. Williamson (Eds.), *The Cambridge history of capitalism* (Vol. 2, pp. 230–263). Cambridge University Press.
OECD. (2016). Household savings. In *OECD Factbook 2015-2016: Economic, environmental and social statistics*. OECD Publishing.
Weber, M. (1992). *The protestant ethic and the spirit of capitalism* (T. Parsons, Trans.). Routledge.

3 Capitalism

Six Blind Men and Capitalism—A Parody[1]

A group of blind men heard that a strange animal, called Capitalism, had been brought to the town, but none of them were aware of its shape and form. Out of curiosity, they said: "We must inspect and know it by touch, of which we are capable." So, they sought it out, and when they found it they groped about it. In the case of the first person, whose hand landed on the trunk, said, "Capitalism is like a free-market." Another, whose hand reached its ear, exclaimed, "Capitalism is like long-term assets used in production." The third blind man, whose hand was upon its leg, declared, "Capitalism is like appropriating wage labor." The fourth blind man, who placed his hand upon its side, said, "Capitalism is like an economic system." The fifth blind man, who felt its tail, said, "capitalism is like private property." The last man felt its tusk and said, "capitalism is like a social system."

Introduction

If we are considering the extinction of capitalism, we must necessarily examine its beginning and its evolution.

The fundamental issue in either a "capitalist," "socialist," or any other economic industrialized system is not whether capital resources are used in production, but who owns the capital resources of production and how those resources are allocated—according to the laws of private property, by the government, or the "people?" There are other issues, of course, but all other issues are secondary and depend first on the ownership of capital resources of production.

There were multiple events associated with the transformation of feudal/agrarian society into capitalism. However, the most important events are the Industrial Revolution and the social transformations accompanying the inventions of the Industrial Revolution, as well as such things as wage-labor, and the "invention" of the capital account and the proliferation of double-entry bookkeeping.

All economies, past and present, are embedded and enmeshed in social relations and the institutions of society (Gemici, 2008; Polanyi, 2001). The

DOI: 10.4324/9781003240969-4

working of the economic system not only influences society but determines how society is perceived and structured as the sides of a triangle determine its angles (Polanyi, 1947). It is thus imperative to understand how the economic system that is called capitalism influences and determines our society and our perceptions of it. Since capitalism is "first and foremost a [sic] historical social system. To understand its origins, its workings, or its current prospects, we have to look at its existing reality" (Wallerstein, 2011, p. 13). Yet, there is a difference between "existing reality" and invalid assumptions about existing reality. Moreover,

> Capitalism is the backbone of contemporary economics… Comprehending economic and social outcomes in the contemporary world thus requires understanding capitalism, its nature, its origin, *variety*, the evolution of particular capitalist economies, and the system as a whole.
>
> (Greif, 2005, p. ix, emphasis added)

This chapter examines briefly the origins and history of capitalism and "types" of capitalism for the purpose of calling attention to the issues involved in how the history and origin of capitalism contributed to the modern (mis)understanding of capitalism and facilitates our understanding of why capitalism as an economic system is extinct, yet continues to be heralded as a global economic system. To that end, we will examine capitalism from different perspectives. First, we will consider definitions and semantics associated with capitalism along with the contention that capitalism is a global system. Since we are examining capitalism from different perspectives there is inevitable overlap between and among the various perspectives in this chapter, as well as with other chapters, because they are placed in different contexts such as capital and its ownership, accounting, profit, and labor.

Next, the origin and history of capitalism will be considered which, for obvious reasons, must be highly selective and extremely abbreviated. The theories of Marx, Sombart, and Weber are considered, followed by those of Yamey, Durkheim, Tawney, Wallerstein, Levy, and Polanyi with sincerest apologies to those both living and deceased whose works are not included here. Marx, Durkheim, and Weber in particular "have provided modern economic sociology with the principle that economic behaviour cannot be separated from social relations centred on the distribution of resources and power, and the social construction of beliefs and institutions" (Radice, 2000, p. 721). Some are included for what they explain; others for what they fail to explain; and still others for what they erroneously explain.

Third, types, forms, varieties, and models of capitalism found in economics, history, and sociology literature are reviewed, including financial capitalism, productive/industrial capitalism, corporate capitalism, and mercantile capitalism. Fourth, the Industrial Revolution is viewed as the fulcrum of the transition from feudalism to capitalism. Finally, capitalism and profit, capitalism and labor, capitalism and the capital account, and capitalism and the spirit of capitalism are considered.

By looking at capitalism from different perspectives, we will better understand what capitalism was, when it came to be the dominant economic and social system, and why, as explained in Chapter 8, it is extinct. As Beckert (2014) observes, "the world we live in cannot be understood without coming to terms with the long history of capitalism—a process that has arguably unfolded over more than half a millennium."

As we begin our examination of capitalism, it must be kept in mind that nowhere has the assumption that capitalism still exists been questioned, challenged, or even debated. Nowhere has it been proven that it still exists. Nowhere has there been any analysis of whether any of the conditions necessary for the existence of capitalism continue to exist.

To say that capitalism exists is the equivalent of the pre-Copernican geocentric view of the solar system. It is a tradition with no basis in fact or law with no explanation much like Tevye's soliloquy, "You may ask, how did this tradition start? I'll tell you—I don't know. But it's a tradition."[2]

Capitalism—Definitions and Semantics

Capitalism is, or rather was, both an economic and social system. "Any and every 'economic' phenomenon is at the same time always a social phenomenon, and existence of a particular kind of 'economy' presupposes a definite kind of society" (Giddens, 1971, pp. 120–121). Melios (2018) is a little more precise: "Capitalism is a specific social structure, or equivalently, a social system, a [sic] historically unique configuration of social relations" (p. 4).

Heilbroner (1985) defined capitalism as, "an economic order marked by the private ownership of the means of production vested in a minority class called 'capitalists,' ..." But he also defined capitalism as, "a social order characterized by a '*bourgeoisie*' culture ..." (p. 79). Capitalism, or what Marx more frequently called the capitalist mode of production, "determines the character of the social, political, and intellectual life" (*Capital*, Vol. I, p. 58).

If we are to consider the extinction capitalism, we must necessarily examine its beginning and its evolution and therefore we must consider the definitions of capitalism[3] and its aberrations, and what are referred to as types of capitalism. However, note that a definition of capitalism is not a definition *per se*. There are too many variables to account for. Thus, to present a definition of capitalism is merely a means to focus our attention and direct the nature of our inquiry.

Capitalism is the "ism" of capital. That is, "the social formation in which we live is described as the 'ism' of capital" (Heilbroner, 1985). The suffix "ism" is defined, in relevant part, as "the action or result of," "the state or quality of," or "the teaching, system or movement of."[4] Thus, "capitalism" is "the action or result of capital," "the state or quality of capital," or "the teaching, system or movement of capital." But not just of capital in the abstract, but the capital resources of production as owned by *bourgeois* capitalists (see Chapter 2 for a discussion of capitalism). Nor is the "ism" of capital the use of capital in production since every industrialized country uses capital in production whether or not it is considered a capitalist economy.

Assuming that all other conditions necessary for capitalism to exist, the "ism" of capital concerns who owns the capital resources of production and how it is allocated. Capitalism is "the state or quality of" capital used by labor in producing commodities and owned by *bourgeois* capitalists[5]; "the teaching, system or movement of" capital used by labor in production and owned by *bourgeois* capitalists; "the action or result of capital" used by labor in production and owned by *bourgeois* capitalists.

One of the principles of economic sociology is that sociologically, economic institutions are social constructions. Languages and culture are important factors in sociological analysis since language and meaning structures play a role in the social construction of economic institutions (Bourdieu, 2005). *Homo economicus* is essentially a cultural phenomenon (Bourdieu, 2005). Social structures influence the economic actions of individuals, economic actions have an element of power, and economic power is the ability to control the resources (Granovetter & Swedberg, 2001). Therefore, the importance of understanding the origin and evolution of capitalism is important to understand the social structures and cultural phenomena associated with capitalism and *homo economicus*.

Capitalism is based on an institutionalized social order (Streek, 2011). But how do we understand economic institutions?

> Institutions further imply historicity and control...Institutions always have a history, of which they are the product. It is impossible to understand an institution adequately without an understanding of the historical process in which it was produced. Institutions also, by the very fact of their existence, control human conduct ...
>
> (Berger & Luckmann, 1966, pp. 54–55)

While capitalism may be (or, more accurately, may have been) an institution, it is (was) not a formal institution or formal organization as is a corporation or government. Democracy is an institution and controls the human behavior of those who are citizens in a democratic political system, but democracy is not a formal institution or formal organization.

Obviously, as with "capitalist," the root of "capitalism" is "capital." But, as explained in Chapter 1, the term "capital" has been so misused that it is now so ambiguous that it has become hostile to any possible relation to ownership of the means of production. The consequence of the ambiguous meaning of "capital" is that the meaning of "capitalism" has become so distorted in both an historical and current context that now economic and social systems are called capitalism that have nothing to do with capital or capitalism.

Laclau (1971) notes well that capitalism is a term that cannot be taken for granted and it is incumbent on all of us to be "well aware of the extensive debates that have occurred over the concept of capitalism" (p. 9). Laclau criticizes Frank's (1967) conception of capitalism because Frank "has defined capitalism so loosely that he is unable legitimately to derive any concrete consequences from it about anything" (p. 15). Laclau does recognize Frank's right to build a model by abstracting "a mass of historical features" and naming it "capitalism," but questions the usefulness of designating such a variety of relations as "capitalism" when those words are normally employed in a different sense (p. 10).

Dobb (1958) agrees, "Capitalism...is a word that those using it employ in a variety of senses, with no little confusion and talk-at-cross-purposes, as a result. There are some even who deny that it can be given precise meaning at all" (p. 5). While it is true that the term is used in a variety of senses, the economic system of capitalism is the ownership of productive capital by *bourgeois* capitalists who are individuals (or partners). Dobb in fact does correctly regard capitalism as a system where productive capital is owned primarily by private individuals but fails to recognize its importance.

Wallerstein (1974) criticizes Laclau's assertion that "the world capitalist system...includes, at the level of its definition, various modes of production" by stating the obvious: "...if it's a matter of definition, then there can be no argument. But then the polemic is scarcely useful since it is reduced to a question of semantics" (p. 392).

In a personal email to the author, David Ellerman, Associate Researcher at the University of Ljubljana (Slovenia), wrote, "When economist Branko Milanovic says that capitalism is alone as the economic system around the world...and you saying it does not exist, then it is clear that words are being used very loosely and the statements are more about the definitions of words than the reality."[6]

But definitions of words have meanings beyond the definitions. Definitions of words shape reality (Berger & Luckmann, 1966; Searle, 1995, 2010). Definitions of words have legal and social meanings and implications.[7] Many U.S. Supreme Court cases have been decided on the definitions of words, and "debates over the meaning of essentially contested concepts goes beyond mere semantics" (Robinson, 2004, p. 1). In other words, a word defined one way shapes one social (and legal) reality. Defined in another way it shapes a different social (and legal) reality. The terms "'feudal' and 'capitalist' are not just convenient words; they are names for concepts whose implications, often unconsciously, affect the user's perception of reality well beyond the immediate context in which the words are used" (Frank, 1967, p. 222).

For example, one of the necessary conditions for capitalism is a free market. But capitalism is almost universally confused with a free-market (free enterprise) economy (e.g., Derks, 2008), with some even going so far as to exclaim, "'capitalism' refers to the 'market system' or 'the free enterprise system'" (Bullock et al., 1999). But free-market economies existed long before capitalism emerged (Chandler, 1984; Elsenhans, 2015; Grassby, 1999) and thus capitalism cannot mean free market. Defining capitalism as a free market shapes our social reality as to what both free markets and capitalism are.

Attempts to reduce a discourse to questions of definitions and semantics are more than just a Humpty Dumpty problem.[8] Often it is an attempt to deflect a debate away from the issues, comparable to an ad hominem attack on a speaker with whom another speaker disagrees but who cannot sustain their argument with logic, or who can offer no legitimate or reasonable counter-argument. Relegating important social, legal, and economic concepts to mere disagreements concerning definitions and semantics reveals a lack of understanding of the social, legal, and economic importance of definitions.

Fifty years ago, Berle (1954) remarked that scholarly studies of capitalism are mere "descriptive clichés" consisting of "little more than a deposit of the verbiage left over from a previous historical age." One can, as a result, expect nothing less than confusion concerning what, where, and when capitalism began and if it still exists.

As with "capital," failure to use "capitalism" with an adjective often compounds the confusion in understanding what is meant by capitalism without an adjective. At the same time, the use of adjectives actually negates the meaning of capitalism, rendering it totally different from what it actually means. Capitalism without an adjective has only one meaning but has been distorted and perverted. It is therefore necessary to consider the use of the term "capitalism" with various adjectives in order to understand the meaning of capitalism, why capitalism with an adjective is not capitalism, and why capitalism is extinct.

Capitalism as a Global System

Wood (1999) declares, "The expansionary drive of capitalism reached a point where today it is virtually universal." Radice (2000) maintains that the trend referred to as globalization involves "a real change in the structures and functioning of world capitalism" (p. 720). But that reveals nothing more than the premise that there is a such a thing not only of capitalism, but world capitalism, the structures and functioning of which involve change as a result of globalization. But on what basis has it ever been established that there is, in fact, capitalism, let alone "world capitalism?"

Wallerstein (1979) questions how and when the capitalist world-economy was first created, why it occurred only in feudal Europe and not elsewhere, and why it occurred at the time it did when earlier attempts failed. But there were no attempts to create capitalism because attempts require intent and capitalism was not planned or guided. Nevertheless, the questions are important because they reveal the universal unproven assumption that there is a capitalist world-economy.

Wallerstein (1974) not only calls capitalism a "world system" but further states

> Capitalism was *from the beginning* an affair of the world-economy and not of nation-states. It is a misreading of the situation to claim that it is only in the twentieth century that capitalism has become "world-wide", although this claim is frequently made in various writings, particularly by Marxists ... capital has never allowed its aspirations to be determined by national boundaries ...
>
> (pp. 401–402, emphasis added)

Nee and Swedberg (2005) assert that "during the last decades of the twentieth century, capitalism expanded its global scope and dominance over economic activity" (p. xxxv). Milanovic (2019) calls capitalism the system that rules the world. Every country, regardless of type of economy, must participate in the world system of capitalism even if that country itself is not a capitalist country (Frank, 1967). Swedberg (2011) sees capitalism not only as the dominant economic system in today's world, but thinks there are few alternatives in sight. "Globalization is the near culmination of a centuries-long process of the spread of capitalist production around the world and its displacement of all precapitalist relations, bringing about a new form of connection between all human beings" (Robinson, 2004, p. 3).

But is it? Is the system that is called the dominate system, a global system, a world system, the system that rules the world, actually capitalism? This question will be answered in Chapter 8, but first the foundation must be established.

Capitalism is broken (Reeves, 2019). Capitalism is imploding (Amin, 2013). Schumpter (2009) asks, "Can capitalism survive?" Levy (2014) concluded that "The 1970s collapse of manufacturing profits in the West is a familiar drama, spelling the end of capitalism's postwar Golden Age, the exhaustion of the Fordist industrial paradigm...Capitalism was once again in crisis" (pp. 172–173). According to Moishe Postone (Hamza & Ruda, 2016), capitalism is prone to crises although, unlike others, he does not believe it will collapse. For over a century, every global financial or economic crisis has been seen by many as a harbinger of the coming collapse of capitalism. It is easy to attribute an economic crisis to capitalism thereby diverting attention from the fact that capitalism does not exist.

When capitalism is considered the dominant global economic system, it is easy to implicate capitalism for every global economic and financial crisis. Capitalism may well be considered as broken, imploding, and in crisis when capitalism is so ill-defined, perverted, and contorted as to make it unrecognizable and therefore misinterpreted.

Any analysis, discussion, debate, or argument of or about capitalism, either for or against capitalism, must necessarily consider both economic and social issues simultaneously. Omitting the economic issues when discussing social issues, or omitting social issues when discussing economic issues, inevitably leads to invalid assumptions and erroneous conclusions. (Of course, incorporating both economic and social issues does not guarantee either valid assumptions or conclusions.) Indeed, one must wonder why anyone would call a system capitalism when it omits both social and economic issues pertaining to capitalism, or that excludes consideration of the ownership of the means of production and the relationship between the ownership of the means of production wage-labor. As Hilton and Hill (1953) comment, capitalist accumulation cannot be understood if the relationship between *bourgeois* capitalists and free wage-labor is ignored.

This chapter is not a dissertation on the history and origin of capitalism. Nor does it propose a new theory on how, when, where, or why capitalism arose. This chapter merely serves the purpose of calling our attention to the issues involved in how the history and origin of capitalism contributed to the current (mis)understanding of capitalists and capitalism and enables us to understand why it is extinct. The rest of this chapter examines very briefly the history, origins, and "types" and "varieties" of capitalism.

Nor does this chapter, or the entire book for that matter, contemplate Marx's political rhetoric concerning the appropriation of surplus value and the exploitation of wage-labor, or class conflict between the proletariat and *bourgeois* capitalists. That is left for others. This chapter merely presents a perspective of capitalism that incorporates its historical, social, and economic origins and context and, by extension, its present day social and economic construction.

The Origin and History of Capitalism

Mielants (2000) sees four major theoretical perspectives on the origins of capitalism: orthodox Marxism, the Brennerian approach, the modernization approach, and world-systems analysis. Orthodox Marxism dates the beginning of capitalism to the late eighteenth century with the Industrial Revolution, with Marxists dating the early roots of capitalism to the 1640s in England. Orthodox Marxism places priority on the means of production as the analytical framework and conceives of capitalism as a rigid dichotomous class struggle between the exploited proletarians and capitalists. The Brennerian approach is also Marxist oriented but focuses on the Middle Ages emphasizing modes of production and class struggle between exploited peasants and exploiter nobility. The modernization approach is based on spiritual or religious values that formed capitalist accumulation, or technological innovations that resulted in Europe's economic dominance in subsequent centuries.

World-systems analysis attempts to answer the questions of how and when the capitalist world-economy was created, why the transition only took place in feudal Europe, and why it happened when it happened. World-systems analysis considers that feudalism was transformed into, and superseded by, capitalism such that for at least two centuries feudalism and capitalism coexisted and converged into a single world-system centered around Europe between 1450 and 1650 (Mielants, 2000).

There were multiple historical processes and events associated with the transformation of feudal/agrarian society into capitalism. Steenland (1975) summarizes Marx's explanation of feudalism as consisting of an economy where wealth is based predominantly on privately owned land; the owners of the land extract the surplus production from the peasantry; production is primarily for use rather than the market; and the peasantry owns their own means of production, including usually a small plot of land.

Unlike what is now known as Marxism, or Communism, capitalism was not planned. There was no "Capitalist Manifesto" to follow or guide the development of capitalism.[9] Capitalism emerged from the coalescence of several historically independent yet interdependent events, all of which were necessary, but none of which was sufficient by itself, or as Wallerstein (1974) describes it, as a series of historical, ecological, and geographic accidents.

It is of course much easier to trace the origin of Marxism, since it obviously began with Marx, than it is to trace the origin of capitalism. It is much more difficult to trace the origin of capitalism because capitalism did not begin with a person. We are thus forced to look at multiple factors across time that took place unevenly in both time and location that contributed to the development of capitalism (Sée, 1928).

Theories of the origin of capitalism include certain aspects of the Christian religion as expressed in the advent of the Protestant Reformation, in particular Calvinism; the "invention" of the capital account and the proliferation of double-entry bookkeeping; the discovery by Europeans of other continents and ways to circumnavigate the globe; colonialism as practiced by European geo-political powers and the rapid expansion of overseas commerce; the invention of the printing press; certain scientific theories and discoveries accompanied by a rational, scientific mindset; population growth; a money-based rather than a barter-based economy; and most important, technological inventions leading to the "Industrial Revolution" in Britain and the United States which resulted in the rise of free wage-labor.

These events and processes have of course presented questions among historians and sociologists of what came first, the chicken or the egg, which preceded the others sequentially, and whether one caused the others. But it is clear that there were multiple events associated with the transformation of feudal/agrarian society into capitalism. Many of the events and processes occurred independently, some interdependently, and some played a more significant role than others.

According to Wallerstein (1974), it was only with the emergence of the modern world-economy in sixteenth-century Europe that saw the full development and economic predominance of market trade. This was the system called capitalism. As a matter of history "the capitalist world-economy has existed for about four or five centuries" (p. 397), i.e., since the Industrial Revolution. The system called capitalism is a world-economy with a single division of labor but with multiple political systems and cultures. Capitalism and a world-economy are two sides of the same coin; one does not cause the other. They are the same indivisible phenomenon but with different characteristics (Wallerstein, 1974). Yet, that is not quite accurate. Capitalism existed before it became what Wallerstein calls a world-economy as did world trade.

Ignoring momentarily who owns the capital, the capitalist mode of production is grounded in the use of productive capital in greater proportion than labor (Giddens, 1971).[10] However, it is not the use of capital in production in just one or even a few companies, but in an economy as a whole. We therefore must look for a time and place when productive capital began to replace labor as the major resource of production; that is, when production became capital intensive vs. labor intensive in the economy as a whole. Furthermore, notwithstanding those who argue to the contrary, capitalism did not begin in Asian or African societies or cultures since the conditions necessary for the development of capitalism did not exist in those cultures; only in Europe. Therefore, it is to Europe that we must look to see what factors contributed to the rise of capitalism there.

The capitalist mode of production is a function of first the ratio of capital to labor. Second, and more important, the capitalist mode of production is a function of who owns the capital as a means of production. The basis of the production of goods (that Marx called commodities) on a large scale can only be accomplished in the capitalistic form of production. "A certain accumulation of capital, *in the hands of individual producers of commodities*, forms therefore the necessary preliminary of the specifically capitalistic mode of production" (*Capital*, Vol. I, p. 440, emphasis added). It is important to note that Marx explicitly equates the accumulation of capital and the capitalist mode of production to individual producers. (Unfortunately, Marx does not specify whether he means the accumulation of financial capital or the accumulation of productive capital.)

Marx assumes that the accumulation of capital occurs during the transition from feudalism, handicraft, and agriculture to capitalistic industry and refers to it as "primitive accumulation" because it is the historic basis, rather than the historic result, of the capitalist mode of production (*Capital*, Vol. I). Primitive accumulation is the historical process of separating the owner of the means of production from labor. Separating labor from ownership of the means of production resulted in the rise of free wage-labor, where labor was able to sell itself to the highest bidder. However, "The minimum amount of [productive] capital...which distinguishes a capitalist from a non-capitalist economy, is never stipulated" (Grassby, 1999, p. 64).

The *Cambridge History of Capitalism*[11] contemplates the appearance of different stages and types of capitalism in Babylonia, ancient Greece, ancient Rome, ancient China, and ancient India, among others. But these examples are neither capitalism, nor stages of capitalism, because they did not result in either primitive accumulation or capital accumulation.[12] The emergence of the capitalist mode of production, and thus capitalism, coincided exclusively with the Industrial Revolution and the decline of European and English feudalism (whether one caused the other is not relevant), among the other things cited in the Introduction to this chapter, and both Marx and Weber recognized the collapse of feudal society as contributing to the rise of capitalism. Wallerstein (1974), Žmolek (2013), and others locate the epicenter of the Industrial Revolution in England and consider the transition from agrarian society to capitalism as having occurred over five centuries following the Industrial Revolution.

In looking for a time when productive capital began to replace labor as the predominate means of production, we must keep in mind that

> There has been no single pattern of capitalist development ... capitalism is a vague concept that can be applied to any society that has developed beyond subsistence agriculture into a market economy ... But most of the characteristics attributed to it ... were clearly a consequence of the Industrial Revolution, which, though battered as a concept and stretched chronologically, still has some merit because it...transformed the economic basis of society.
>
> (Grassby, 1999, p. 63)

Multiple dozens of books and hundreds of articles in history, economics, and sociology have been written attempting to explain the origin and history of capitalism and it would be foolish and futile, not to mention arrogant, to try to explain either the history or the origin of capitalism here. The title of this section is not intended to convey the impression that the origin and history of capitalism is known, understood, or agreed upon. Nor is it the purpose of this chapter to provide a comprehensive review of those works, and certainly not to resolve the conflicting theories of how, why, or where capitalism originated, or the economic or historical validity of those theories.

The purpose of this section is merely to identify in an extremely brief manner some of the more prominent theories of capitalism and its history and origins in order to place capitalism and the types of capitalism in context, and to understand the meaning and nature of capitalism and why it is extinct. A few paragraphs will thus suffice merely to highlight the pertinent issues concerning the economic and social issues of capitalism.

An examination of the origin and history of capitalism cannot be done without considering the three most important authors on capitalism—Karl Marx, Werner Sombart, and Max Weber—since it was these three that introduced the topic of capitalism into social theory (Granovetter & Swedberg, 2011). All that follow them are either commentaries, interpretations, or criticisms of their theories. Therefore, I begin with an examination of their works. However, before I review their theories of capitalism and its origins, readers are reminded that capitalism, i.e., the capitalist mode of production, is not a function of the actual use of physical capital as a means of production. Although the capitalist mode of production requires the use of physical capital in greater ratio than labor in an economy as a whole, capitalism is not solely a function of the use productive capital in greater proportion than labor. Giddens (1971) concludes his analysis of Marx by emphasizing, "in short, in Marxist socialism, capital does not disappear; it is merely administered by society and not by individuals" (p. 204).

Karl Marx

Marx rarely used the term "capitalism." He uses the term twice in *Volume I*. First, he explains the period of capitalism as the time "when social wealth becomes to an ever-increasing degree the property of those who are in a position to appropriate continually and ever afresh the unpaid labour of others" (*Capital*, Vol. I, p. 414). Second, he states, "the constant tendency of capital is to force the cost of labour back towards this zero…[which] betrays the innermost secret soul of English capitalism" (*Capital*, Vol. I, p. 421). But a labor cost of zero is essentially slavery.

He uses the term four times in *Volume II*, twice in connection with its abolishment. He uses the term three times in *Volume III*, mostly in relation to profit and surplus value. The first is, "the rise in the rate of surplus-value and the fall in the rate of profit are but specific forms through which growing productivity of labour is expressed under capitalism" (*Capital*, Vol. III, p. 169).

Continuing, Marx states

> Since the aim of capital is not to minister to certain wants, but to produce profit …a rift must continually ensue between the limited dimensions of consumption under *capitalism* and a production which forever tends to exceed this immanent barrier. Furthermore, *capital consists of commodities*, and therefore over-production of capital implies over-production of commodities.
>
> (*Capital*, Vol. III, p. 180, emphasis added)

Rather than "capitalism," Marx prefers to use the term "capitalist mode of production" or "capitalist production." He uses "capitalist mode of production" 44 times in *Volume I*, 22 times in *Volume II*, and 184 times in

Volume III. A few examples serve to illustrate his use and meaning of the capitalist mode of production. Not surprisingly, much of his exposition of the capitalist mode of production deals with labor vs. machines as reflected in the section entitled *The Strife Between Workman and Machine.*

> The wealth of those societies in which the capitalist mode of production prevails, presents itself as 'an immense accumulation of commodities' ...
>
> (*Capital*, Vol. I, p. 27)

> This point [the simultaneous employment of a large number of wage-labourers] coincides with the birth of capital itself...on the one hand, the capitalist mode of production presents itself to us historically, as a necessary condition to the transformation of the labour-process into a social process ...
>
> (*Capital*, Vol. I, p. 233)

> The production and the circulation of commodities are the general pre-requisites of the capitalist mode of production...
>
> (*Capital*, Vol. I, p. 245)

> ... since machinery is continually seizing upon new fields of production, its temporary effect is really permanent. Hence, the character of independence and estrangement which the capitalist mode of production as a whole gives to the instruments of labour ... is developed by means of machinery ...
>
> (*Capital*, Vol. I, p. 289)

Marx was, of course, wrong that "this point coincides with the birth of capital itself" since capital as a resource of production is anything made, created, manufactured, or produced by humans to be used by humans in producing commodities to produce food (hunting, or planting and harvesting, for example) and clothing and is therefore thousands of years old.

However, Marx is not considering capital merely as a resource of production, but capitalists owning and substituting capital for labor as a means of production and separating capital from labor. While he was imprecise in the use of his language, it is clear that he regarded the Industrial Revolution as the actual birth of capitalism.

> The basis of the production of commodities can admit of production on a large scale in the capitalistic form alone. A certain accumulation of capital, in *the hands of individual producers of commodities*, forms therefore the necessary preliminary of the specifically capitalistic mode of production.
>
> (*Capital*, Vol. I, p. 440)

> With the accumulation of capital, therefore, the specifically capitalistic mode of production develops, and with the capitalist mode of production the accumulation of capital. Both these economic factors bring about … change in the technical composition of capital by which the variable constituent [variable capital, i.e., labor] becomes always smaller and smaller as compared with the constant [physical capital].
>
> (*Capital*, Vol. I, p. 440)

Werner Sombart

Sombart is regarded as responsible for originating the thesis that the system of double-entry bookkeeping, first disseminated by Luca Pacioli in 1494 but invented much earlier, "played an important part in releasing, activating, stimulating or accentuating the 'rationalistic pursuit of unlimited profits,' *an essential element in the capitalistic spirit*" (Yamey, 1964, p. 117, emphasis added). Indeed, "ever since the rise of double-entry bookkeeping in late medieval Italy, the basic contributions of accounting to capitalism have remained constant" (Levy, 2014, p. 174). (Problems caused by the contributions of accounting to capitalism are discussed in Chapter 6.)

Sombart argued that the system of double-entry bookkeeping "was an active catalyst in the economic expansion that occurred in Europe following the close of the Middle Ages…and in the role that it played in *transforming medieval man's attitude toward* economic life" (Winjum, 1971, p. 333, emphasis added). The development of double-entry bookkeeping introduced the capital account into the accounting system (Winjum, 1971).[13] Sombart (2019) attempted to synthesize the economic history of Europe, and emphasized the role and significance of the "spirit of capitalism," later adopted by Max Weber, and how the spirit of capitalism and double-entry bookkeeping influenced the evolution of modern capitalism (Winjum, 1971).

> (1) Double entry contributed to a *new attitude toward economic life* … The goals of the enterprise could be placed in a specific form and the *concept of capital* was made possible. (2) This new spirit of acquisition was aided and propelled by the refinement of economic calculations [which] made it possible for the entrepreneur to pursue profits rationally …
>
> (Winjum, 1971, pp. 335–336, emphases added)

Sangster (2016) presents evidence and a persuasive argument that double-entry bookkeeping was first used by bankers in the early thirteenth century in Florence. Be that as it may, whether the origin of double-entry bookkeeping is found in medieval bankers or merchants is not dispositive of its role in the development of capitalism since neither bankers nor merchants are in any sense capitalists either now or historically. While as an historical note it is important for understanding the history of accounting, and especially double-entry bookkeeping, to understand how, when, where, and why double-entry bookkeeping originated, the important issue is its use to separate personal wealth from business profit and capital, and to separate business capital from personal wealth. Double-entry bookkeeping was imported centuries later into capitalist development as Pacioli's treatise on its use was proliferated by the invention of the printing press invented a short time prior to the time Pacioli's treatise was written.

Sangster et al. (2018) studied how profit was determined in medieval times. The double-entry method was used in account books, although not in the form we know today, between 1383 and 1386 by an international merchant, Francesco Datini, a century prior to Pacioli's tome. Profit or loss was calculated on each transaction and subsequently consolidated in an overall profit or loss. This reveals at least two things.

First, notwithstanding church teachings to the contrary, profit was pursued by merchants long before the advent of capitalism and the capitalist spirit. Second, profit was calculated prior to the advent of capitalism, albeit perhaps not rationally.

Max Weber

Weber is probably best known for his 1904 *The Protestant Ethic and the Spirit of Capitalism* (Collins, 1980). For Sombart, capitalism developed primarily as a result of capital accounting with double-entry bookkeeping. For Weber, who borrowed from Sombart the importance of double-entry bookkeeping as well as the "spirit of capitalism" (discussed below), the development of the spirit of capitalism was more the result of the Protestant Reformation, especially Calvinism, than of double-entry bookkeeping (Collins, 1980). In other words, both Weber and Sombart agree that the development of double-entry bookkeeping was an essential component of the emergence of capitalism but differ over how essential was its role. Furthermore, Weber emphasized much more heavily than Sombart the meaning and importance of the spirit of capitalism in the rational pursuit of profit.

Weber (1978) describes capital accounting as

> the valuation and verification of opportunities for profit…by means of a valuation of the total assets (goods and money) of the enterprise at the beginning of a profitmaking venture, and the comparison of this with a similar valuation of the assets still present and newly acquired at the end of the process ….
>
> (p. 91)

The means of profit-making "are those goods and other economic advantages which are used in the interests of economic profit-making" (p. 91). It must be understood that there is an implicit assumption that the difference in the value between beginning balance and ending balance is the result of transactions. The difference in value could, for example, be the result of inflation with no transactions taking place.

Weber explains the necessity of separating the business entity from the individual owner of the entity for the development of capitalism, which is of course only possible with the invention of the capital account. While the pursuit of profit is rational,

> The tendency to separate the sphere of private affairs from the business is thus not fortuitous. It is a consequence of the fact that, from the point of view of business interest, the interest in maintaining *the private wealth of the owner* [of the business] is often irrational.
>
> (p. 98, emphasis added)

But Weber clarifies this distinction.

> The sharp distinction between the budgetary unit (the household) and the profit-making enterprise *should also be clearly brought out in the terminology* [emphasis added]. The purchase of securities on the part of a private investor who wishes to consume the proceeds is not a "capital-investment," but a "*wealth*-investment ..." A money loan made ... to a consumer and one to an entrepreneur for business purposes are quite different ... The bank is investing capital [cash] and the entrepreneur is borrowing capital [cash]...
>
> (p. 99, emphases in original)

> The factory today is a category of the capitalistic economy. Hence in the present discussion the concept "factory" will be confined to a type of establishment which is at least potentially under the control of a profit-making firm with fixed capital...with a high degree of mechanization of the work process by the use of mechanical power and machinery...the concept "factory" will ... be limited to organized workshops where the material means of production are fully appropriated by *an owner* ...
>
> (p. 135, emphasis added)

Capitalism is not just a system for means of production using capital resources. "Capitalism is a concept that comes from the social sciences, *used to refer to a certain perceived way of thinking in an economic system* ... It is not a concept that originated in the world of business, as accounting did" (Chiapello, 2007, p. 276, emphasis added). Economic historian T.S. Ashton reminds us that the changes from a feudal system to a capitalist system were not industrial only; they were also social and intellectual (Ashton, 1968) as firmly established by Weber.

Weber and Marx both agree that

> Mechanization dominates the capitalist mode of production. There is set in motion the constant impetus towards technological modification which becomes the hallmark of capitalism. The development of increasingly more complicated and expensive machinery is a primary factor in the centralisation of the capitalist economy upon which Marx lays so much stress …
>
> (Giddens, 1971, p. 34)

Regardless of its critics, Weber's thesis is still the only comprehensive theory of the origins of capitalism because it accounts for most, if not all, institutional and individual motivational conditions for world-transforming capitalism (Collins, 1980).

> The enduring legacy of Weber's scholarship is perhaps not so much the Protestant ethic thesis, but the view that mechanisms motivating and facilitating *today's capitalism* are rooted not in the materialistic domain of incremental capital accumulation, but in the realm of *institutional structures.*
>
> (Nee & Swedberg, 2007, p. 5, emphasis added)

Others

Emile Durkheim, Basil Yamey, Richard Tawney and, more recently, Immanuel Wallerstein and Jonathan Levy, Karl Polanyi, among others, contributed significantly to the discourse on capitalism. However, they, as their predecessors, although otherwise very insightful, missed the mark and merely followed the beaten path of accepting capitalism as an established social and economic fact.

Emile Durkheim

Durkheim's contribution to attempting to understand capitalism was much narrower than Marx, Sombart, or Weber. Durkheim focused mostly on the division of labor within capitalist societies with his 1893 *The Division of Labor in Society*, considered the most important of his works with respect to the economy and society. He does acknowledge that the division of labor is not, as of the date of his writing, a recent phenomenon, but its importance was not socially recognized until the end of the eighteenth century.

It is doubtful anyone would argue against the importance of the division of labor in any society or economic system. But the division of labor is irrelevant when considering capitalism. The division of labor is not the defining characteristic of capitalism. Nor does capitalism exist as a result of the division of labor. Free labor is a characteristic of the capitalist mode of production, but a division of labor existed in pre-capitalist society and still exists in non-capitalist societies (Sée, 1928).

Durkheim notes that the tendency of industry is to advance to more powerful machines and great concentration of capital resulting in an extreme division of labor. But this is true regardless of the economic system be it capitalism, socialism, or Marxism.

Since the resources of production are land, labor, and capital, the division of labor as a resource of production is no different than the division of capital as a resource of production—steam powered machines, electric powered machines, computers. Capital is capital regardless of how it is divided. Likewise, labor is labor, i.e., humans, regardless of how it is classified, blue collar or white collar (or what accountants calls direct labor and indirect labor), or slaves. The division of labor merely classifies labor according to the functions performed. Different divisions of labor do not transform labor, or any division within labor, into something other than labor.

The division of labor within labor adds nothing to our understanding of the meaning or evolution of capitalism.

Basil Yamey

Yamey (1949) rejected the thesis that double-entry bookkeeping was a catalyst for the rise and progress of capitalism. Yamey found that there was little evidence that many merchants used double-entry bookkeeping to keep track of their capital and profits. Accounting practices at the time do not suggest the comparison of profits and capital, or the separation of the owner and the enterprise. While Yamey agrees that double-entry bookkeeping could contribute toward the systemization of business life, he concludes that the role of systematic bookkeeping in the development of capitalism is limited.

Assuming Yamey's evidence and argument are historically accurate, both are off point. Merchants, while they use capital, were not, and are not, *bourgeois* capitalists. That merchants' use of double-entry bookkeeping may have been limited is not an argument that double-entry bookkeeping was not a significant factor in the development of capitalism. It was the *bourgeois* capitalists' adoption of double-entry bookkeeping, separating individual wealth from business capital that, together with Calvinist doctrine, altered the attitude of both *bourgeois* capitalists and labor that enabled the spirit of capitalism to take root and grow.

Richard Tawney

Tawney (1926) regarded England as the most important arena during the sixteenth and seventeenth centuries where the transformation of society from a religious explanation to a naturalistic explanation, i.e., the secularization of social and economic philosophy, was the earliest, swiftest, and most complete. Even though it was a secularization of social and economic philosophy, such a transformation would have laid the groundwork for the coming Industrial Revolution and the spirit of capitalism where, contrary to prior church teachings, the rational pursuit of profit was sanctioned by the Calvinistic branch of the Reformation.

Tawney posits that

> if capitalism means the direction of industry by the owners of capital for their own pecuniary gain, and the social relations which established themselves between [the owners of capital] and the wage-earning proletariat whom they control, then capitalism had existed on a grand scale in medieval Italy and medieval Flanders. If by capitalist sprit is meant the temper which is prepared to sacrifice all moral scruples in the pursuit of profit, it had been only too familiar to the saints and sages of the Middle Ages...It was predominantly Catholic cities which were commercial capitals of Europe, and Catholic bankers who were its leading financiers.
>
> (p. 93)

Yet this is not entirely accurate since there was no free wage-earning proletariat until the Industrial Revolution was well under way. Nor was there a rational calculation of profit until the invention of double-entry bookkeeping and the capital account. To be sure there had been capital, both financial and productive, as well as a pursuit of profit for centuries. However, the mere existence of financial and productive capital and the pursuit of profit do not translate into the capitalist mode of production.

As perceptive as is Tawney's work, he neglects to consider the thread that ties together financial capital and productive capital, owners of financial capital and productive capital, and the spirit of capitalism. Tawney avoids discussing the role of double-entry bookkeeping and the capital account, focusing rather on the relationship of the Christian religion and capitalism, comparing and contrasting Catholicism with that of the Reformers, Luther, Calvin, and the Church of England, with respect to their economic teachings. While Luther was "convinced that serfdom was the necessary foundation of society" (p. 102), it was Calvinism that possessed a comparatively novel and important characteristic in that its social ethic was built on the assumption of advanced economic organization which differed from Catholicism, Lutheranism, and the Church of England. Capital, credit, banking, and large-scale commerce and finance were a necessary part of practical and business facts of life, thus conferring a previously unrecognized legitimacy on the rational pursuit of profit that subsequently became enhanced by the Industrial Revolution and the resulting birth of capitalism. Calvinism was

> designed to liberate economic energies, and to weld a disciplined social force the rising *bourgeoisie*, conscious of the contrast between its own standards and those of a laxer world...the issue which was at stake was not merely convenience or self-interest, but the will of God.
>
> (pp. 119–120)

In Tawney's words, "Calvin did for the *bourgeoisie* ... what Marx did for the proletariat" (p. 120).

Immanuel Wallerstein

Wallerstein (1974), a strong proponent of the system of capitalism as a world system, declares, "There are today no socialist systems in the world-economy any more than there are feudal systems because there is only one world-system. It is a world-economy and it is by definition capitalist in form" (p. 415). Historically, the genesis of the capitalist system is found in late fifteenth century Europe. "The system expanded in space overtime to cover the entire globe by the late 19th century, and it still today covers the entire globe" (p. 19).

Wallerstein (1974) looks at the historical evolution of the capitalist world-economy and analyzes the stages in the evolution of capitalism as a world system. He theorizes that the emergence of the European world-economy between 1450 and 1640 was made possible by an historical conjuncture: the crisis of feudalism, climatic changes, and a geographic and demographic expansion. Following the collapse of the Hapsburg dream of a world-empire in 1557, the capitalist world-economy was an established system that became almost impossible to unbalance. At that time, a stage of industrial rather than of agricultural capitalism begins. Subsequently, industrial production comprised an ever larger percentage of world gross production and world gross surplus. The rise of industrial manufacturing created for the first time a large-scale urban proletariat and free wage-labor.

For Wallerstein, not only capitalism as a global system, but the very existence of capitalism, is an incontrovertible assumption. Yet, as so many others, he does not actually discuss what capitalism is, which would allow readers to judge for themselves whether capitalism is a global system or that capitalism actually exists.

Jonathan Levy

Levy (2014) contests the Sombart/Weber thesis which claims that double-entry bookkeeping made possible the separation of the profit and loss statement from the capital account and points out that scholars and historians of early modern accounting have illustrated that, "it ain't necessarily so."[14] "In practice," says Levy, "well until the nineteenth century, double-entry bookkeeping failed to realize its logic—the separation of the profit and loss statement from the capital" (p. 182).

But that is not quite accurate. First, in the Sombart/Weber thesis it was not that the primary purpose of double-entry bookkeeping to separate profit from capital, but to separate the capital of the business (including profit) from the personal wealth of the owner(s). Even if double-entry bookkeeping was not widely used to separate profit from capital, it made possible the separation of personal wealth from the capital of the business via the capital account and contributed significantly to the conception of capital and the change in attitude toward the pursuit of profit and the measurement of profit.

Second, Levy contends that, "double-entry bookkeeping…emerged from the complex forms of partnership and debt that constituted merchant capital in late medieval Italian city-states—which created the need for new forms of accountability" (p. 178). (See Chapter 2 for a discussion of merchant capital.) Accountability naturally pertains to profit and the distribution of profit. But, while it is indisputable that Italian merchants used double-entry bookkeeping in order to distribute profits to the partners, Sangster et al. (2014) established that double-entry bookkeeping actually originated with Italian banks, which was then subsequently incorporated into merchant bookkeeping. (It should be noted again that banks are not capitalists since they produce nothing although they facilitate obtaining financial capital by providing loans.) The method of double-entry bookkeeping used by bankers was subsequently adopted by merchants and then by capitalists over centuries.

Karl Polanyi

Polanyi (2001) suggests that it was the merchants of the eighteenth century who fostered the factory system through the introduction of elaborate machines and factories that required specialization and continued long-term investment, which in turn intensified specialization. Capitalism required the use of double-entry bookkeeping. The merchant evolved into the industrial capitalist along with the use of double-entry bookkeeping. Industrial production requires a continuous supply of factors of production, which inexplicably, and with no explanation, Polanyi considers to be "land, labor, and *money* (emphasis added),"[15] thereby not only invalidating Marx's $M \rightarrow C \rightarrow M \rightarrow C$ cycle but the factors of production themselves. It has already been shown that money is not a factor of production. Money is not even financial capital unless it is intended to be used to acquire productive capital.

One Other

There are, of course, many others too numerous to include here who have advanced theories of capitalism, including its origins, its "types," "forms," or "varieties," its characteristics, and its current significance. But time and space preclude the inclusion of other writers' concepts and theories of capitalism. However, one additional author does deserve honorary mention here as a courtesy, not because he adds anything to an understanding of capitalism, but because of his total disregard for the meaning of capitalism—Milton Friedman. One of Friedman's more influential works, *Capitalism and Freedom*, first published in 1962, actually had almost nothing to say about capitalism in spite of the title. Rather, it is merely an apologetic for a system that he merely assumes to exist and relates it to freedom (undefined).

Friedman presents a series of essays to explain his view of such things as the relationship between economic freedom and political freedom, the role of government in a free society, and the distribution of income. Friedman is essentially equating capitalism to economic freedom and free markets, as well as to political freedom, extolling the virtues of economic freedom and free markets as corollaries to capitalism. Whether there is any validity to his views regarding the relationship between government and freedom and capitalism is beyond the point. The point is that nowhere does he relate capitalism to capital, capitalists, or the ownership of the means of production.

Like those who both preceded and followed him, Friedman implicitly assumes not only that capitalism exists, but everyone knows it exists. The existence of capitalism is taken for granted; a premise taken as a given; an axiom that needs no proof.

Types, Forms, Varieties, and Models of Capitalism

There are several varieties of capitalism (Walker, 2010, p. 137). Except there aren't. There are different forms of capitalism in different countries (Streek, 2011; Whitley, 1999). Except there aren't. There are multiple varieties of capitalism (Hall & Soskice, 2001). Except there aren't.

Huber (2020, 2021) provides a comprehensive, but not exhaustive, list of "types" of capitalism labeled as capitalism that are referred to in the literature. But that is all they are. Labels. Labels without conceptual substance or validity. They are not really types or varieties of capitalism. There is only one "type" of capitalism—capitalism. No adjective is needed. Nevertheless, we must consider other "types" of capitalism in order to understand why there are no types.

In Hall and Soskice's (2001) *Varieties of Capitalism: The Institutional Foundations of Comparative Advantage*, there are 14 chapters in three parts that include discussions of labor politics, monetary policy, welfare state, social policy patterns of the labor market in Britain and Germany, politics of decentralized cooperation in Germany and France, coordination and restructuring in French industry, corporate governance in Germany and the UK, macro varieties of capitalism and strategic management in European airlines, and national varieties of standardization. But nowhere do any of the authors assembled by Hall and Soskice actually discuss capitalism.

Zukin and DiMaggio's (1990) *Structures of Capital: The Social Organization of the Economy* includes 15 chapters divided into five parts: theory building in sociology, forms of organization, finance capital, capitalist states, and entrepreneurship. Together they cover game theory, economic theories of organization, bureaucracies, control of corporations, financial hegemony, business and politics in the U.S. and the U.K., political choice and the logics of capital, social wage-labor expansion, American management, technical autonomy in British plants, and immigration. Yet, for all this, there is not actually anything about capital, capitalists, or capitalism. There is nothing about actual structures of capital, either financial capital or the resource of production. As with Hall and Soskice, no authors actually discuss capitalism.

Nee and Swedberg's (2005) *The Economic Sociology of Capitalism* collected works from 16 authors covering such things as the economic sociology of capitalism; capitalism and economic growth; the modernity of postindustrial capitalism; venture capital and modern capitalism; circuits within capitalism; brain circulation and capitalist dynamics; the globalization of stock markets and the convergence of corporate governance; and comparing tax regimes in advanced capitalist countries. Their 2007 *On Capitalism* collection includes works on anticultural capitalism; the spirit of American capitalism; income inequality; political capitalism; international financial institutions; corruption; spiritual capital; political economy and religion in Max Weber's spirit of capitalism; dynamics of belief; analytical individualism; and public intervention in promoting growth. Yet we are again left with the question, what is capitalism and where is the evidence that it still exists?

Whether it is the literature contained in the works of Hall and Soskice, Zukin and DiMaggio, or Nee and Swedberg, many of their collections are accompanied by elaborate tables, graphs, and charts (and some not so elaborate) but nevertheless suffer from the same absence regarding what capitalism is. To a person, none engage in any explanation of what capitalism is or any argument that capitalism exists. Capitalism is merely accepted as an established, indisputable fact.

There is a saying that if something looks like a duck, quacks like a duck, and walks like a duck, then it must be a duck. In this case, it can be said that it does not look like a duck, quack like a duck, or walk like a duck, but it is nevertheless a duck. That is, even though it does not look like capitalism, quack like capitalism, or walk like capitalism, economists, sociologists, anthropologists, and others still call it capitalism. While a rose by any other name would smell as sweet, calling a tulip a rose does not make it a rose.

Types of Capitalism

Some types of capitalism referred to in the literature roughly correspond to types of capital. But there are actually no "types" of capitalism, contrary to what other authors suggest. For example, Chandler (1984) states

> In the late nineteenth and early twentieth centuries, a *new type of capitalism* emerged. It differed from traditional *personal capitalism* in that basic decisions concerning the production and distribution of goods and services were made by … managers who had little or *no equity ownership in the enterprises they operated.*
>
> (p. 473, emphases added)

But Chandler's "new type of capitalism" that differed from "traditional *personal capitalism*" is not capitalism. There can be no capitalism without capitalists owning the means of production.

Neal (2016) asks, "What are the salient features of modern capitalism?" He identifies four elements common to all variants of capitalism: private property, enforceable contracts, markets with responsive prices (presumably "free markets"), and supportive governments. He recognizes that capital as a resource of production is embodied in each of the four elements and goes on to explain that capital must be long-lived (what in accounting is referred to as "long-term assets") and must be productive (p. 2). By definition that excludes financial capital (money) since financial capital is not a long-lived asset and is not productive (see Chapter 2).

Neal notes that scholarly literature has described several types of capitalism, including agrarian capitalism, industrial capitalism, financial capitalism, monopoly capitalism, state capitalism, and crony capitalism. One important type of capitalism omitted by Neal is welfare capitalism that Hicks and Kenworthy (2003) and Esping-Andersen (1990) categorize as socialist (social democratic), liberal (residual), and conservative (corporatist). Another type of capitalism that Neal omits is corporate capitalism (Smith, 1965). Amin (2013) refers to "contemporary capitalism," "historic capitalism," and "abstract capitalism." Chandler (1984) refers to personal capitalism, family capitalism, group enterprise capitalism, and managerial capitalism. Yet, while listing the types described in the literature, Chandler does not explain how any of the types are actually capitalism.

Weber (1978) refers to political capitalism, trade capitalism, rational capitalism, market capitalism, industrial capitalism, colonial capitalism, early, ancient, modern, slave capitalism, bourgeois capitalism, mercantilistic or mercantile capitalism, imperialist capitalism, and patrimonial capitalism. Mielants (2000) accepts the proposition that "*forms of capitalism*—commercial, industrial, banking—already existed in thirteenth century Florence" (p. 250, emphasis added). Whatever may be said about commercial or industrial capitalism, there can be no such thing as banking capitalism. Banks are merely financial intermediaries channeling money from savings to producers of commodities, whether capitalists or corporations.

Relevant to the purposes of this book and consistent with financial (money) capital and industrial (physical) capital as a resource of production are financial capitalism and industrial capitalism. In spite of the various labels, there is only one type of capitalism. While "capitalism" has acquired many adjectives on its journey to the present, thus requiring frequent clarification in this book, those adjectives serve only to detract from a full understanding of capitalism as it is found in history, sociology, corporate law, economics, finance, and accounting.

Financial Capitalism

Financial capitalism is a function of financial capital. But does financial capitalism actually exist? Is financial capitalism actually a social and economic system constructed on the private ownership of the means of production? Obviously not.

Financial capital is obviously important because it is used to acquire productive capital. But just because financial capital is important, it should not be confused with capital.

As discussed in Chapter 7, securities laws are concerned with financial capital, the funds that corporations raise when they issue securities to the public in an IPO. The entire intent of the securities laws is to keep the capital markets functioning efficiently, thus reflecting the importance of financial capital. However, financial capital is just money, albeit money that is intended to be used to acquire productive capital, and money is not a resource of production as is capital. Thus, financial capitalism has nothing to do with capitalism or the means of production.

Michie (2014) considers financial capitalism as the dominant economic system in the nineteenth century. "What made securities central to financial capitalism was the growing importance of joint-stock companies … It was in the nineteenth century that joint-stock companies began go play a central role in economic activity" (p. 235), which Marx was well aware of, when in the United States corporations were created by mere registration, rather than government (or royal) charter.

Importantly, "In financial capitalism the investment became center stage, with everything directed towards maximizing the returns obtained from the security" (Michie, 2014, p. 236). But the return from the security is not directly correlated to the performance of the company, but to the movement of the price of the security in the market according to the Financial Asset Pricing Model.[16] Thus, "… financial capitalism increasingly came to characterize capitalism itself, rather than referring simply to the use of [money] capital provided by the owners of a business or borrowed from their immediate circle of family, friends, and business associates" (p. 261).

> "Financialization" unleashed a new pattern of economic development, as *Western capitalism* sought to transcend the industrial crisis of the 1970s through financial profit making…But the shift entailed not only a purging of fixed capital …with a subsequent reallocation of capital to financial activity. It also entailed an utterly *"different definition of profit."* When the profit rate exhibited a tendency to decline, in other words, capitalists redefined what profit was.
>
> (Levy, 2014, p. 173, emphases added)

Financial capitalism is not capitalism regardless of its label. Capitalism is the use of the capital resource of production and the social construct built on the private ownership of the capital resource of production by *bourgeois* capitalists who are individual capitalist entrepreneurs. Financial capital is not a resource of production. It produces nothing. Labor cannot use financial capital to produce anything.

Productive/Industrial Capitalism

Just as financial capitalism is a function of financial capital, productive (industrial) capitalism is a function of productive (industrial) capital; i.e. capital resources of production. But of course, industrial capitalism needs no adjective. It is just "capitalism."

Productive capital has existed for thousands of years, beginning with simple stone tools. Then, with the advent of factories and other technological inventions, mere productive capital was transformed into industrial capital by *bourgeois* capitalists replacing labor with machines, and thus transformed into industrial capitalism. Industrial capitalism is the heart and soul of Marx's capitalistic mode of production, with the United States as the penultimate standard of the capitalist spirit although it first appeared in England.

Industrial enterprise requires, among other things, an organization consisting of free wage-labor (those who sell their labor to the highest bidder) and which depends upon the possibility of correct profit-making calculations. Industrial capitalism, i.e., capitalism, requires "the continuity, trustworthiness and objectivity of the legal order, and on the rational, predictable functioning of legal and administrative agencies" (Weber, 1978, p. 1095); in other words, industrial capitalism requires a concomitant supporting legal and social structure.

Industrial or productive capitalism, or just "capitalism," is comprised first and foremost of physical capital in the form of machines in factories as the means of production replacing labor. Second, industrial capitalism requires private ownership of capital by *bourgeois* capitalists and the use of wage-labor. Third, related to the second, it requires that the ownership of the financial capital be the same as the owners of capital in order for them to acquire productive capital.

Corporate Capitalism

"Corporate capitalism" has become a popular term in the literature. It is included here only for the purpose of proving there is no such thing as corporate capitalism.

Joint-stock companies as the precursor of the corporation known today were well known and Marx admits that he is aware not only of the relationship of corporations to the capitalist mode of production, but also of the nature and role of stock exchanges.

> *The stock-company business*, which *represents the abolition of capitalist private industry* on the basis of the capitalist system itself *and destroys private industry* as it expands and invades new spheres of production ... Since property here exists in the form of stock, its movement and transfer become purely a result of gambling on the stock exchange, where the little fish are swallowed by the sharks and the lambs by the stock-exchange wolves. There is antagonism against the old form in the stock companies, in which social means of production appear as private property; but the conversion to the form of stock still remains ensnared in the trammels of *capitalism*; hence, instead of overcoming the antithesis between the character of wealth as social and as private wealth, *the stock companies merely develop it in a new form.*
>
> (*Capital*, Vol. III, p. 317, emphases added)

Unfortunately, Marx stops short of following his awareness that corporations represent the abolition of capitalist private industry and destroy private industry to its obvious and logical conclusion—the destruction and abolition of capitalism. His failure thus undermines his entire thesis.

The joint-stock company did not develop capitalism in a new form. There can be no new form. There has never been a new form since its origin. While it is true that "property here exists in the form of stock," the property that is owned by shareowners is just that—shares—not the means of production (see Chapter 5).

"Corporate capitalism" as developed in the United States encompassed the "private ownership of the means of production, increased participation of the state in the political economy, centralization of the major institutions, imperialism, efficiency, and functionalism," and was a transition from traditional *laissez-faire* between 1870 and 1900 (Smith, 1965, p. 401). But increased participation of the state in the political economy, centralization of the major institutions, imperialism, efficiency, and functionalism can be, and in fact has been, done without corporations whose shares are on a public exchange, just not on as large a scale.

Perrow (2002) traces the beginning of corporate capitalism back to 1837 when Connecticut became the first state to allow incorporation by registration rather than by special charter (an important step in the march of capitalism toward extinction). Johnson (2010), on the other hand, suggests the foundations of corporate capitalism are found in nineteenth-century Britain.

According to Smith (1965), "corporate capitalism" was the progeny of American ideological sociologists. Charter members and presidents of the American Sociological Association were "dedicated capitalists in their ideologies" who "recommended capitalism, but the corporate form" (p. 402). Noteworthy is Smith's assessment that,

> The impending and imminent threats to the essential nature of the capitalist system served as a very strong impetus to the development of

> sociology. Sociology as part of the general movement endeavoring to reform and maintain capitalism provided an ideological justification for the corporate form of capitalism.
>
> (p. 415)

Once the term "corporate capitalism" was popularized, it was assumed that corporate capitalism actually exists. Like capitalism itself, corporate capitalism was (and is) accepted as a given, with no regard to corporate law or property law, propagated through the decades with no critical analysis of the legitimacy of the underlying assumptions. However, there are several insurmountable problems inherent in the theory of corporate capitalism.

The first and most important problem is that there is no such thing as "corporate capitalism." In order for there to be "corporate capitalism," there must be "corporate capitalists" which has no meaning. It would transform corporations into capitalists, and corporate capitalists simply do not exist. "Corporate capitalism" would make corporate capitalism a function of corporate capital, which also has no meaning.

A second problem which infects almost every work addressing corporation and shareowner relationships, explained more fully in Chapter 5, is the mistaken assumption that owners of the shares of a corporation own the corporation, extending even into the more egregiously mistaken assumptions that shareowners own the assets of the corporation (including either as beneficial owners or residual owners), and directors are agents of shareowners. (See *Corporate Law and the Theory of the Firm: Reconstructing Corporations, Shareholders, Directors, Owners, and Investors*.)

Regardless whether the roots of corporate capitalism are found in Britain or the U.S., the key to corporate capitalism is what Johnson calls "companification," which is "the substitution of an impersonal corporate legal entity for the sole proprietorship or partnership [which] has long been seen by economic analysts and commentators as *the* defining element of modern capitalism" (p. 106, emphasis in original). While it is true that impersonal corporate legal entities have been substituted for the sole proprietorship or partnership capitalist entrepreneur, the substitution actually destroyed *bourgeois* capitalists and capitalism as explained in Chapter 8. All who subscribe to the notion of corporate capitalism have in common is their substitution of *bourgeois* capitalist entrepreneurs with corporations. But if we attempt to substitute the meaning of *bourgeois* capitalist entrepreneurs with corporations, we are confronted with the Humpty Dumpty problem.[17]

Capitalism is a social and economic system consisting of capital as the means of production and the ownership of capital by individual (or partner) *bourgeois* capitalist entrepreneurs, as opposed to, e.g., Marxism where capital is owned by "the people" (or government). There simply is no such thing as "corporate capitalism" which Marx himself concedes: "To be a capitalist, is to have not only a *purely personal*, but a social status in production" (*Manifesto*, p. 23).

Mercantile Capitalism

Mercantile capitalism, or merchant capitalism, may be the most important "type" of capitalism because it is considered by many as a precursor of capitalism. While production obviously took place under a mercantilist economy, as it did in any economic system throughout history, production cannot be accomplished using "merchant capital" under mercantile capitalism the way that production is accomplished using capital under capitalism. Under mercantile capitalism, capital did not replace labor the way capital replaced labor during and following the Industrial Revolution. If labor is not replaced by capital, it is not capitalism regardless of the adjective used to describe it. Mercantile capitalism did not exist anymore than financial capitalism or corporate capitalism exist. However, it must be included in our examination of capitalism because it is so commonly accepted as legitimate.

Marx had somewhat to say about merchant capitalism, merchant capitalists, and merchant capital. Marx assumes "the entire transaction ... takes place between two kinds of capitalists—the money-capitalist and the industrial or merchant capitalist" (*Capital*, Vol. III, p. 239) which on its face appears to recognize two kinds of capitalists in contradistinction to his numerous other references to capitalists as owners of the means of production (industrial capitalist) who bought free wage-labor. Industrial capitalists cannot be the same as merchant capitalists because, being merchants, merchant capitalists do not own the means of production.

Marx in fact later, in an apparent contradiction, states

> we have become acquainted with a rate of profit only for merchant capital. For only merchant and usurers' capital had existed up to that time; industrial capital was yet to be developed. Production was still predominantly in the hands of workers owning their own means of production, whose work therefore yielded no surplus-value to any capital.
>
> (*Capital*, Vol. III, p. 642)

Marx differentiates merchant capital from industrial capital and what merchants do, or don't do: "*merchant's capital* (the first form of which is always money, since the merchant as such does not create any 'product' or 'commodity') ..." (*Capital*, Vol. II, p. 257, emphasis in original). Furthermore, while merchants owned some productive capital, the capital owned by the merchants did not replace labor as it did under a capitalist mode of production, as seen by the fact that mercantile capitalists and the mercantile "mode of production" did not raise the wrath of Marx as did *bourgeois* capitalists and the capitalist mode of production. The labor hired by merchants mostly owned their own capital (i.e., instruments of production).

To say that the transition to capitalism occurred unevenly over a relatively long period of time in different regions, and that agrarian feudalism, mercantilism, and capitalism co-existed for at least part of that time (at least two centuries according to Mielants (2000)) is to state the obvious. Mielants judiciously asks, "who can really tell for sure when one system profoundly takes over (incorporates) the other one(s) at a specific moment in time?" (p. 241). After all, it is not as if capitalism occurred on June 17, 1508 at 03:00 GMT in England. But just because the time and place of the transition to capitalism cannot be pinpointed with any degree of accuracy, or the stages cannot be delineated with precision, does not mean there was no transition or that there were no stages. To say there was a transition, whether discrete stages or a continuous process, is in fact the whole point. That transition was not direct and could not possibly have been direct. It was a convergence of a "series of historical accidents" over a period of time—unplanned, undirected, unguided.

Prior to the eighteenth century, "merchant capitalism" and other precapitalist systems were the main focus. The capitalist mode of production did not become dominant until the latter part of the eighteenth century (Lis & Soly, 1997).

According to Van Zanden (1993), "merchant capitalism" designates "the phase in the development of capitalism in which the merchant-entrepreneur dominated. The entrepreneur combined commercial activities with intervention in the production process, and thus in labor relations." However, others argue that "merchants in general and wholesalers in particular did their best to avoid production until the mid-eighteenth century" (Lis & Soly, 1997). While mercantilism is a system, "mercantile capitalism" is not. While there are (or rather were) mercantilists, there are not (were not) mercantile capitalists regardless of the label. To combine "mercantile" and "capitalist" is the equivalent of mixing oil and water. They are both held in one container, but do not mix.

Other questions arise as to the meaning of "merchant capitalism." Why put "merchant" before "capital" or "capitalist?" Does merchant capital differ from productive capital, or even financial capital? Do merchant capitalists differ from *bourgeois* capitalists? If there is a difference, then there is no merchant capital or merchant capitalist. To say "merchant capitalists" is merely to say "merchants who own capital," which really does not say anything. Capital is always owned by someone (or something, like the state, or a corporation). Capital owned by merchants is still capital. The difference lies not only in who owns the capital but how it is used. Capital owned by merchants (or "merchant capitalists") did not replace labor. Capital owned by *bourgeois* capitalists did replace labor, a fundamental requirement for the existence of capitalism.

In spite of all the debate regarding merchant capitalism, unlike with capitalism itself, "no theoretical explanation is available for the structure and dynamics of merchant capitalism" (Lis & Soly, 1977).

Forms, Varieties, and Models of Capitalism

Radice (2000) alleges that models of capitalism "can *focus narrowly on the production and exchange of goods and services*, or extend to include any and all aspects of society; they can be sectoral or economy-wide; they can be local, national, regional or global" (p. 729, emphasis added). But, of course, the production and exchange of services is not capitalism since the production and exchange of services does not contemplate capital or its ownership.

Radice further alleges that institutional variations in capitalism can be considered through the lens of historical political economy because "capitalism has *always* been a global system..." (p. 725). Yet, while capitalism can be considered through the lens of historical political economy, Radice offers no explanation of how this gives rise to variations in capitalism.

The regimes of capital, and therefore of capitalism, present a wide variety of forms (Heilbroner, 1985). "That capitalist economies might take diverse forms has been long recognised by some scholars" (Crouch, 2005, p. 439). There are models of European capitalism (market models, managed models, and state models), Japanese models, German, American (or Anglo-American), French, Dutch, Swiss, and Scandinavian, among others. The diversity of forms, or approaches, are different but all see some form of capitalism superseding earlier forms (Crouch, 2005). Heilbroner speaks of European and Japanese capitalism.

Just as Hicks and Kenworthy (2003) and Esping-Andersen (1990) suggest there are varieties or worlds of "welfare capitalism," Streek (2011) proposes there are "varieties of capitalism" and "varieties of approaches" to capitalism. But then, in his explanation of the varieties of capitalism, he substitutes "four models of capitalist variety" which is not the same. Streek's four models of capitalist variety are (1) social embeddedness; (2) the power resource model; (3) the historical-institutionalist model; and (4) the nationalist-functionalist model.

Streek characterizes the social embeddedness of capitalist variety as, "the persistence of capitalist diversity in societies' cultural traditions and formal and informal social structures or networks" (p. 427). The power resource model of capitalist variety is politically based rather than culturally or social-structurally based. The historical-institutionalist model of capitalist variety emphasizes the role of inherited institutions as both constraints and opportunities for economic action. Finally, Streek explains the rationalist-functionalist model of capitalist variety as the outcome of a search for economic advantage.

But not surprisingly, none of the models of capitalist variety is related to *bourgeois* capitalists or the private ownership of the capital resource of production. Furthermore, Streek fails to relate any "models of capitalists variety" to any of the "varieties of capitalism." He fails to specify how any model of capitalists corresponds to any variety of capitalism. Finally, he fails to give any consideration to the ownership of capital.

In 2001, Peter Hall and David Soskice edited a volume entitled *Varieties of Capitalism: The Institutional Foundations of Comparative Advantage*. Yet, rather than attempting to explain what capitalism is (or isn't), or to identify or distinguish its characteristics historically or currently, they just assume that it *is*, i.e., that capitalism exists. They then embark on a tangent in which they do not actually discuss capitalism.

Hall and Soskice's collection of papers pertain only to corporations—corporate strategy; corporate governance; neo-corporatism; corporate finance and the financial system; corporate networks; and corporate structures. In other words, in their (and their contributors') framework, capitalism is, for all practical purposes, solely a function of corporations whose shares are traded in the public. Thus, the varieties of capitalism are a function of the varieties of corporations and corporate strategy which vary according to country.

Hall and Soskice explain their "varieties of capitalism" approach to political economy as a terrain of actors who seek to advance their interests in a rational way by interacting with others. The actors may be individuals, firms, producer groups, or government, where "firms" are equated to corporations whose shares are traded in the public. They then explain that a firm-centered political economy regards companies, again equated to corporations whose shares are traded in the public, as crucial actors in a "capitalist economy." Their concept of the firm is "relational;" that is, firms have "core competencies" or "dynamic capabilities" for developing, producing, and distributing goods which depend on the quality of their relationships. Accepting as true that firms have "core competencies" or "dynamic capabilities" for developing, producing, and distributing goods which depend on the quality of their relationships, that has nothing to do with capitalism.

Like Streek's, Hall and Soskice's "varieties of capitalism" falls apart insofar as they attempt to apply "varieties" to "capitalism." While their framework is worthy of application in a corporate strategy field, it is out of place within a context of capitalism. To suggest there are varieties of capitalism simply multiplies the confusion as to what capitalism is and presents a distorted concept of capitalism by ignoring capital, the ownership of capital, and capitalists. A "capitalist economy" is one that depends on *bourgeois* capitalists who own the means of production, i.e., the capital resources of production. Nowhere in their framework are capitalists considered as the foundation of a capitalist economy. The only time they use the term "capitalist" is in "capitalist economy." Furthermore, they never take into account the actual means of production and its ownership.

In addition, there are more egregious "models of capitalism." Bremmer (2011), McNally (2013), and Wang and Rowley (2017) and others use the term "state capitalism" to refer to capitalism in East Asian countries, particularly China, while Livingstone (1976) applies the term "corporate capitalist states," as well as "corporate capitalist," to the United States, Canada, Australia, Western Europe, and Japan.

Bremmer, e.g., defines "state capitalism" as "a form of bureaucratically engineered capitalism… in which the state dominates markets primarily for political gain" (p. 43). There are models of capitalism referred to as state capitalism found in Brazil, Russia, India, and China that maintain government ownership and control of key enterprises and financial institutions (McNally, 2013). "Corporate capitalist states" implies at once that there are "corporate capitalists," and "capitalist states," neither of which can exist without twisting the terms beyond recognition.

But "state capitalism" is an oxymoron. If the state (the government) in an industrialized economy owns the means of production, it is not capitalism. Such a misuse of terms is simply an application of the Humpty Dumpty principle, the equivalent of making words mean what they want them to mean, or calling a tulip a rose.

The Industrial Revolution—The Fulcrum of the Transition to Capitalism

While there were many, the most important events and processes relevant to the consideration of the origin of capitalism are the technological inventions that define the "Industrial Revolution" in Britain and the United States, along with the social transformations accompanying those inventions—free wage-labor (the proletariat), the "invention" of the capital account, and the proliferation of double-entry bookkeeping.

Consider that at one time there was no capitalist mode of production. Then, at some point in time, there was a capitalist mode of production. The inevitable conclusions is that whatever the mode of production was prior to the emergence of the capitalist mode of production, and whenever and wherever the arrival of the capitalist mode of production occurred, there was something that brought about the transition. We can in fact conclude there was a period of transition (which some refer to as stages)—a tipping point or point of no return so to speak—when production in an economy (generally considered to be a nation) became capital intensive vs. labor intensive, when primitive accumulation became capitalist accumulation, and when *bourgeois* capitalists and proletariat were formed, all without planning or guidance. That period of transition encompassed the coalescence of various historically independent yet interdependent events the most important of which are the "invention" of the capital account, the proliferation of double-entry bookkeeping, and, most important, the technological inventions leading to the "Industrial Revolution" in Britain and the United States.[18]

Therefore, to see the Industrial Revolution as the fulcrum of the transition to capitalism, we can engage in a "but for" analysis. In other words, could the capitalist mode of production, i.e., capitalism, *not* have developed "but for" any one particular historical event or process? Can any one historical event or process be identified as a tipping point or point of no return in which society was transformed from a non-capitalist mode of production into a capitalist mode of production? The most persuasive argument favors technological inventions leading to the "Industrial Revolution" in Britain and the United States as the tipping point or point of no return when the balance shifted from agrarian feudalism or mercantilism to capitalism, since all the other events and processes—e.g., banking, double-entry bookkeeping, colonialism and the arrival of Europeans in the Western Hemisphere, etc.—already existed and could have staggered and stumbled ahead historically without the technological inventions that brought about the Industrial Revolution, and without capitalism becoming the dominant mode of production. No other historical event or process could have produced the *bourgeois* capitalist and proletariat classes characteristic of capitalism. It was the Industrial Revolution and the ownership of capital by *bourgeois* capitalists that resulted in the mechanization of the production process that replaced labor.

Capitalism and Accounting, Profit, Labor, the Capital Account, and the Spirit of Capitalism

Capitalism does not exist without capital and the spirit of capitalism. The Soviet Union became heavily industrialized but there was obviously no spirit of capitalism (Allen, 2003). Nor does capitalism exist without profit, in particular the pursuit of profit. The spirit of capitalism is essentially the rational pursuit of profit by *bourgeois* capitalists who own the capital resources of production. However, neither the pursuit of profit nor the use of capital implies the existence of capitalism since both exist without capitalism. Capitalism and profit-seeking may be conjoined but they are not synonymous.

Capitalism, Accounting, and Profit

Accounting has two aspects. One is the recording of transactions known as double-entry bookkeeping addressed here. Double-entry bookkeeping gives rise to a balance sheet where assets equals debt plus equity, and every transaction is recorded twice—once on each side of the balance sheet. (The actual process is irrelevant here.) The second is financial reporting dealt with in Chapter 6.

Aho (2005) argues that double-entry bookkeeping originated in the High Middle Ages (ca. 1,000 CE–1,250 CE). Similarly, Sangster (2016) argues that double-entry bookkeeping was used by bankers in thirteenth century. Double-entry bookkeeping appeared in several Italian cities simultaneously dating from at least 1327 and which spread as the result of Pacioli's (1494) *Summa* and the invention of the printing press.

If Aho and Sangster are correct, double-entry bookkeeping appeared before capitalism and there is no reason to believe that its use would not have continued and expanded without the development of capitalism. It is also possible that capitalism may have developed without double-entry bookkeeping, but without double-entry bookkeeping and the capital account there would not have been an efficient method to keep track of profit or equity and thus the development of capitalism would have been severely retarded. If capitalism and the use of double-entry bookkeeping and the capital account were plotted on a scattergram, there would no doubt be an almost perfect correlation. But as every economist and accountant (and maybe a few lawyers) knows, correlation is not causation. *Bourgeois* capitalists simply adopted double-entry bookkeeping and the capital account which facilitated the rational pursuit of profit and the separation of business assets from personal wealth.

"The history of profit is a history of power" (Levy, 2014). Therefore, since "capitalism refers to the organization of production in terms of a search for the realization of profit for privately owned [productive] capital ..." (Giddens, 1971; Scott, 1979), the history of capital is also a history of power. If the private owners of capital, i.e., *bourgeois* capitalists, seek profit, they seek power.[19] But how does a capitalist know whether she has earned a profit?

Profit can only be calculated scientifically using accounting thus accounting is implicit in Marx's formulation of surplus value. Indeed, "At the core of Marx's mode of production is a calculative mentality" (Bryer, 2000, p. 137). Although he said little about accounting per se, Marx's well-known maxim, "The hand-mill gives you society with the feudal lord; the steam mill, society with the industrial capitalist" establishes that, since industrial capitalists are concerned with profit, double-entry bookkeeping became inseparable from capitalism. That is, "From Marx's perspective, the signature for the social character of capital is double-entry bookkeeping" (Bryer, 2000) because in order to accumulate profit or capital, capitalists must calculate the price of commodities and represent the exchange-value of the commodities in monetary terms in an account. There is no way to rationally calculate profit absent double-entry bookkeeping.

Profit, while existing and pursued apart from capitalists and capitalism, is inexorably linked to capital, and thus the spirit of capitalism, capitalists, and capitalism. But profit in medieval, feudal, and mercantilist periods was not a mere definition as it is today (see Chapter 6). Profit, in general, was the money that consisted of the price of the commodities sold minus the cost of the commodities produced, with some exceptions not relevant here. Money that was used to acquire additional physical capital was, and still is, financial capital, while money used by the owner for personal reasons was not capital in any form, but savings as part of her wealth. Prior to the invention of the capital account profit was simply part of the wealth of the owner(s), as was the capital. After the capital account was invented, profit was part of the money value of the assets of the business that was owned by the individual or partners as measured by the change in their value as the result of transactions, which was part of the owner's (or owners') equity.

> Capital accounting is the valuation and verification of opportunities for profit...by means of a valuation of the total assets (goods and money) of the enterprise at the beginning of a profitmaking venture, and the

> comparison of this with a similar valuation of the assets still present and newly acquired at the end of the process ....
>
> (Weber, 1978, p. 91)

Beams (2008) sees the "*driving force of capitalism is* not production for use or need, or even production for the market as such, but the *accumulation of capital—the making of profit*" (p. 5, emphasis added). Beams is thus equating the making of profit to the accumulation of capital, which was, of course, Marx's contention. But if profit is not money, it is not capital, either financial or productive. Since profit is added to equity, equity is not capital.

Although he does correctly state that "*Money, as capital, is used to purchase the means of production*" (p. 5, emphasis added), Beams' equating the making of profit to the accumulation of capital is troublesome. First, profit does not actually exist. Profit is merely a calculation. While there was a time when profit was money, profit for decades has actually been just a definition—revenue minus the costs of production (land, labor, and capital, operation, and distribution) equals net income, i.e., profit. What constitutes revenue and expenses has been defined since 1973 by the Financial Standards Accounting Board in the U.S. (or the equivalent standard setting body in other countries). The profit is then added to the retained earnings of the corporation. Retained earnings is neither money, nor financial capital, nor productive capital.

Second, combining "the *accumulation of capital—the making of profit*" with "*Money, as capital*" reveals that Beams considers profit to be money and therefore money to be capital, which makes profit capital, which is contrary to Fisher's (1912) celebrated *The Nature of Capital and Income*. But profit is neither money nor financial capital. Financial capital is money intended to be used to acquire productive capital, i.e., the means of production.[20] There is "a palpable difference between the circulation of money as capital, and its circulation as mere money" (*Capital*, Vol. I).

Profit-seeking has been a motivation for engaging in any given industry and type of economy throughout history. There are preindustrial societies where people are just as obsessed with profit and making money as they are in capitalist societies (Granovetter & Swedberg, 2011). But double-entry bookkeeping allowed profit to be put into the specific form of a definite sum of money. It was this abstraction of profit that made the concept of capital possible (Yamey, 1949) because the invention of double-entry bookkeeping was accompanied by the introduction of the "capital account." Although originally used by bankers (Sangster, 2016), double-entry bookkeeping was adopted by individual merchants and partnerships to reflect the "capital" contributed to (invested in) the firm by the owner(s) and to keep track of profit.

> Double-entry bookkeeping, for instance, emerged from the complex forms of partnership and debt that constituted merchant [financial]

> capital in late medieval Italian city-states—which created the need for new forms of accountability ... Double-entry bookkeeping was designed for long-distance maritime trade. A ship went out and months later, if not years, it came back. Upon the event, profits were calculated and distributed to partners, investors, and creditors.
>
> (Levy, 2014, pp. 178–180)

While double-entry bookkeeping was used in long-distance maritime trade, Sangster (2016) finds evidence it was actually designed by bankers prior to that time. Thus, it appears that double-entry bookkeeping and the capital account was later adopted and modified by merchants and maritime traders.

Along with all the other conditions, capitalism was enabled by the capital account since the capital account permitted the separation of personal wealth of the owner(s) of the enterprise from the enterprise assets and allowed the rational calculation of the profit of the enterprise. The profit earned by the enterprise became part of the wealth of the owner(s) even though enterprise profit was separated from the wealth of the owner(s) by the capital account since the capital account itself was the equity of the owner(s) of the enterprise. The profit was retained within the enterprise until the owner(s) withdrew it. Until then, the profit was merely part of the net assets, i.e., the equity, of the enterprise and thus the wealth of the owner.

Connell-Smith (1951) found that in practice double-entry accounting was rarely taken advantage of in its entirety. Furthermore, in spite of what appeared as meticulous entries, accounts may have been infrequently balanced (Carruthers & Espeland, 1991; Coleman, 1963). Critics of Weber and Sombart point to this as evidence that there was no connection between the development of capitalism and accounting (Carruthers & Espeland, 1991). However, that misses the point.

First, one of the consequences of rationality is that symbols of rationality become tools of legitimation even if decoupled from practice. Double-entry bookkeeping and the capital account are symbols of rationality. Double-entry bookkeeping and the capital account legitimized business activities, even if the actual accounts did not conform exactly to the requirements of double-entry bookkeeping and the capital account (Carruthers & Espeland, 1991). Furthermore, whether double-entry accounting was rarely taken advantage of in its entirety, or accounts may have been infrequently balanced, does not mean there was no connection between the development of capitalism and accounting.

While perhaps not a cause of the rise of capitalism, Meyer (1986) and Carruthers and Espeland (1991) see "a causal efficacy to double-entry bookkeeping that served to transform the ways in which business was interpreted and understood, which in turn contributed to the rise of capitalism." To provide an account is to provide a classificatory scheme. It is conceptual, a cognitive device that provides a method to sort and order society. Accounts frame an economic reality in a particular way. That is, it is the classification scheme, and not the numbers or the balances per se, that renders double-entry bookkeeping and the capital account a fundamental characteristic of capitalism.[21]

> In the last resort the factor which produced capitalism is the rational permanent enterprise, rational accounting, rational technology and rational law, but again not these alone. Necessary complementary factors were the rational spirit, the rationalization of the conduct of life in general, and a rationalistic economic ethic.
>
> (Weber, 1981, p. 354)

Conceptually, the accumulation of capital, one of the fundamental principles of Marx's critique of political economy, does not make sense. Capital is not "accumulated." Marx rightly equated money with profit in the M → C → M cycle[22] since profit was historically money, but the money accumulated by the *bourgeois* capitalist's became financial capital used to acquire productive capital. *Bourgeois* capitalists do not accumulate machines. While *bourgeois* capitalists may accumulate profit, they can only acquire machines (capital) using the financial capital obtained at start up plus the profit received by selling commodities.

Levy (2014) cites Justice Edwards' ruling in *United Steel Workers of America v. United States Steel Corporation*: "with a different definition of profit," the "outcome of an accounting analysis could be made to be non-profitability" (p. 175).[23] Unlike the profit of the "Merchants of Venice" and the capitalists that emerged with the Industrial Revolution, where profit for the most part was indeed money, profit today is a definition.

Fisher (1912) is credited with shedding light on the difference between capital and income. But he not only added no small confusion to the concept of capital and capitalism, he destroyed one of the foundational requirements of capitalism. In fact, Fisher does not even mention capitalism, an oddity given that capitalism is dependent on capital and income (profit-seeking).

Fisher defines capital as "a fund, or a stock of wealth" and income as "a flow," the income, or profit that reflects the difference between beginning and ending balances which, like Schrödinger's cat, is both true and false at the same time. First, it is true because capital exists at a point in time, a stock so to speak. But it is false because capital is not wealth. Capital pertains strictly to business enterprises. It is used by labor to produce commodities. Wealth pertains strictly to individuals. Thus, a fundamental requirement of capitalism, that capital is a resource of production, has been destroyed and thus capitalism ceases to exist in a Fisherian framework.

While income may be a flow from the beginning of a specified period of time to the end of that period of time, it is not the difference between the beginning and end that constitutes profit unless there were transactions. There may be a difference between the value at the beginning and end simply because of a change in valuation methods or inflation, neither of which is income.

Fisher, unlike Sombart and Weber, defines the "capital account" as "synonymous with the balance sheet," which is "a *person's* assets and liabilities" (emphasis added), while he defines the "capital balance" as the "difference between assets and liabilities" on a balance sheet, which is nothing other than the net assets, or equity. These are, of course, contradictions. A capital account cannot be a balance sheet. A capital account is the equity account which records the monetary value of the net assets, both financial capital and productive capital. Defining the capital account as a person's assets and liabilities negates the purpose for which the capital account was created—to separate personal wealth from enterprise assets.

That Fisher does not distinguish individual wealth from enterprise assets as do Sombart and Weber is an unfortunate omission since, while money is a part of wealth it is not financial capital if it is not intended to be used to acquire physical capital resources of production by an enterprise. More important, however, is that by not distinguishing individual wealth from enterprise capital he annihilates a key component of capitalism and thus capitalism itself. While both businesses, regardless of the form, and individuals have balance sheets, the balance sheet of individuals has nothing to do with capital which is only relevant to production.

Consider that it is virtually impossible for any business in the long run to produce something merely to sell it for something of the same value. Selling something produced for something of equal value would not provide the producer with the resources to replenish the capital necessary for the production of future commodities. Profit is simply the difference between the value of something sold, and the value of something received in exchange, i.e., surplus value or exchange value in Marx's terms. Marx, Weber, Fisher—all recognize this. What is done with the profit—accumulated by *bourgeois* capitalists or distributed to labor—is a distinction between capitalism and Marxism. However, it cannot be overemphasized that profit simply cannot be distributed because profit is merely an equation, a definition. As I tell my students, you cannot go the supermarket and buy a loaf of bread with profit; you must use money.

As previously alluded to, the pursuit of profit is a bedrock of capitalism but has existed since production of commodities has existed, whether for use of the market, for thousands of years. Yet, until the Protestant Reformation and the Enlightenment (the Age of Reason and rationalist philosophy), and the Industrial Revolution the pursuit of profit was often constrained by religious or spiritual prohibitions, in particular the Catholic Church. The Protestant Reformation freed business owners from many of the constraints placed on profit seeking by the Catholic Church and allowed the rational pursuit of profit to progress. There were still limitations placed on the pursuit of profit, just different limitations, and less strict. The Enlightenment and Industrial Revolution removed most religious or spiritual principals guiding the pursuit of profit and the floodgates were opened for essentially what amounted to the pursuit of profit unlimited except by the market forces.

Capitalism and Labor

The process of capitalist accumulation cannot be understood if one leaves out of the calculation the relation between *bourgeois* capitalists and labor (Hilton & Hill, 1953) since the purpose of capital is to improve the productivity of labor, although Marx, Weber, and others argue it does not just improve the productivity of labor, but replaces labor.

Both Weber and Durkheim have much to say about the division of labor within society. But the division of labor within capitalism is not relevant for purposes of capitalism. The division of labor—factory worker or manager—is nothing more than distinguishing types of labor that are associated with production which, while important for some purposes, contributes nothing to an analysis of capitalism, owners of capital, or free wage-labor.

Neither capital nor land *do* anything. It is labor does things, whether slave or free. "Labour is alone productive" (Harvey, 1982, p. 104). "Labor works on land *through* capital, not on capital nor with capital. The place of each of the factors in the productive process is sharply distinguished" (Hicks, 1974, p. 311, emphasis in original).[24]

Capital is created by humans but tends to remain at rest unless acted upon by an outside force—labor. Labor, whether slave or free, is not created by humans. It is impossible for capital to do anything without human labor. Granted that a machine may be run by a computer program, the program is created by humans. Labor or slaves may or may not use capital. Picking cotton by slaves did not require the use of capital. In fact, picking cotton by labor was eventually accomplished by machines in the first half of the twentieth century. Capital not only increases the productivity of labor, and at times replaces labor whether free or slaves.

Feudalism precludes economies based on slave labor. The peasant does possess some means of production and some traditional rights. Thus, he is not a slave. At the same time, a peasant is not free wage-labor (Steenland, 1975). Of course, feudalism was accompanied by its own unique set of political, legal, and military relationships and institutions. However, meticulous details of what constituted feudal/agrarian society and means of production are beyond the scope this book.

But capitalism cannot be based on slave labor either. That is, while *bourgeois* capitalists may depend on raw materials supplied by slave owners produced by slave labor, as occurred in the American south prior to the Civil War, the very nature of the capitalist mode of production requires free wage-labor such that the absence of free wage-labor, such as slave labor, contravenes the essence of capitalism. Slaves are "merely" forced labor with a wage rate of zero.

Levy (2014) suggests that slaves were capital assets ("a chief task of profit under capitalism is to organize capital's inherent temporal motion. Posing the problem this way leads to the temporal logics of the changing forms of capital—the biological life cycle of the slave ..." p. 171), as do Ransom and Sutch ("The southern [U.S.] plantation system, though, was an unusual species of capitalism in which the capital assets were land and slaves rather than physical or financial capital," 1988, p. 134).

But Levy and Ransom and Sutch are wrong to classify slaves as capital. Since there can of necessity be only three resources of production (land, labor, and capital), once you introduce humans into production, whether slave or free, then you are automatically introducing labor into the production function which of course is necessary to produce anything. Calling slaves "forms of capital" does not in fact transform slaves into forms of capital. Slaves are still labor, even if the wage rate is zero.

Capitalism introduced two new social classes—the *bourgeois* capitalists and the proletariat who are the free wage-labor. Any discourse of capitalism therefore necessarily requires a consideration of the relationship of capital, the ownership of capital, and labor. It is only free wage-labor using capital that makes capitalism, capitalism, assuming all the other necessary conditions are present. "The *prevalence* of wage labour differentiates capitalism from previous social systems. It is a relation between the owner of the means of production (the capitalist) and the worker...The *wage relation* is therefore the *first fundamental characteristic of capitalism*" (Melios, 2018, p. 12, emphasis in original).

Capitalism continues to refer the accumulations of the efforts of past labor, at least by the critics of capitalism, an argument originally put forth by Marx. But if this were all, Wallerstein (2011) points out, then even Neanderthals could be labelled as capitalist, since they, too, had accumulated stocks that incarnated past labor. What distinguishes the system called capitalism is that capital came to be used in a very special way. Past accumulations became capital to the extent they were used to accumulate more (Wallerstein, 2011), accomplished by the M → C → M → C cycle.

Laclau (1971) sees the existence of free wage-labor as the defining characteristic of a capitalist mode of production. "The fundamental economic relationship of capitalism is constituted by the *free* labourer's sale of his labour-power ..." (pp. 10–11, italics in original).

Like profit, capital must be calculable. Capital must be quantifiable on the balance sheet. It can be kept, sold, traded, used to settle claims, or expire or depreciate. Capital cannot be labor. At the same time, labor cannot be capital. Labor is quantifiable on the income statement because of the wage-rate incorporated into the cost of commodities produced and sold.

Referring to slaves, a type of labor, as capital is a prime example of a different definition of both labor and capital resulting in a negation of the meaning of labor, capital, and capitalism. By using different definitions of labor and capital you immediately get caught in a logic trap. Consider that if you transform labor (slaves) into a "form of capital" you are then necessarily defining capital as a "form of labor" (slaves) which is clearly illogical, an example of circular reasoning. You can just then as easily define actual capital (machines) as a "form of labor."[25] One could just as easily define labor (slaves) as land, or land as capital, or as labor. Where does it end? Definitions are far from a matter of semantics.[26]

Obviously, there are different divisions, classes, or types of labor within labor, but all are still labor. If it is human and used for the production of commodities (whether free or slave), it is labor regardless of its classification (in accounting it is referred to as direct labor and indirect labor). The labor resource of production is labor regardless of its classification; it is not capital, and it is not land.

Like Laclau, Wallerstein (1974) also sees the defining characteristic of a social system as the division of labor. But in capitalism it is not the division of labor within, between, or among labor as Durkheim suggests. It is the division (separation) of labor from the ownership of the means of production. The change in attitude was not only in the mind of *bourgeois* capitalists in pursuing profit, but also in the mind of labor itself who became detached from the ownership of production and thus became free to sell their labor to the highest bidder.

Capitalism and the Capital Account

Early mercantile voyages were usually chartered for just one voyage after which the firm was dissolved and assets were liquidated. Profits and capital were divided among the investing partners according to their percentage of financial contribution (Carruthers & Espeland, 1991; Heilbroner, 1985).[27]

The development of joint-stock companies required additional accounts. Investors relied on accounts to provide the necessary information about their investment (Carruthers & Espeland, 1991). For example, the capital account was used to record transactions in shares of the East India Company at least as far back as 1600 using the double-entry method. A ledger was kept by the company and each shareowner had a separate account to keep a record of the amount each shareowner invested in the enterprise as well as each shareowner's share of the profits (Beams, 2008; Carruthers & Espeland, 1991). The company was rechartered in 1657 as a permanent, ongoing enterprise, rather than just a per voyage charter. Subsequently, dividends were only paid out of profits since capital had to be preserved to allow the firm to continue operations. It was therefore critical to separate capital and profits which was accomplished by using double-entry accounting and the capital account (Carruthers & Espeland, 1991; Coleman, 1963; Winjum, 1971). Unlike what occurs today in corporations whose shares are traded in the public, where profit is added to the equity of the corporation and then may or may not be distributed to shareowners, profit was distributed very quickly to the investors in the venture based on the amount invested in the venture.

However, today individual owners of shares of corporations do not have separate capital accounts recording the amount paid for the shares of individual shareowners. There is today, in fact, no "capital account" recording the investment of shareowners. There is instead a "common stock account" that records the amount of cash the corporation receives in an IPO. There is instead only a stock ledger used to record the number of shares owned by each shareowner. [28] Dividends are paid our of corporate equity based on the number of shares owned, not on the amount paid by the purchasers of the shares when issued. It is referred to as the capital account out of deference to tradition, not because the capital account records the amount invested by owners of shares. Profits are not shared by shareowners according to the amount invested in the stock. In fact, profits are not shared by shareowners at all since shareowners have no say in how profits are used or distributed.

As commercial networks increased in size and geography, double-entry bookkeeping was diffused from Italy throughout Western Europe and England. Once double-entry bookkeeping was sufficiently diffused, adherence to the principles of double-entry bookkeeping was maintained because every business operated within the same network as other businesses (Carruthers & Espeland, 1991). Double-entry bookkeeping acquired a "taken-for-granted quality of institutionalized practices" (Carruthers & Espeland, 1991; DiMaggio, 1988, pp. 4–5). It took centuries for double-entry accounting to diffuse throughout Europe (Carruthers & Espeland, 1991; Winjum, 1971) providing further evidence that feudalism and mercantilism co-existed with capitalism until feudalism and mercantilism disappeared and capitalism became dominant. Moreover, a centuries long process for capitalism to fully develop must be placed in the context with the development of double-entry bookkeeping. Neither entered history in a fully developed form. They evolved together, with one facilitating the development of the other.

The capital account was nothing other than an account to show the initial investment, i.e., the amount of money the merchant contributed to the firm or venture plus profit from selling goods minus liabilities. Thus, it is not the invention of double-entry bookkeeping per se, but the invention of the "capital account" to separate personal assets and wealth from business assets and capital as an integral part of double-entry bookkeeping that became a fundamental part of the development and expansion of capitalism.

It is essential to understand that the capital account was not itself capital since capital is the resource of production, or in the case of financial capital, the means of acquiring the resource of production. Referring to the equity account as capital is an error that has persisted for some 600 years. It not only confuses, but equates, equity with capital itself. But as previously noted, equity does not equal either financial capital or productive capital or the total of both.

As a prelude to Chapters 5 and 6, although an error, if one insists that the equity account of corporation is the capital account,[29] it must be understood that just as equity is the equity of the corporation, the capital account is the *corporation's* capital account, not the capital account of the owners of the shares, and not the capital account of *bourgeois* capitalists. Shareowners of corporations whose shares are traded in the public do not own either the financial capital, the productive capital, the equity of the corporation, or the corporation itself.

As previously noted, the "capital account" merely shows equity, which is the net monetary value of total financial capital and productive capital. As shown in Chapter 6, assets minus liabilities equals equity (net assets). For simplicity, if an enterprise has $1,000,000 in productive capital, $500,000 in debt, and $500,000 in equity (the "capital account"), we are now confronted with the paradox that the "capital account" (equity) of $500,000 does not equal the total financial capital and productive capital of the enterprise, $1,000,000.

We encounter other conceptual as well as terminological problems with the capital account. The entire right side of the balance sheet is also referred to as the firm's "capital structure" (i.e., debt plus equity).[30] But what happens when we consider assets minus liabilities equals equity? The balance sheet still balances, but the firm's "capital" (the entire right-hand side of the balance sheet) has been shattered by simple arithmetic. The net value of the firm's equity (the capital account), $500,000, is now the total capital of the firm's productive capital, $1,000,000. That is, the total value of the capital, the right side of the balance sheet, is equal not only to the left side of the balance sheet, but to the net value of the firm, the equity (the capital account) as well. $1,000,000 equals $500,000! Voldemort would be proud.

A further twist is seen in that if the firm's assets are entirely physical capital, then subtracting part of the firm's capital structure (liabilities) from the total assets (physical capital) still leaves capital (equity). Capital minus capital equals capital! Thus, to define "capital" with either the entire right side of the balance sheet or the equity account cannot be justified either by definition or math except by changing definitions to fit into a preconceived narrative.

There is simply no link between the equity of the corporation (the capital account) and the corporation's financial capital or its capital resources of production. To continue to call the equity account capital is misleading. To refer to the entire right side of the balance sheet as the capital structure is even more misleading. The "capital account," equity, merely shows the net value of the financial capital plus productive capital minus liabilities, not the value of the financial capital plus productive capital.

Prior to double-entry bookkeeping and the development of the capital account, the monetary value of capital, both financial and productive, was recorded by single entry; no debit or credit. With the invention of double-entry bookkeeping and the capital account (the monetary value of capital), both productive capital and financial capital were recorded as an entry on the debit side. But the monetary value of productive capital and financial capital was also recorded as an entry on the credit side, in the capital account (ignoring debt). The capital account and the entries in the capital account were not capital which was represented by the entries on the debit side.

Obviously, all entries are the monetary values of something, but the recording of productive assets or financial assets represents the monetary value of those assets, while the recording of the equity (or a liability) represents nothing more than a concept, a definition, a legal obligation (in the case of debt), or the result of an equation. Unlike asset accounts, liability and equity accounts do not represent physical things.

The value of capital must be accounted for, but merely recording the value of the capital as an asset reveals nothing about the relationship of the owner of the capital to the capital and its value. Enter the capital account. With double-entry bookkeeping and the capital account, now not only is the value of the capital itself accounted for, but the relationship of the owner of the capital is accounted for—the equity of the owner of the capital which is the corporation—through the credit side of the balance sheet.

Consider further a simple case of banks. Banks receive money from owners of the banks (in the case of medieval banks) or owners of shares of the banks, which they then lend to borrowers. But we know that the money received by banks is not financial capital because it is not used to acquire physical capital since banks do not produce commodities. It is obviously not physical capital. So now the capital structure of the banks does not equal any capital assets.[31]

Of course, critics will say my analysis is wrong because "capital" means one thing in one context, and another thing in another context. But such criticism merely proves my point. It is dishonest, it is disingenuous, it is deceptive, it is duplicitous, to change the meaning of words to suit a preconceived narrative. To claim different meanings of capital in different contexts is a one-way excursion into Wonderland, or the Wizarding World, and serves no purpose other than to perpetuate the myth that capitalism exists.

Capitalism and the Spirit of Capitalism

Weber uses the expression spirit of capitalism to describe the attitude which seeks profit rationally and systematically (Giddens, 1971). "... *attitude* of mind has on the one hand found its most suitable expression in capitalistic enterprise, while on the other the enterprise has derived its most suitable motive force from the *spirit of capitalism*" (Weber, 1992, p. 28, emphases added). But the "capitalist spirit" or "spirit of capitalism," which Weber calls an "attitude," is nothing more than a social construct and, as an attitude, a psychological condition. An attitude is

> a relatively enduring and general evaluation of an object, person, group, issue, or concept on a dimension ranging from negative to positive. Attitudes provide summary evaluations of target objects and are often

> assumed to be derived from specific beliefs, emotions, and past behaviors associated with those objects.[32]

Moreover, "Any and every 'economic' phenomenon is at the same time always a social phenomenon, and existence of a particular kind of 'economy' presupposes a definite kind of society" (Giddens, 1971, pp. 120–121), which is, of course, the social construct of capitalism erected on the capitalist mode of production.

It is not by chance that there is no "spirit of feudalism;" no "spirit of mercantilism;" no spirit of financial capitalism, of corporate capitalism, of mercantile capitalism, or spirit of any other "type" of capitalism. The spirit of capitalism was born out of the Industrial Revolution facilitated by the Protestant Reformation and the rational pursuit of profit using double-entry bookkeeping and the capital account. Yet, the spirit of capitalism is both more, and other, than the spirit of pursuing profit since the pursuit of profit existed centuries prior to the period in which the spirit of capitalism appeared. The spirit of capitalism is the rational pursuit of profit enabled by the capital account and sanctified by a new theology introduced by the Calvinist branch of the Protestant Reformation,[33] which ran counter to that of the Catholic Church because Calvinism accepted the acquisition of riches as legitimate (Sée, 1928).

Chapter Summary

In this chapter, I surveyed the theories of Karl Marx, Werner Sombart, and Max Weber, as well as Emile Durkheim, Basil Yamey, Richard Tawney, Immanuel Wallerstein, Jonathan Levy, and Karl Polanyi concerning the origins, history, and extent of capitalism, and the capital and profit that are an inherent part of capitalism. It was seen that not one modern writer from any discipline who claims that capitalism exists and is a global system has offered any evidence or argument that capitalism does actually still exist, let alone that it is a global system.

Capitalism evolved over a long period of time unevenly in various countries in Europe beginning with the Industrial Revolution. The historical processes and events that converged to transition from agrarian feudal and mercantilist society include the Protestant Reformation; the "invention" of the capital account and the proliferation of double-entry bookkeeping; the discovery by Europeans of other continents and ways to circumnavigate the globe; colonialism as practiced by European geo-political powers and the rapid expansion of overseas commerce; the invention of the printing press; certain scientific theories and discoveries accompanied by a rational, scientific mindset; population growth; a money-based rather than a barter-based economy; and most important, technological inventions leading to the "Industrial Revolution" in Britain and the United States which resulted in the rise of free wage-labor.

With the arrival of the Industrial Revolution accompanied by the introduction of the capital account, the concept of capital, rational profit seeking through double-entry bookkeeping, the separation of the business from the individual's personal life, and the formation of the *bourgeois* capitalists and proletariat classes, the spirit of capitalism and thus capitalism itself was born. The spirit of capitalism, i.e., the social construct of capitalism as the ownership of productive capital by *bourgeois* capitalists and the rational pursuit of profit, was based only and entirely on the ownership of productive capital by *bourgeois* capitalists separate and apart from the individual's ownership and use of his personal assets which constituted his savings and wealth.

In this chapter, I also reviewed the types, forms, varieties, and models of capitalism found in economic, history, and sociology literature. No one has attempted to argue that types, forms, varieties, and models of capitalism are in fact capitalism. No one has justified what makes their version of capitalism, capitalism. That capitalism still exists and is a global system, and that it exists in various types and forms, is merely asserted; accepted as an axiom.

There is only one type of capitalism—the economic and social system where the use of capital is the predominant mode of production and the capital is owned by *bourgeois* capitalists. "Financial capitalism," "corporate capitalism," "mercantile capitalism," and other "types" of capitalism are not types or forms of capitalism regardless of their labels.

There are some who maintain that the definition of capitalism is a matter of semantics. It was shown in this chapter that it is anything but a matter of semantics. Definitions have social, economic, and legal ramifications. The definition of capitalism has been perverted and contorted which has caused a false belief that capitalism still exists.

Notes

1 *Six Blind Men and an Elephant*. https://en.wikipedia.org/wiki/Blind_men_and_an_elephant.
2 From Jerry Bock and Sheldon Harnick's 1964 production of *Fiddler on the Roof*.
3 Defining "capitalism" is as elusive as defining "church" or "family." Nevertheless, we can consider factors that must be present in capitalism in order to constitute capitalism and accept the presence of those factors as definitions of capitalism.
4 Oxford Advanced Learner's Dictionary. https://www.oxfordlearnersdictionaries.com/us/definition/english/ism_2.
5 *Bourgeois* is an adjective. *Bourgeoisie* is a noun.
6 Personal email from David Ellerman to author March 9, 2021.
7 For example, "employee" and "independent contractor" are definitions that have economic as well as legal meanings. One cannot be substituted for the other without legal consequences.
8 Humpty Dumpty is a character in Lewis Carroll's *Alice in Wonderland*, who claims words mean what he wants them to mean.

9 Recent publications purporting to be "capitalist manifestos" are nothing more than an apology (in the theological sense) for capitalism, free-markets, and democracy. See, e.g., Kelso and Adler (2011), Wolfram (2013), Kiyosaki (2014), Rajan and Zingales (2013), Mishin (2020), and Haque (2011).

10 That is, a production function where $q = f(k, l)$, where q is quantity produced, k is capital, and l is labor, $k > l$ and land is fixed. Production functions specify the degree of substitution of capital for labor.

11 *Cambridge History of Capitalism*, Volumes I and II, Ed. By Larry Neal and Jeffrey G. Williamson. Cambridge: UK: Cambridge University Press.

12 See Wallerstein (1974) for an in-depth explanation of the stages of capitalism.

13 Obviously, there is more than one capital account—common stock, preferred stock, etc. For convenience all capital accounts are simply referred to as "the capital account."

14 *Porgy and Bess* by George Gershwin "It Ain't Necessarily So," Act 2, Scene 2.

15 While financial capital (money) is necessary to acquire resources of production, there is no production function $q = f(\text{labor, money})$. Money cannot be substituted for labor.

16 See Huber (2021) *Economics, Capitalism, and Corporations: Contradictions of Corporate Law, Economics, and the Theory of the Firm* for an explanation why the Financial Asset Pricing Model is erroneously referred to as the Capital Asset Pricing Model.

17 If one insists that corporations have replaced the *bourgeois* capitalist entrepreneur, then it must be conceded that shareowners do not own corporations or the means of production which renders void the argument of separation of ownership and control of corporations and directors as agents of shareowners, a pillar of the theory of the firm.

18 For a more detailed summary of the events contributing to the advent of capitalism, see Wm. Dennis Huber, *Economics, Capitalism, and Corporations: Contradictions of Corporate Law, Economics, and the Theory of the Firm*, Routledge, 2021.

19 In *The Social Structures of the Economy*, Bourdieu (2005) identifies several types of capital, including social capital, symbolic capital, and cultural capital. However, he also includes "commercial capital" that he defines as sales power related to the distribution network thus equating "capital" with power. Unfortunately, *The Social Structures of the Economy* is dedicated to the housing market, which is a good resource for policy making and implementation, but lacking in actual analysis of the social structures of the economy.

20 To see that neither profit nor equity is financial capital, one need only look at any balance sheet of any corporation to see that equity (including all outstanding stock plus retained earnings) does not equal cash and cash equivalents.

21 Even today, there are frequently errors in corporate financial statements requiring restatements.

22 See *Economics, Capitalism, and Corporations: Contradictions of Corporate Law, Economics, and the Theory of the Firm.*

23 631 F.2d 1264 (6th Cir. 1980).

24 I am not sure how important the distinction is between through, on, and with, but the distinction between labor, land, and capital is of the utmost importance.

25 Perhaps when robots and AI become more sophisticated robots can be classified as labor.

26 Also, plantations were not corporations whose shares were traded in the public and therefore not subject to reporting standards. Such enterprises could, essentially, categorize anything that they wanted as capital assets.

27 Sée (1928) explains that the Company of the Merchants Adventurers was created in 1553 with 240 shares at £25 sterling each. The joint effort was limited to a single voyage after which the profits were shared in proportion to the amount invested by each of the associates.
28 In double-entry accounting, there would be a debit to the Cash and a credit to one Common Stock account for all stock issued in an IPO regardless of the number of shares purchased by shareowners or the price paid.
29 Although there are several equity accounts—common stock, preferred stock, retained earnings—for simplicity all equity accounts are referred to simply as the equity account.
30 See, e.g., Baker and Martin (2011), *Capital Structure and Corporate Financing Decisions: Theory, Evidence, and Practice.*
31 Banks, of course, own physical assets in the form of land and buildings. But land and buildings are not productive capital.
32 *Attitude*, APA Dictionary of Psychology, https://dictionary.apa.org/attitude.
33 *The Protestant Ethic and the Spirit of Capitalism* would have been more appropriately named *The Protestant Sprit and the Ethic of Capitalism*, and perhaps would have been so, if Weber would have had more theological training.

Bibliography

Aho, J. (2005). *Confession and bookkeeping.* State University of New York Press.

Allen, R. C. (2003). *Farm to factory: A reinterpretation of the Soviet Industrial Revolution.* Princeton University Press.

Amin, S. (2013). *The implosion of contemporary capitalism.* Monthly Review Press.

Ashton, T. S. (1968). *The Industrial Revolution: 1760-1830.* Oxford University Press.

Baker, H. K., & Martin, G. S. (2011). *Capital structure and corporate financing decisions: Theory, evidence, and practice.* Wiley.

Beams, N. (2008). *The world economic crisis: A Marxist analysis.* Retrieved from http://tomweston.net/WorldCrisis.pdf

Beckert, S. (2014). Slavery and capitalism. *The Chronicle of Higher Education: The Review.* Retrieved from https://www.chronicle.com/article/slavery-and-capitalism/?cid2=gen_login_refresh&cid=gen_sign_in

Berger, P. L., & Luckmann, T. (1966). *The social construction of reality: A treatise on the sociology of knowledge.* Random House.

Berle, A. A., Jr. (1954). *The 20th century capitalist revolution.* Harcourt Brace & World, Inc.

Berle, A. A., & Means, G. C. (1991). *The modern corporation and private property* (2nd ed.). Routledge.

Bourdieu, P. (2005). *The social structures of the economy.* Polity Press.

Bremmer, I. (2011). *The end of the free market: Who wins the war between states and corporations?* Portfolio.

Brenner, R. (1977). The origins of capitalist development: A critique of Neo-Smithian Marxism. *New Left Review, 104*, 25–92. Retrieved from https://newleftreview.org/issues/i104/articles/robert-brenner-the-origins-of-capitalist-development-a-critique-of-neo-smithian-marxism

Bryer, R. A. (2000). The history of accounting and the transition to capitalism in England. Part one: Theory. *Accounting, Organizations and Society, 25*(2), 131–162. Retrieved from https://www.sciencedirect.com/science/article/pii/S036136829900032X

Bullock, A., Trombley, S., & Lawrie, A. (Eds.). (1999). *The new Fontana dictionary of modern thought*. HarperCollins.

Carruthers, B. G., & Espeland, W. N. (1991). Accounting for rationality: Double-entry bookkeeping and the rhetoric of economic rationality. *American Journal of Sociology, 97*(1), 31–69. Retrieved from https://www.jstor.org/stable/2781637

Chandler, A. D. Jr. (1984). The emergence of managerial capitalism. *The Business History Review, 58*(4), 473–503. https://doi.org/10.2307/3114162

Chiapello, E. (2007). Accounting and the birth of the notion of capitalism. *Critical Perspectives on Accounting, 18*, 263–296. https://doi.org/10.1016/j.cpa.2005.11.012

Coleman, D. C. (1963). *Sir John Banks: Baronet and businessman*. Clarendon.

Collins, R. (1980). Weber's last theory of capitalism: A systematization. *American Sociological Review, 45*, 925–942. Retrieved from https://pages.nyu.edu/jackson/class.analysis/readings/Collins–WebersGenEconHist.pdf

Connell-Smith, G. (1951). The ledger of Thomas Howell. *Economic History Review*, 3, 363–370. https://doi.org/10.2307/2599993

Crossick, G., & Haupt, H.-G. (2016). *The petite bourgeoisie in Europe 1780-1914: Enterprise, family and independence*. Routledge.

Crouch, C. (2005). Models of capitalism. *New Political Economy, 10*(4), 339–456. https://doi.org/10.1080/13563460500344336

Derks, H. (2008). Religion, capitalism and the rise of double-entry bookkeeping. *Accounting, Business & Financial History, 18*(2), 187–213. https://doi.org/10.1080/09585200802058735

DiMaggio, P. J. (1988). Interest and agency in institutional theory. In L. G. Zucker (Ed.), *Institutional patterns and organizations* (pp. 3–21). Ballinger.

Dobb, M. (1958). *Capitalism yesterday and today*. Lawrence and Wishart.

Durkheim, E. (1893). *The division of labor in society* (G. Simpson, Trans.). The Free Press of Glencoe. Retrieved from https://archive.org/details/in.ernet.dli.2015.126617/page/n1/mode/2up

Elsenhans, H. (2015). *Saving capitalism from the capitalists: World capitalism and global history*. SAGE Publications.

Esping-Andersen, G. (1990). *The three worlds of welfare capitalism*. Polity Press.

Fisher, I. (1912). *The nature of capital and income*. The MacMillan Company.

Frank, A. G. (1967). *Capitalism and underdevelopment in Latin America: Historical studies of Chile and Brazil* (rev. ed.). Monthly Review Press.

Friedman, M. (1962). *Capitalism and freedom*. University of Chicago Press.

Gemici, K. (2008). Karl Polanyi and the antinomies of embeddedness. *Socio-Economic Review, 6*, 5–33. https://doi.org/10.1093/ser/mwl034

Giddens, A. (1970). Marx, Weber, and the development of capitalism. *Sociology, 4*(3), 289–310. https://doi.org/10.1177/003803857000400301

Giddens, A. (1971). *Capitalism and modern social theory: An analysis of the writings of Marx, Durkheim, and Max Weber*. Cambridge University Press.

Granovetter, V., & Swedberg, R. (2001). *The sociology of economic life* (2nd ed.). Westview Press.

Granovetter, V., & Swedberg, R. (2011). Introduction. In M. Granovetter & R. Swedberg (Eds.), *The sociology of economic life* (3rd ed., pp. xiii–xli). Routledge.

Grassby, R. (1999). *The idea of capitalism before the Industrial Revolution*. Rohman & Littlefield, Inc.

Greif, A. (2005). Institutions, markets, and games. In V. Nee & R. Swedberg (Eds.), *The economic sociology of capitalism* (pp. ix–xxxi). Princeton University Press.

Hall, P. A., & Soskice, D. (Eds.). (2001). *Varieties of capitalism: The institutional foundations of comparative advantage*. Oxford University Press.

Hamza, A., & Ruda, F. (2016). An interview with Moishe Postone: That capital has limits does not mean that it will collapse. *Crisis & Critique*, *3*(3), 500–517. Retrieved from https://thecharnelhouse.org/wp-content/uploads/2018/03/Moishe-Postone-That-Capital-Has-Limits-does-Not-Mean-that-It-Will-Collapse-2016.pdf

Haque, U. (2011). *The new capitalist manifesto: Building a disruptively better business*. Harvard Business Review Press.

Harvey, D. (1982). *The limits to capital*. Basil Blackwell Publisher Ltd.

Heilbroner, R. (1985). *The nature and logic of capitalism*. W. W. Norton.

Hicks, A., & Kenworthy, L. (2003). Varieties of welfare capitalism. *Socio-Economic Review*, *1*(1), 27–61. https://doi.org/10.1093/soceco/1.1.27

Hicks, J. (1974). Capital controversies: Ancient and modern. *The American Economic Review*, *64*(2), 307–326. Retrieved from https://www.jstor.org/stable/1816058?seq=1#metadata_info_tab_contents

Hilton, R. H., & Hill, C. (1953). The transition from feudalism to capitalism. *Science & Society*, *17*(4), 340–351. Retrieved from https://www.jstor.org/stable/40400217

Huber, W. D. (2020). *Corporate law and the theory of the firm: Reconstructing shareholders, directors, owners, and investors*. Routledge.

Huber, W. D. (2021). *Economics, capitalism, and corporations: Contradictions of corporate law, economics, and the theory of the firm*. Routledge.

Johnson, P. (2010). *Making the market: Victorian origins of corporate capitalism*. Cambridge University Press.

Kelso, L. O., & Adler, M. J. (2011). *The capitalist manifesto*. Literary Licensing, LLC.

Kiyosaki, R. (2014). *Capitalist manifesto: How entrepreneurs can save capitalism*. The Rich Dad Company.

Laclau, E. (1971). Feudalism and capitalism in Latin America. *New Left Review*, *67*(1). Retrieved from https://newleftreview.org/issues/i67/articles/ernesto-laclau-feudalism-and-capitalism-in-latin-america

Levy, J. (2014). Accounting for profit and the history of capital. *Critical Historical Studies*, *1*(2), 171–214. Retrieved from http://www.jstor.org/stable/10.1086/677977

Lis, C., & Soly, H. (1997). Different paths of development capitalism in the Northern and Southern Netherlands during the Late Middle Ages and the Early Modern Period. *Review*, *XX*(2), 211–242. Retrieved from https://www.jstor.org/stable/40241399

Livingstone, D. W. (1976). On hegemony in corporate capitalist states: Material structures, ideological forms, class consciousness, and hegemonic acts. *Sociological Inquiry*, *46*(3-4), 235–250. https://doi.org/10.1111/j.1475-682X.1976.tb00768

Lukács, G. (1971). *History and class consciousness: Studies in Marxist dialectics* (R. Livingstone, Trans.). The MIT Press.

Marx, K. (1990). *Capital, A critique of political economy* (Vol. 3). Penguin Classics.

Marx, K., & Engels, F. (1848). *Manifesto of the Communist Party*. Retrieved from https://activistmanifesto.org/assets/original-communist-manifesto.pdf

McNally, C. A. (2013). How emerging forms of capitalism are changing the global economic order. *Analysis from the East-West Center, 107*. Retrieved from https://scholarspace.manoa.hawaii.edu/bitstream/10125/26953/api107.pdf

Melios, J. (2018). *The origins of capitalism as a social system: The prevalence of an aleatory encounter*. Routledge.

Meyer, J. W. (1986). Social environments and organizational accounting. *Accounting, Organizations and Society*, *11*(4-5), 345–56. https://doi.org/10.1016/0361-3682(86)90006-1
Michie, R. (2014). The rise of capitalism from ancient origins to 1948. In L. Neal & J. G. Williamson (Eds.), *The Cambridge history of capitalism* (Vol. 2, pp. 230–263). Cambridge University Press.
Mielants, E. (2000). Perspectives on the origins of merchant capitalism in Europe. *Review (Fernand Braudel Center)*, *23*(2), 229–292. Available from http://www.jstor.org/stable/40241485
Milanovic, B. (2019). *Capitalism, alone: The future of the system that rules the world*. Harvard University Press.
Mishin, D. N. (2020). *The capitalist manifesto*. Independently published.
Neal, L. (2016). Introduction. In L. Neal & J. G. Williamson (Eds.), *The Cambridge history of capitalism* (Vol. 1, pp. 1–23). Cambridge University Press.
Nee, V., & Swedberg, R. (2005). Introduction. In V. Nee & R. Swedberg (Eds.), *The economic sociology of capitalism* (pp. xxxv–xlvii). Princeton University Press.
Nee, V., & Swedberg, R. (2007). Introduction. In V. Nee & R. Swedberg (Eds.), *On capitalism*. Stanford University Press.
Novak, M. (1990). *The spirit of democratic capitalism*. Madison Books.
Pacioli, L. (1494). *Summa de arithmetica, geometria, proportioni et proportionalita*. Paganinus de Paganinis.
Pacioli, L., Geijsbeek, J. B., Manzoni, D., Pietra, A., Mainardi, M., Christoffels, J. Y., Stevin, S., & Dafforne, R. (1914). *Ancient double-entry bookkeeping: Lucas [sic] Pacioli's treatise (A.D. 1494–the earliest known writer on bookkeeping)*. J.B. Geijsbeek.
Perrow, C. (2002). *Organizing America: Wealth, power, and the origins of corporate capitalism*. Princeton University Press.
Polanyi, K. (1947). Our obsolete market economy: Civilization must find a new thought pattern. *Commentary*, *3*, 109–117. Retrieved from https://www.ocf.berkeley.edu/˜immer/polanyiobsolete.pdf
Polanyi, K. (2001). *The great transformation: The political and economic origins of our time*. Beacon Press.
Radice, H. (2000). Globalization and national capitalisms: Theorizing convergence and differentiation. *Review of International Political Economy*, *7*(4), 719–742. Retrieved from https://www.jstor.org/stable/4177368
Rajan, G., & Zingales, L. (2013). *Saving capitalism from the capitalists: Unleashing the power of financial markets to create wealth and spread opportunity*. Harper Collins Publishers.
Ransom, R. & Sutch, R. (1988). Capitalists without capital: The burden of slavery and the impact of emancipation. *Quantitative Studies in Agrarian History*, *62*(3), 133–160. Retrieved from www.jstor.org/stable/3743211
Richard Reeves, R. (2019). Yes, capitalism is broken. To recover, liberals must eat humble pie. The Guardian. Retrieved from https://www.theguardian.com/commentisfree/2019/sep/25/broken-capitalism-liberals-economy-politics
Robinson, W. I. (2004). *A theory of global capitalism: Production, class, and state in a transnational world*. Johns Hopkins University Press.
Sangster, A. (2016). The genesis of double entry bookkeeping. *The Accounting Review*, *91*(1), 299–315. https://doi.org/10.2308/accr-51115

Sangster, A., Kuter, M., Gurskaya, M., & Andreenkova, A. (2018). The determination of profit in medieval times. In T. Antipova & A. Rocha (Eds.), *Information technology science*. Springer.

Schumpter, J. A. (2009). *Can capitalism survive?* Harper Collins.

Scott, J. T. (1979). *Corporations, classes, and capitalism*. Hutchinson.

Searle, J. (1995). *The construction of social reality*. The Free Press.

Searle, J. (2010). *Making the social world: The structure of human civilization*. Oxford University Press.

Sée, H. (1928). *Modern capitalism: Its origin and evolution*. Adelphi Co.

Smith, D. L. (1965). Sociology and the rise of corporate capitalism. *Science & Society*, *29*(4), 401–418. Retrieved from https://www.jstor.org/stable/40401148

Sombart, W. (2019). *Modern capitalism* (Vol. 1, K. Alistair Nitz, Trans.). K.A. Nitz.

Steenland, K. (1975). Notes on feudalism and capitalism in Chile and Latin America. *Latin American Perspectives*, *2*(1), 49–58. Retrieved from https://www.jstor.org/stable/2633410

Streek, W. (2011). E plurbus unum? Varieties and commodities of capitalism. In M. Granovetter & R. Swedberg (Eds.), *The sociology of economic life* (3rd ed., pp. 419–455). Routledge.

Swedberg, R. (2011). Max Weber's central text in economic sociology. In M. Granovetter & R. Swedberg (Eds.), *The sociology of economic life* (3rd ed., pp. 62–77). Routledge.

Tawney, R. H. (1926). *Religion and the rise of capitalism: A historical study*. Verso.

Toms, S. (2009). Capitalism. In J. R. Edwards & S. P. Walker (Eds.), *The Routledge companion to accounting history* (pp. 342–352). Routledge.

Van Zanden, J. L. (1993). *The rise and decline of Holland's economy: Merchant capitalism and the labour market*. Manchester Univ. Press.

Walker, M. (2010). Accounting for varieties of capitalism: The case against a single set of global accounting standards. *British Accounting Review*, *42*(3), 137–152. https://doi.org/10.1016/j.bar.2010.04.003

Wallerstein, I. (1974). The rise and future demise of the world capitalist system: Concepts for comparative analysis. *Comparative Studies in Society and History*, *16*(4), 387–415. Retrieved from https://www.jstor.org/stable/178015

Wallerstein, I. (1979). *The capitalist world-economy*. Cambridge University Press.

Wallerstein, I. (2011). *Historical capitalism with capitalist civilization*. Verso.

Wang, B. X., & Rowley, C. (2017). Business networks and the emergence of *Guanxi* capitalism in China: The role of the 'invisible hand'. In J. Nolan, C. Rowley, & M. Warner (Eds.), *Business networks in East Asian capitalisms: Enduring trends, emerging patterns* (1st ed., pp. 93–118).

Weber, M. (1978). *Economy and society: An outline of interpretive sociology* (E. Fischoff, & H. Gerth et al., Trans.). In G. Roth & C. Wittich (Eds.). University of California Press.

Weber, M. (1981). *General economic history* (F. Knight, Trans.). Routledge.

Weber, M. (1992). *The protestant ethic and the spirit of capitalism* (T. Parsons, Trans.). Routledge.

Whitley, R. (1999). *Divergent capitalisms*. Oxford University Press.

Winjum, J. O. (1971). Accounting and the rise of capitalism: An accountant's view. *Journal of Accounting Research*, *9*(2), 333–350. Retrieved from https://www.jstor.org/stable/2489937

Wolfram, G. (2013). *A capitalist manifesto: Understanding the market economy and defending liberty*. Dunlap Goddard Publishing LLC.
Wood, E. (1999). *The origin of capitalism: A longer view*. Monthly Review Press.
Yamey, B. S. (1964). Accounting and the rise of capitalism: Further notes on a theme by Sombart. *Journal of Accounting Research*, *2*, 99–113.
Žmolek, M. A. (2013). *Rethinking the industrial revolution: Five centuries of transition from agrarian to industrial capitalism in England*. Haymarket Books.
Zukin, S., & DiMaggio, P. (1990). *Structures of capital: The social organization of the economy*. Cambridge University Press.

Part II

Corporations and Corporate Law

Part II looks at the history and nature of corporations and the functions of corporations in the economy. It then examines corporate statutory law with particular emphasis on U.S. corporate law focusing on Delaware corporate law.

Corporations existed prior to corporate statutory law per se. However, today the vast majority of corporate law is a function of statutory law, with relatively little a function of common law.[1]

Corporations and corporate law are an inherent part of securities laws, which are considered in Chapter 7. A basic understanding of corporations and corporate law, therefore, is essential in understanding securities laws and how corporate law and securities laws contributed to the extinction of capitalists and capitalism.

Corporate law and securities laws are substantially similar in other countries, particularly Anglo-American countries that share similar legal systems, with respect to the issues considered in this book.

Note

1 Principles of common law applied to corporations are seen in issues concerning fiduciary duty, which is beyond the scope of this book.

DOI: 10.4324/9781003240969-5

4 Corporations

Introduction

In 1991, Ronald Coase was awarded the Noble Prize in Economics for his work introducing the nature of the corporation, which he referred to as the "firm," as an explanation for why corporations exist. In his 1937 work, he concluded that "the main reason why it is profitable to establish a firm would seem to be that there is a cost of using the price mechanism" (p. 390). He then uses the concept of transaction costs to explain the nature and limits of firms, concluding that the reason firms exist is in order to reduce transaction costs. Still not finished, in 1990 he continued to emphatically explain "transaction cost considerations undoubtedly explain why firms come into existence."

To be fair, his work on the nature of the corporation was not about the nature of the corporation *per se* in spite of its title because he explicitly ignored the corporation as a legal entity, an approach that has continued to this day. Nevertheless, in a case of "a rose by any other name," the firm as he envisions it can be nothing other than a corporation whose share are traded in the public, which leads to a very convoluted and distorted concept on what a corporation is, why it exists, and what it does. There is no firm to suppress the price mechanism unless the firm is a corporation whose shares are traded in the public.

This chapter considers the nature of corporations and the reasons why corporations are formed as well as their function and role in the economy and society as a prelude to corporate law. That role and function determine why capitalists and capitalism are extinct.

It should be noted here that there are more types of firms than just large corporations whose shares are traded in the public. Partnerships, for example, are often referred to as "firms" (see, e.g., Morrison & Wilhelm Jr, 2004). Family businesses, including small, family-owned corporations, are also called "firms" (see, e.g., Burkart et al., 2003). But the nature of the firm as structured by Coase (1937), Jensen and Mecking (1976), and others considered here is the corporation whose shares are traded in the public.[1] Therefore, "firm," "enterprise," or "corporate firm" as used here refers exclusively to corporations whose shares are traded in the public unless otherwise stated.

DOI: 10.4324/9781003240969-6

The Nature and Characteristics of the Corporate Firm

Since 1819 corporations in the United States have been referred to in legal, accounting, and economics literature and by the U.S. Supreme Court, although not by state corporate statutes, as "fictitious persons." But corporations as fictitious persons began much earlier in Europe. In the early sixteenth century, a corporation as a fictitious person was firmly established in English law.[2]

In *Trustees of Dartmouth College v. Woodward*, U.S. Supreme Court Chief Justice Marshall considered a corporation as existing only in law. Specifically, Justice Marshall wrote

> An aggregate corporation, at common law, is a collection of individuals, united into one collective body under a special name and possessing certain immunities, privileges and capacities in its collective character which do not belong to the natural persons composing it. Among other things, it possesses the capacity of perpetual succession, and of acting by the collected vote or will of its component members, and of suing and being sued in all things touching its corporate rights and duties. It is, in short, *an artificial person, existing in contemplation of law …*
>
> (emphasis added)[3]

Justice Marshall is, of course, discussing the corporation as a legal entity, which is explained in Chapter 5. But it is the artificiality of the corporation as a person that constitutes what Coase considers a firm as distinct from the corporation as a legal entity. Yet, the two are one and the same and to separate them has no economic or legal justification.

Coase (1937) asks, what is a firm and why does a firm exist? He begins by defining a firm as "consist[ing] of the system of relationships which comes into existence when the direction of resources is dependent on an entrepreneur" (p. 393). But entrepreneur necessarily means individual proprietorships and partnerships since a corporation cannot be an entrepreneur. Coase thinks that "it is not possible to draw a hard and fast line which determines whether there is a firm or not. There may be more or less direction. It is similar to the legal question of whether there is the relationship of master and servant or principal and agent" (p. 392).

However, the existence of a corporate firm is not *similar to* the legal question of whether there is a relationship of master and servant or principal and agent which must take various factor into consideration. The existence of a corporate firm *is* a legal question, but it is not similar to the legal question of whether there is the relationship of master and servant or principal and agent. Unlike the question of whether there is the relationship of master and servant or principal and agent, it *is* possible to draw a hard and fast line which determines whether there is a firm or not, and in fact a hard and fast line must be drawn. A corporate firm does not exist unless there is a corporation. A firm is either a corporation or it is not. A corporation either has shares traded in the public, or it does not.

While a court may have to consider various facts and circumstances to decide whether there is a relationship of master and servant or principal and agent, the only fact a court must look at in order to decide whether there is a corporation is whether the state has issued a corporate charter. The only fact that a court must look at to decide whether the corporation is one whose shares are traded in the public is whether the Securities and Exchange Commission has authorized the corporation to issue shares to the public and whether the corporation has actually issued shares to the public.

Coase understands that the firm may "imply control over another person's property as well as over their labour" (p. 404) and perceives the identity of employer-employee relationship and the economic concept of the firm to be "*sufficiently close for an examination of the legal concept* to be of value in appraising the worth of the economic concept" (p. 403, emphasis added). However, it is *not* "sufficiently close" because the corporate firm controls labor. It does not control the property of others since the corporation is itself the owner of the property. Such is the confusion generated when one ignores corporate law and property law.

Coase suggests that the distinguishing mark of the firm is the suppression of the price mechanism which works interfirm but not intrafirm. "The main reason why it is profitable to establish a firm would seem to be that there is a cost of using the price mechanism" (p. 390) which are greatly reduced within the firm.

Coase uses "firm" (i.e., corporation) interchangeably with "entrepreneur" which has no logical, legal, or economic validity and further contributes to the vast confusion that exists regarding the existence of capitalism.

> The operation of a market costs something and by forming an organisation and allowing some authority (*an "entrepreneur"*) to direct the resources, certain marketing costs are saved. The *entrepreneur* has to carry out his function at less cost.
>
> (p. 392, emphases added)

Coase unwaveringly argued that

> Resources are not employed in those uses where they make the most valuable contribution...because of the existence of what has come to be called transaction costs...*firms emerge* because they are able to achieve some of those more productive arrangements of factors of production.
>
> (Coase, 1990, p. 10, emphasis added)

and emphatically states "transaction cost considerations undoubtedly explain why firms come into existence" (p. 11).

But this makes no legal sense. Corporations do not "emerge." They do not "come into existence." They do not self-create. They do not appear out of nowhere. Although corporations are created *ex nihilo*,[4] they are created by people and the reason people create firms is not to reduce costs.

People simply do not get together and say, "let's create a firm." Nor do they say, "let's create a corporation and then operate it as a firm." In this context, of course, corporations whose shares are traded in the public often form other corporations as subsidiaries of which they are the sole owners of the shares of the subsidiary. But that does not alter the purposes for forming a corporation. On the contrary, it reinforces it. A corporation whose shares are traded in the public does not say, "let's create a new firm" but, "let's create a new corporation."

People create corporations first to allow a large number of individuals to combine their savings by transferring their savings to a corporation by purchasing shares in the corporation in order for the corporation to acquire a large amount of financial capital in order to acquire physical capital in order to produce and sell a greater amount of commodities thereby making a greater profit. Reducing costs, including transaction costs, is a result, not the purpose, of creating firms. Second, people create corporations to avail themselves of limited risk[5] (see Chapter 5).

People simply do not get together and say, "Let's create a corporation to reduce costs." Reducing costs is simply not their primary motivation. Corporations need large amounts of capital (Milhaupt, 1998). Therefore people say, "Let's create a corporation in order to pool our financial capital and to limit our risk of loss in order to increase production and sales (and profit)."

Corporations are often created by *bourgeois* capitalist entrepreneurs who are individuals or partnerships who own all the assets (the financial capital and the physical capital means of production) of the corporation which is merely an extension or alter ego of the individuals who own the shares of the corporation. However, once the corporation issues shares to the public, the *bourgeois* capitalist entrepreneur ceases to exist since they no longer own the means of production.

Hart and Moore (1990) "identify a firm with the assets it possesses and take the position that ownership confers residual rights of control over the firm's assets" (p. 1120). They emphasize that the approach they take makes a distinction between ownership in the sense of possession and ownership in the sense of entitlement to an asset's profit stream.

The first problem presented by their argument is that the "firm" does not possess assets. It is the corporation as a legal entity that possess the assets. If the firm is different from the corporation, the firm cannot possess the assets.

The second problem is that they "take the position that ownership confers residual rights of control over the firm's assets: the right to decide how these assets are to be used ..." (p. 1120). They correctly "suppose that the sole right possessed by the owner of an asset is his ability to exclude others from the use of that asset. That is, the owner of a machine can decide who can and who cannot work on that machine..." (p. 1121). This, in turn, leads them to conclude that the owner of the machine allows the owner to indirectly control over labor.

While it is obvious that the owner of a machine controls the workers who use the machine, the owner of the machine is not a person when the subject of their analysis is the corporation that owns the capital resources of production. The owner of the machine is the corporation, while the person who has control over the worker is the supervisor, manager, foreperson, etc., who has no ownership rights in the machine.

Without explaining what is capitalism, what is a capitalist, what is a "capitalist setting," what is a "capitalist economic institution," or what private ownership means with respect to shareowners, corporations, and corporate property, Putterman (1993) states,

> *In a capitalist setting, the existence of an owner or owners who hold the right of control* [over assets], *the right to net revenue, and the right to alienate* is an aspect of business organization that is usually taken for granted [and] private ownership can be presumed ...
>
> (p. 244)

The confusion here is endless. First, while a capitalist (alone or with partners) holds the right of control over assets and revenue, shareowners do not. Only the corporate firm holds the right of control over assets and revenues as the owner of the assets. Furthermore, only the corporation has a right to net revenue, not the shareowners. Third, only the corporation has the right to alienate its property, not the shareowners.

But his error does not stop there. It is true that, "In most business firms, decision-making rights are held by persons who are also financial risk-bearers and suppliers of funds. The holders of these rights are known as the owners of the firm" (p. 245). But that refers to sole proprietorships and partnerships which in terms of numbers are greater than corporations whose shares are traded in the market and therefore are "most business firms." However, it is not true of corporations whose shares are traded in the market. By law, shareowners are not "owners of the firm." By law, shareowners are not entitled to the profit stream of the corporation (see Chapter 5).

With respect to corporations whose shares are traded in the public, to consider the firm as different from the corporation is futile.. To separate the firm from the corporation essentially treats the corporation as if it does not exist.

Corporations and Capital Resources of Production

The allocation of scarce resources is a function of the legal structure of society (Banner, 2011). But capitalism has nothing to do with the allocation of scarce resources; nor, for that matter, does socialism, communism, or

Marxism. The allocation of scarce resources takes place regardless of the type of legal, economic, or social system that a society has chosen, that has evolved, or that has been imposed upon it by force. It is the method by which resources are allocated that differs according to the legal, economic, or social system of the society—by the laws of private property and the market, or by the government. Here we are concerned only with the economic system of capitalism and the relation of corporations and the extinction of capitalism.

A corporation whose shares are owned entirely by a single person or a small number of persons can be said to be owned by the shareowners. The corporation is merely an extension, or "alter ego," of the shareowners. Although the corporation is the legal owner of capital, both financial and productive, it can be said that the owner of the shares is the owner of the capital who merely uses the corporate form to operate her business. Assuming that the corporation is a manufacturer of commodities, and not a mercantile business or financial intermediary, the corporation is a "capitalistic enterprise" since its owner in essence owns the means of production. The owner is a *bourgeois* capitalist. The *bourgeois* capitalist owner directs the allocation of the resources of production owned (land, capital) or hired (wage labor) by the corporation and decides the production function.

However, as explained in Chapter 5, and in more detail in *Corporate Law and the Theory of the Firm: Reconstructing Corporations, Shareholders, Directors, Owners, and Investors*, when a corporation "goes public" the corporation is no longer an extension or alter ego of the shareowners. Shareowners do not own the corporation. They own shares of stock that grants certain rights, none of which pertain to claims against the corporation or ownership rights in the corporation. It is now the corporation that owns all the capital, both financial and productive; that owns all the assets, both total and net (i.e., equity); and has the exclusive right to allocate the resources of production and decide on the production function.[6]

The property rights approach to the theory of the firm "relies on the idea that...the firm's *owner* has the right to decide who uses the firm's assets" (Hart, 1989, p. 1771). But he then says, "one of the weaknesses of the property rights approach ... is that it does not take account of the separation of ownership and control present in *large, publicly held corporations*" (p. 1773, emphasis added). Hart explains that "Although *owners* (shareholders) typically retain some control rights...in practice *they* delegate many others to *management*, at least on a day-to-day basis" (p. 1773, emphases added). But changing the analysis from the single owner of a corporation to a corporation whose shares are publicly traded on an exchange alters the legal parameters of the corporation and the owner thereby changing the relationships and the economic dynamics which Hart neglects to take into account. "The world of law shapes the reality of economic and financial dynamics in an essential way [that is] contrary to the ajuridical approaches of most theories of the firm" (Biondi et al. 2007, p. 7).

Hart and Moore (1990) identify a firm according to the assets it possesses and take the position that ownership of assets confers residual rights of control over the assets which means the right to decide how the assets will be used. This is partly right and partly wrong. It is partly right because according to the law of property firms own the assets. It is partly wrong because the concept of residual rights applies only to shareowners who by law are not permitted to say how corporate assets will be used (although shareowners have no residual rights, see Chapter 5 and *Corporate Law and the Theory of the Firm: Reconstructing Corporations, Shareholders, Directors, Owners, and Investors*).

Hart and Moore continue, "The entrepreneur-organizer, who let us assume is the chief operating officer [COO] and sole repository of control of the corporation, does not find his authority residing in common stockholders…" (p. 789). By corporate statutory law authority does not reside in common stockholders, and the COO is not an entrepreneur and certainly not the sole repository of control of the corporation. That function, by law, resides with the board of directors.

Fama (1980) recognizes that dispelling the notion that a firm is owned by its shareowners is "important because it is a first step toward understanding that control over a firm's decisions is not necessarily the province of security holders. The second step is setting aside the equally tenacious role in the firm usually attributed to the entrepreneur" (p. 290).

Chapter Summary

This chapter highlighted some of the more relevant characteristics of corporations as they relate to the allocation of the resources of production, in particular capital resources of production, and to capitalists and therefore to capitalism.

Corporations can have no "spirit of capitalism," a necessary element of the social system of capitalism. Corporations can have no ideologies.

Once created, the purpose of a corporation becomes undertaking projects that would not be possible for individuals first, because of the amount of physical capital is greater than what individuals alone could provide and second, because the degree of risk involved is greater than what individuals could bear

Berle (1954) summarizes his previous thesis regarding the separation of ownership and control of corporations (Berle & Means, 1991) by stating the corporation is "incapable of being owned by any individual or small group of individuals" (p. 30). He goes on to explain that "when an individual invests capital in the large corporation, he grants to the corporate management all power to use that capital to create, produce, and develop…" (p. 30). It is partly right because it again recognizes, although not explicitly, that there are no longer *bourgeois* capitalist entrepreneurs. It is partly wrong because, as I previously established, individuals do not invest in corporations; they invest in the shares of the corporation which then becomes the financial capital of the corporations. Their ownership of shares is savings and wealth, not capital.

Berle correctly recognizes that a corporation obtains it financial capital in the market. "… the corporate entrepreneur from time to time had to go into the markets seeking funds: to add this plant, to increase the size of his existing business…" (p. 36). However, while it is true the corporations must obtain their financial capital in the market, it is not the "corporate entrepreneur" who does so, but the corporation. There is, in every legal, economic, finance, or accounting respect, no such thing as a "corporate entrepreneur" when dealing with corporations whose shares are traded in the market. An entrepreneur is an individual, not a corporation. Berle is fully aware that capitalist entrepreneurs are individuals and that corporations are not capitalist entrepreneurs: "The capital is there; and so is capitalism. The waning factor is the capitalist. He has somehow vanished…He is not extinct; roughly a billion dollars a year…is invested by him…" (p. 39). But Berle was again partly wrong because capitalism is not there either.

Notes

1 Many firms in the world are controlled by their founders, or by the founders' families and heirs. Such family ownership is nearly universal among privately held firms, but is also found among publicly traded firms. In Western Europe, South and East Asia, the Middle East, Latin America, and Africa, many publicly traded firms are family controlled (Claessens et al., 2000; European Corporate Governance Network, 2001; La Porta et al., 1999). Even in the United States and the United Kingdom, some of the largest publicly traded firms, such as Wal-Mart Stores and Ford Motor, are controlled by families. However, many of these family-controlled firms are merchants, not producers of commodities.

2 Sir Edward Coke (1552–1634), *Institutes of the Laws of England*, 7 volumes, published posthumously by London: E. & R. Brooke, 1794.

3 Trustees of Dartmouth College v. Woodward, 17 U.S. 518 (1819).

4 *Ex nihilo* is Latin "out of nothing" usually used in a theological sense. Unlike sole proprietorships and partnerships, corporations have no antecedent existence.

5 As I explained in *Corporate Law and the Theory of the Firm: Reconstructing Corporations, Shareholders, Directors, Owners, and Investors*, "limited risk" is mistakenly referred to as "limited liability." However, according to corporate law shareholders have no liability whatsoever. They have limited risk of loss the maximum amount of which is the amount they paid for their shares. Furthermore, in the event of liquidation, the corporation loses its equity, but the equity is the corporation's, it is not the shareowners' equity. The maximum amount shareowners lose in liquidation is the amount they paid for their shares when the market price drops to zero.

6 It is not the corporation per se that decides on what resources to allocate and what production function to use since the corporation exists merely as a piece of paper through the corporate charter. It is the corporate directors that make such decisions through the officers and management hired by the directors who make such decisions as agents of the corporation, not of the shareowners. To say that the corporation decides on the allocation of resources is merely for convenience.

Bibliography

Banner, S. (2011). *American property: A history of how, why, and what we own.* Harvard University Press.

Berle, A. A., Jr. (1954). *The 20th century capitalist revolution.* Harcourt Brace & World, Inc.

Berle, A. A., & Means, G. C. (1991). *The modern corporation and private property* (2nd ed.). Routledge.

Biondi, Y., Canziani, A., & Kirat, T. (2007). Coming back to the enterprise. In Y. Biondi, A. Canziani, & T. Kirat (Eds.), *The firm as a legal entity: Implications for economics, accounting and the law* (pp. 3–8). Routledge.

Burkart, M., Panunzi, F., & Shleifer, A. (2003). Family firms. *Journal of Finance, 58*(5), 2167–2201. https://doi.org/10.1111/1540-6261.00601

Claessens, S., Djankov, S., & Lang, L. (2000). The separation of ownership and control in East Asian corporations, *Journal of Financial Economics, 68*, 81–112. https://doi.org/10.1016/S0304-405X(00)00067-2

Coase, R. H. (1937). The nature of the firm. *Economica, 4*(16), 386–405. https://doi.org/10.1111/j.1468-0335.1937.tb00002.x

Coase, R. H. (1990). Accounting and the theory of the firm. *Journal of Accounting and Economics, 12*(1-3), 3–13. https://doi.org/10.1016/0165-4101(90)90038-6

European Corporate Governance Network (ECGN). (2001). F. Berea & M. gvBecht (Eds.), *The control of corporate Europe.* Oxford University Press.

Fama, E. F. (1980). Agency problems and the theory of the firm. *Journal of Political Economy, 88*(2), 288–307. https://doi.org/https://doi.org/10.1086/260866

Hart, O. D. (1989). An economist's perspective on the theory of the firm. *Columbia Law Review, 89*(7), 1757–1774. Retrieved from http://www.jstor.org/stable/1122818

Hart, O. D., & Moore, J. (1990). Property rights and the nature of the firm. *Journal of Political Economy, 98*(6), 1119–1158. https://doi.org/10.1086/261729

Huber, W. D. (2020). *Corporate law and the theory of the firm: Reconstructing corporations, shareholders, directors, owners, and investors.* Routledge.

Huber, W. D. (2021). *Economics, capitalism, and corporations: Contradictions of corporate law, economics, and the theory of the firm.* Routledge.

Jensen, M. C., & Meckling, W. H. (1976). Theory of the firm: Managerial behavior, agency costs and ownership structure. *Journal of Financial Economics, 3*, 305–360. https://doi.org/10.1016/0304-405X(76)90026-X

La Porta, R., Lopez-de-Silanes, F., Shleifer, A., & Vishny, R. (1998). Law and finance. *Journal of Political Economy, 106*, 1113–1155. https://doi.org/10.1086/250042

Milhaupt, C. J. (1998). Property rights in firms. *Virginia Law Review, 84*(6), 1145–1194. Retrieved from https://www.jstor.org/stable/1073696

Morrison, A. D., & Wilhelm, W. J. Jr. (2004). Partnership firms, reputation, and human capital. *American Economic Review, 94*(5), 1682–1692. https://doi.org/10.1257/0002828043052367

Putterman, L. (1993). Ownership and the nature of the firm. *Journal of Comparative Economics, 17*, 243–263. Retrieved from https://EconPapers.repec.org/RePEc:eee:jcecon:v:17:y:1993:i:2:p:243-263

5 Corporate Law

Introduction

Arthur Levitt, Jr., former Chairman of the Securities Exchange Commission, asserted, "The principle that shareholders own the companies in which they invest—and are the ultimate bosses of those running them—is central to modern capitalism" (Levitt, 2008). This echoes Friedman's (1970) well-known declaration that, "In a free-enterprise, private-property system, a corporate executive is an employee of the owners of the business. He has direct responsibility to his employers. That responsibility is to conduct the business in accordance with their desires." Unfortunately, neither Levitt's nor Friedman's proclamation that shareowners own corporations have any basis in corporate law.

Booth (2001) questions who owns a corporation. He notes that some theories are so widely accepted it is forgotten they are theories. For Booth, one theory that is so widely accepted that it is forgotten it is a theory is the theory that a corporation is owned by its stockowners. This theory, he says, "has proved useful as a way of organizing our thoughts about corporation law. It has helped us define the duty owed by directors and officers to the corporation and to the stockowners" (p. 147). And that is precisely the problem. The theory that has organized our thoughts is that shareowners own corporations. Yet, absolutely no proof or argument based on property law or corporate statutory law (except for Huber, 2020) that shareowners own corporations has, to this point, been offered.

Corporate law determines the legal structure of the corporation. Corporate law determines the relationships between corporations and shareowners. Corporate law in conjunction with property law determines the ownership of corporate property (its assets) and therefore the allocation of scarce resources of production. It is thus imperative to understand the relationship of property law to corporate law in order to understand how, and why, capitalists and capitalism became extinct.

Up until the early nineteenth century, corporations were formed by an act of a sovereign (e.g., a king) or an act by a legislative body that issued a charter limiting their purpose to that which would be beneficial to the public or

DOI: 10.4324/9781003240969-7

the nation as a whole. Beginning in the early nineteenth century in the U.S., corporations could be formed by merely filing the proper paperwork that allowed them to be formed for "any legal purpose." This was the beginning of the end of capitalists as the number of corporations increased and their shares became more widely traded in the market.

Shareowners are precluded by statutory law from owning corporate property. Statutory corporate law confers on corporations the sole right to own all corporate assets, including its financial capital and productive capital. It also explicitly prohibits shareowners from managing the corporation, vesting management of the corporation in a board of directors.

This chapter, indeed the entire book, is concerned only with corporations whose securities are traded in the public, not privately held corporations. Securities laws govern the issuance and trading of securities by corporations whose securities are traded in the public, which is covered in Chapter 7. *Bourgeois* capitalists may form a corporation as an alter-ego as a means of reducing risk and limiting liability. *Bourgeois* capitalists are individuals or partnerships who, unlike shareowners in publicly traded corporations, actually do own the corporation.

> It has long been possible for an individual to incorporate his business even though it still represents his own investment, his own activities and his own business transactions; he has in fact merely created a legal alter ego by setting up a corporation as the nominal vehicle ...[1]
>
> (Berle & Means, 1991, p. 5)

This chapter surveys corporate statutory laws and explores how corporate statutory law contributed to the extinction of capitalists and therefore capitalism. The emphasis is on U.S. corporate law although corporate statutory laws are similar in countries that adopt Anglo-American laws. Corporate statutory laws govern the creation and management of the corporations and the relationship of shareowners and corporations.

Creation of a Corporation

As Levy (2014) explains, for centuries corporations had been defined according to sovereignty. In the U.S., after the adoption of the Constitution in 1789, state legislatures granted corporate charters. The propertied basis of corporations was private, but charters were granted only if they fulfilled some public purpose such as constructing a turnpike. The language of the charters held the corporation to a public account. The purpose of corporations was restricted by their charters. A banking corporation, for instance, could not turn around and build a railroad simply because doing so would increase the corporation's profits.

Then, "in the second half of the nineteenth century, the legal personality of American corporations transformed. Public expectations were increasingly abolished" (Levy, 2014, p. 190). They became private actors while maintaining limited liability for shareowners. States began to enact general incorporation laws which allowed corporations to be created free from the legislative chartering process while at the same time allowing corporations to pursue profit anywhere and giving them perpetual existence. The language of corporate charters replaced "public purpose" with "lawful purpose," which meant profit.

Thus, corporations can only be created in the U.S. pursuant to state corporation statutes. In 1837 Connecticut became the first state to enact legislation that allowed incorporation by registration rather than by sovereign or legislative charter (Perrow, 2002). Pressured by competition, other states soon followed Connecticut and enacted incorporation by registration statutes so that now all jurisdictions have substantially similar statutes for the creation of corporations. Countries that follow the legal principles of Anglo-American law have similar statutes.

Incorporation by registration marked a significant milestone in the downward spiral to the extinction of capitalists and thus of capitalism. Incorporation by registration allows a corporation to be formed "for any legal purpose" and to issue any number of shares to the public stated in the corporate charter or articles of incorporation. Incorporation by registration also opened the floodgates for issuing shares to the public and the trading of shares on an exchange, both of which existed prior to incorporation by registration but incorporation by registration removed many of the limitations and restrictions on issuing shares to the public. (Issuing shares to the public is subject to securities laws explained in Chapter 7.)

In the U.S., each state has its own statute governing the creation and operations of corporations as a result of the Tenth Amendment to the U.S. Constitution.[2] Delaware is the most popular state in which Fortune 500 corporations are incorporated.[3] Therefore, the Delaware General Corporation Law will be used as a reference point, with comparisons to the New York Business Corporation Law.

Delaware General Corporation Law[4] sets forth the requirements for creating a corporation:

> Any person, partnership, association or corporation, singly or jointly with others, and without regard to such person's or entity's residence, domicile or state of incorporation, may incorporate or organize a corporation under this chapter by filing with the Division of Corporations in the Department of State a certificate of incorporation which shall be executed, acknowledged and filed in accordance with § 103 of this title.[5]

The New York Business Corporation Law, on the other hand, limits the formation of a corporation to natural, not artificial, legal, or fictitious persons.

> Incorporators. One or more natural persons of the age of eighteen years or over may act as incorporators of a corporation to be formed under this chapter.[6]

Corporate Existence, Governance, and Operations

Corporate Existence

In all jurisdictions, corporations begin their existence and operation when the articles of incorporation are filed with the secretary (or department) of state, not when shares are issued or assets are transferred to the corporation.

In Delaware, once the certificate of incorporation is filed in accordance with the Delaware General Corporation Law, the corporation begins its existence.

> Upon the filing with the Secretary of State of the certificate of incorporation, executed and acknowledged in accordance with § 103 of this title, the incorporator or incorporators who signed the certificate, and such incorporator's or incorporators' successors and assigns, shall, from the date of such filing, be and constitute a body corporate, by the name set forth in the certificate, subject to § 103(d) of this title and subject to dissolution or other termination of its existence as provided in this chapter.[7]

The New York Business Corporation Law is more emphatic.

> Upon the filing of the certificate of incorporation by the department of state, the corporate existence shall begin ...[8]

It is important to note that the corporation exists without assets, without shares, and without shareowners. Significantly, the corporation begins its existence and its governance structure is in place prior to the election of the directors by the shareowners. There are in fact no shares outstanding at this time so there are no shareowners to elect the directors.[9] The duties of directors to the corporation begin at the time the directors are named in the articles of incorporation and filed, or when they are appointed by the incorporators in the certificate of incorporation filed with the state.

In Delaware, unless otherwise stated in the certificate of incorporation, the corporation has a perpetual existence.[10] Likewise in New York, a corporation has perpetual existence unless otherwise stated in the articles of incorporation.[11]

Corporate Governance

Corporate governance must be in accordance with corporate statutory law. Common law[12] only enters into the interpretation of corporate governance when statutory law is ambiguous or silent.

The Delaware General Corporation Law provides that, "The business and affairs of every corporation organized under this chapter *shall be managed by or under the direction of a board of directors*" (emphasis added).[13] "Managed by or under the direction of a board of directors" necessarily includes decisions on how to acquire and allocate financial capital and productive capital.

In New York, "the business of a corporation *shall be managed under the direction of its board of directors* ..." (emphasis added).[14]

In Delaware, if shareowners' voting rights are not denied, after incorporation and the directors are either named in the articles of incorporation or elected by the incorporators, "Directors shall be elected by a plurality of the votes" present at an annual meeting.[15]

In New York, initial directors are not named in the certificate of incorporation. If shareowners' voting rights are not denied, after the articles of incorporation are filed, "an organization meeting of the incorporator or incorporators shall be held within or without this state, for the purpose of...electing directors to hold office until the first annual meeting of shareholders..."[16]

Note that under both the Delaware General Corporation Law[17] and the New York Business Corporation Law,[18] after the certificate of incorporation is filed, if directors are not named in the certificate of incorporation, the incorporators must hold an organizational meeting to elect directors until the first annual meeting of shareowners is held at which time the shareowners elect directors. Either way, the corporation has begun its existence and it is important to understand at this point that whether the directors are named in the articles of incorporation, or are appointed by the incorporators, it is the unelected directors who are in control, governing, and managing the corporation. For example, in Delaware,

> If the persons who are to *serve as directors until the first annual meeting of stockholders* have not been named in the certificate of incorporation, the incorporator or incorporators, *until the directors are elected, shall manage the affairs of the corporation and may do whatever is necessary and proper to perfect the organization of the corporation,* including the adoption of the original bylaws of the corporation and the election of directors.[19]

That undeniably demonstrates the fact that the corporation is operational and corporate governance is in place prior to shareowners owning shares, and therefore directors are not agents of shareowners since there are no shareowners.

Corporate Operations

As noted above, the Delaware General Corporation Law and the New York Business Corporation Law both provide that the corporation is to be managed by or under the direction of a board of directors whether or not the directors of the corporation have been elected by the shareowners in the organizational meeting.

In order for there to be shareowners, the initial directors must issue shares. Shareowners must pay for the shares the price determined by the directors in an arm's length transaction. When shareowners purchase shares, they are not purchasing x/n% of the corporation[20] or x/n% of the assets of the corporation. They are purchasing x/n% of the shares issued by the corporation where x is the number of shares they purchase and n is the total number of shares issued. They are purchasing a set of rights as determined by the articles of incorporation and the terms of the class of stock which they are purchasing.

In addition to property (limited to cash in the case of purchasing shares issued in an IPO, see Chapter 7), according to contract law consideration can include a surrender of rights. That is, of course, what happens when shareowners purchase shares in an IPO. In addition to the cash paid, shareowners surrender their rights to decide how to allocate their assets (cash) in exchange for obtaining other rights and a set of expectations (discussed below).

In all jurisdictions, as with corporate existence, corporate operations begin when the articles of incorporation are filed with the secretary (or department) of state, not when assets are transferred to the corporation. (See Huber, 2017, for a novel argument that a not-for-profit corporation never began operations because no assets were transferred to the corporation.) Indeed, the corporation cannot issue shares or receive assets unless there are first directors and it has begun operations.

The initial directors must issue shares in order for there to be shareowners. While shares and shareowners are not necessary to begin operations, issuing shares is necessary in order to receive the financial capital when shareowners purchase stock in the IPO. Prior to stock being issued, the corporation can, e.g., borrow, or at least arrange to borrow once shares are issued. It can also sign contracts.

Only the directors may issue stock on behalf of the corporation. Under the Delaware General Corporation Law the initial board of directors, who have not been elected by shareowners, "may authorize capital stock to be issued for consideration consisting of cash, any tangible or intangible property or any benefit to the corporation, or any combination thereof."[21] The shares issued by the corporation need not be evidenced by a certificate (i.e., a piece of paper).[22]

> Every corporation may issue 1 or more classes of stock or 1 or more series of stock within any class thereof, any or all of which classes may be of stock with par value or stock without par value and which classes or series may have such voting powers, full or limited, or no voting powers, and such designations, preferences and relative, participating,

> optional or other special rights, and qualifications, limitations or restrictions thereof, as shall be stated and expressed in the certificate of incorporation or of any amendment thereto, or in the resolution or resolutions providing for the issue of such stock adopted by the board of directors pursuant to authority expressly vested in it by the provisions of its certificate of incorporation.[23]
>
> The consideration, as determined pursuant to § 153(a) and (b) of this title, for subscriptions to, or the purchase of, the capital stock to be issued by a corporation shall be paid in such form and in such manner as the board of directors shall determine...The board of directors may determine the amount of consideration for which shares may be issued by setting a minimum amount of consideration...[24]

The New York Business Corporation Law contains similar provisions

> Consideration for the issue of shares shall consist of money or other property, tangible or intangible; labor or services actually received by or performed for the corporation or for its benefit or in its formation or reorganization; a binding obligation to pay the purchase price or the subscription price in cash or other property...[25]

Even Berle and Means (1991) knew that purchasing shares in an IPO was a contract. In exchange for the shares and the rights conferred by the shares, purchasers agree to surrender certain of their rights—the right to decide which corporate resources to purchase or sell; the right to decide how to allocate corporate resources. Berle and Means understood that a shareowner of a large corporation "so far surrenders his wealth to those in control of the Corporation that he had exchanged the position of independent owner for one in which he may become merely a recipient of the wages capital" (Berle & Means, 1991).

Berle and Means go on to explain, "In place of actual physical properties over which the owner could exercise direction and for which he was responsible, the owner now holds a piece of paper representing a set of rights and expectations with respect to an enterprise" (p. 64). They continue, "It follows from all the foregoing that the shareholder in the modern corporate situation has surrendered a set of definite rights for certain indefinite expectations" (p. 244).

In order for the corporation to earn profit it must operate, which means it must produce. It uses the financial capital it received from issuing shares to acquire productive capital. It then, through its directors, officers, and managers, decides on a production function—the combination of free wage-labor and capital (assuming it owns or leases land)—and hires the free wage-labor. All of this is done without shareowner involvement.

Corporate Ownership

There is an almost universal belief in academic and legal literature and judicial opinions that shareowners own corporations, ranging from outright owners, to residual owners, to beneficial owners. Shareowners as residual owners or beneficial owners was refuted in *Corporate Law and the Theory of the Firm: Reconstructing Corporations, Shareholders, Directors, Owners, and Investors*, but since shareowners as residual owners or beneficial owners is not directly related to capitalists and capitalism it will not be repeated here other than to say that residual owners or beneficial owners cannot be *bourgeois* capitalists.

However, shareowners as owners of corporations bears repeating here because it is directly related to capitalists and capitalism and the extinction of capitalists and capitalism. Unlike partners in a partnership, shareowners do not have an ownership right in the corporation's property in which they own shares the way partners have an ownership right in partnership property where the net assets of the partnership are owned by the partners in proportion to their partnership interest. That is, partners own the partnership and thus partners have an ownership right in the partnership property. Shareowners, on the other hand, do not own either the corporation or corporate property. Partners can sell their interest in the partnership property to others (subject to agreement of the other partners). Shareowners only own shares which is not an ownership right in the corporate property. When shareowners sell their shares, they are not selling an ownership right in the corporate property.

Corporation Rights

Corporate rights are extremely broad. First, a corporation has the right to sue and be sued as a corporation; i.e., as an entity in the name of the corporation.

The Delaware General Corporation Law provides that

> Every corporation created under this chapter shall have power to…Sue and be sued in all courts and participate, as a party or otherwise, in any judicial, administrative, arbitrative or other proceeding, in its corporate name…[26]

Thus, e.g., if a corporation sustains economic damages, it is the corporation that must bring the action to recover damages, not the shareowners. If the corporation causes injury, the injured party must sue the corporation, not the shareowners.

Furthermore, if a director causes the injury, the plaintiff must sue the corporation as the principal of the director, not the shareowners as principals, which would be the case if directors were agents of the shareowners since principals are responsible for the acts of their agents.

New York grants similar rights.

> Each corporation, subject to any limitations provided in this chapter or any other statute of this state or its certificate of incorporation, shall have power in furtherance of its corporate purposes...(2) To sue and be sued in all courts and to participate in actions and proceedings, whether judicial, administrative, arbitrative or otherwise, in like cases *as natural persons.*
>
> (emphasis added)[27]

In addition to the right to sue and be sued, corporations have very expansive powers. The Delaware General Corporation Law grants

> In addition to the powers enumerated in § 122 of this title, every corporation, its officers, directors and stockholders shall possess and may exercise all the powers and privileges granted by this chapter or by any other law or by its certificate of incorporation, together with any powers incidental thereto, so far as such powers and privileges are necessary or convenient to the conduct, promotion or attainment of the business or purposes set forth in its certificate of incorporation.[28]

In New York, corporations shall "have and exercise all powers necessary or convenient to effect any or all of the purposes for which the corporation is formed."[29]

Corporations and Corporate Property

The Delaware General Corporation Law is very explicit in explaining the relationship of a corporation to corporate property.

> Every corporation created under this chapter shall have power to... *Purchase*, receive, take by grant, gift, devise, bequest or otherwise, lease, or otherwise acquire, *own*, hold, improve, employ, use and otherwise deal in and with real or personal property, or any interest therein, wherever situated, and to *sell*, convey, lease, exchange, transfer or otherwise dispose of, or mortgage or pledge, *all or any of its property and ass*ets, or any interest therein, wherever situated.
>
> (emphases added)[30]

The New York Business Corporation Law is more exhaustive.

> (a) Each corporation...shall have power in furtherance of its corporate purposes ... (4) To *purchase*, receive, take by grant, gift, devise, bequest or otherwise, lease, or otherwise acquire, *own*, hold, improve, employ, use and otherwise deal in and with, real or personal property, or any

> interest therein, wherever situated; (5) To *sell*, convey, lease, exchange, transfer or otherwise dispose of, or mortgage or pledge, or create a security interest in, all or any of its property, or any interest therein, wherever situated; (6) To *purchase*, take, receive, subscribe for, or otherwise acquire, own, hold, vote, employ, sell, lend, lease, exchange, transfer, or otherwise dispose of, mortgage, pledge, use and otherwise deal in and with, bonds and other obligations, shares, or other securities or interests issued by others, whether engaged in similar or different business, governmental, or other activities; (7) To *make contracts*, give guarantees and incur liabilities, borrow money at such rates of interest as the corporation may determine, issue its notes, bonds and other obligations, and secure any of its obligations by mortgage or pledge of all or any of its property or any interest therein, wherever situated. (8) To lend money, invest and reinvest its funds, and take and hold real and personal property as security for the payment of funds so loaned or invested.
>
> (emphases added)[31]

Assets are owned by the corporation. Liabilities are owed by the corporation. Therefore, we may ask, if the corporation owns the assets, how is the net assets, i.e., the equity, magically transformed into *shareowners'* equity? Assets minus liabilities equals net assets which, of course, equals equity. If shareowners do not own the assets or owe the liabilities, how can shareowners own the net assets, i.e., the equity? How is the *corporation's* equity magically transformed into *shareowners'* equity? Transforming the net assets which are owned by the corporation into net assets owned by shareowners is worthy of anything coming out of Wizarding World!

The California Supreme Court in 1941 in *Miller v. McColgan* relied on the U.S. Supreme Court ruling in *Rhode Island Hospital Trust Co. v. Doughton*.[32]

> The owner of the shares of stock in a company is not the owner of the corporation's property. He has a right to his share in the earnings of the corporation, as they may be declared in dividends arising from the use of all *its* property. In the dissolution of the corporation he may take his proportionate share in what is left, after all the debts of the corporation have been paid and the assets are divided in accordance with the law of its creation. But he does not own the corporate property...The interest of the shareholder entitles him to participate in the net profits earned by the bank in the employment of *its* capital, during the existence of its charter, in proportion to the number of his shares...
>
> (emphases added)

But the California Supreme Court went further:

> [L]et us first consider the nature of this property—corporate stock—and the status of corporations and shareholders. [1] It is fundamental,

of course, that the corporation has a personality distinct from that of its *shareholders, and that the latter neither own the corporate property nor the corporate earnings.* The shareholder simply has an *expectancy* in each, and he becomes the owner of a portion of each only when the corporation is liquidated by action of the directors or when a portion of the corporation's earnings is segregated and set aside for dividend payments on action of the directors in declaring a dividend. This well-settled proposition was amplified in Rhode Island Hospital Trust Co. v. Doughton, 270 U.S. 69, 81 [46 S. Ct. 256, 70 L. Ed. 475], wherein appears the following cogent language: "The owner of the shares of stock in a company is not the owner of the corporation's property. He has a right to his share in the earnings of the corporation, as they may be declared in dividends arising from the use of all its property. In the dissolution of the corporation he may take his proportionate share in what is left, after all the debts of the corporation have been paid and the assets are divided in accordance with the law of its creation. But he does not own the corporate property."

(emphasis added)

That corporate property, i.e., its financial capital and productive capital, is owned by the corporation and not the shareowners was confirmed by the U.S. Supreme Court in *Rhode Island Hospital Trust Co. v. Doughton*. "The owner of the shares of stock in a company is not the owner of the corporation's property."[33] Moreover, "shareholders … neither own the corporate property nor the corporate earnings."[34]

The equity of a corporation is the net assets of the corporation (assets minus liabilities equals equity, discussed more fully in *Economics, Capitalism, and Corporations: Contradictions of Corporate Law, Economics, and the Theory of the Firm*), which arises in the first instance when the corporation issues shares and subsequently by retained earnings. But the equity is not owned by the shareowner. It is owned by corporation. The shareowner only has a right to receive net assets when the corporation is liquidated and the net assets are required by law to be distributed to the shareowners.

The Delaware General Corporation Law provides that "The directors of every corporation, subject to any restrictions contained in its certificate of incorporation, *may* declare and pay dividends upon the shares of its capital stock …"[35] Thus, not only do directors have no duty to declare dividends, shareowners have no right to receive a dividend until it is declared by the directors. Thus, receiving a dividend is no more than a mere expectation or hope.

When a partnership suffers a loss, the loss is distributed among the partners' capital accounts. However, when a corporation suffers a loss, the loss is not distributed among the shareowners' capital accounts because they have no capital accounts.

Shareowners' Rights

Shareowners have very limited rights. Shareowners normally have a right to vote on directors, amending the corporate charter, mergers, and dissolution. Shareowners have no right to receive dividends since declaration of dividends is discretionary with the board of directors. They have no right to share in corporate profits. They have no right to manage the corporation or to acquire or allocate resources of production. They have no right to accumulate profits or capital, whether financial or physical.

Chapter Summary

This chapter reviewed basic corporate law—the creation, ownership, existence, and governance of corporations. Corporations exist prior to shareowners. Corporations are governed prior to shareowners. Shareowners only own a percentage of outstanding shares, not a percentage of the corporation. Shareowners are prohibited by corporate law and property from owning corporate property. Shareowners are prohibited by corporate law from managing the corporation or allocating its resources.

Corporate statutory law provides that corporations own all their capital to the exclusion of shareowners. However, the fact that corporations own capital does not transform corporations into capitalists. Capital is owned by the government in Marxist-based economies, but that does not make the government a capitalist. To refer to a corporation as a "capitalist enterprise" or "capitalist corporation" is an oxymoron. Corporations cannot be capitalists.

If, as has been claimed in economic and legal literature and judicial opinions (although with no supporting arguments or evidence), shareowners are residual owners of corporations, then they cannot be *bourgeois* capitalists who must be the actual owners of capital. *Bourgeois* capitalists own both the productive capital and the corporation as an alter ego (i.e., a corporation whose shares are not traded in the public). If, as has been alleged in economic and legal literature and judicial opinions, shareowners are beneficial owners of corporations, then again they cannot be *bourgeois* capitalists who are actual owners of capital. *Bourgeois* capitalists own both the productive capital and the corporation as an alter ego. Beneficial owners are prohibited by trust law from owning the trust property, be it capital or a corporation. Legal title to trust property is vested in the trustee. (See *Corporate Law and the Theory of the Firm: Reconstructing Corporations, Shareholders, Directors, Owners, and Investors.*)

If shareowners were *bourgeois* capitalists, what does that say about day-traders who own shares for less than a day, or flash-traders or own shares for a few minutes? What does that say about trusts that own shares for a beneficiary? Who is the *bourgeois* capitalist? The trust as the legal owner, or the beneficiary as the beneficial owner?

So, who is left to be *bourgeois* capitalists? Corporations? It is true, of course, that according to property law and corporate statutory law corporations own the financial capital and productive capital as do *bourgeois* capitalists. But it takes more than ownership of productive capital to make a *bourgeois* capitalist.

As seen in Chapter 2, *bourgeois* capitalists invest their own money in the enterprise. Of course, they may borrow, but before they borrow they must invest their own money. The source of the money they invest in the enterprise is from their personal wealth, i.e., their savings. The money they invest in the enterprise becomes the financial capital of the enterprise that the enterprise uses to acquire productive capital. The enterprise assets are separate from the personal wealth of the *bourgeois* capitalist even though the *bourgeois* capitalist owns both. Furthermore, the profit the enterprise earns, and accumulates, is just that—the profit of the enterprise enabled and separated from the owner by the capital account. Yet, although it is separate, the *bourgeois* capitalist owns the profit as well as the capital as part of her wealth.

By corporate statutory law, the profit of the corporation is just that—the profit of the corporation, not the shareowners. It is not owned by the shareowners and it is not part of the shareowners' wealth. Furthermore, by corporate statutory law none of the corporation's initial financial capital was its own as the financial capital of the *bourgeois* capitalist is hers. The initial financial capital of the corporation was acquired in its entirety from outside the corporation by issuing shares (ignoring debt).

Notes

1 *The Modern Corporation and Private Property* was first published in 1932 when sexist language was the norm.
2 "The powers not delegated to the United States by the Constitution, nor prohibited by it to the States, are reserved to the States respectively, or to the people." U.S. Constitution, Amendment X. The Constitution does not delegate to the United States the authority to create corporations.
3 Sixty-two percent of Fortune 500 companies are incorporated in Delaware. Delaware Division of Corporations. Annual Report Statistics.
4 More than two-thirds of the Fortune 500 and 80% of all firms that go public are incorporated in Delaware. Delaware Division of Corporations. Annual Report Statistics. https://corpfiles.delaware.gov/Annual-Reports/Division-of-Corporations-2019-Annual-Report.pdf.
5 Delaware General Corporation Law §101.
6 New York Business Corporation Law Sec. 401.
7 Delaware General Corporation Law § 106.
8 New York Business Corporation Law Sec. 403.
9 Delaware General Corporation Law § 106. "Commencement of corporate existence. Upon the filing with the Secretary of State of the certificate of incorporation, executed and acknowledged in accordance with § 103 of this title, the incorporator or incorporators who signed the certificate, and such incorporator's or incorporators' successors and assigns, shall, from the date

of such filing, be and constitute a body corporate, by the name set forth in the certificate, subject to § 103(d) of this title and subject to dissolution or other termination of its existence as provided in this chapter."

10 Delaware General Corporation Law § 102(b)(5).

11 New York Business Corporation Law Sec. 402(a)(9).

12 The role of common law in corporate governance is explained in *Corporate law and the theory of the firm: Reconstructing corporations, shareholders, directors, owners, and investors.*

13 Delaware General Corporation Law § 141(a).

14 New York Business Corporation Law Sec. 701.

15 Delaware General Corporation Law § 216.

16 New York Business Corporation Law Sec. 404(a).

17 Delaware General Corporation Law § 108, "Organization meeting of incorporators or directors named in certificate of incorporation. (a) After the filing of the certificate of incorporation an organization meeting of the incorporator or incorporators, or of the board of directors if the initial directors were named in the certificate of incorporation, shall be held, either within or without this State, at the call of a majority of the incorporators or directors, as the case may be, for the purposes of adopting bylaws, electing directors (if the meeting is of the incorporators) to serve or hold office until the first annual meeting of stockholders or until their successors are elected and qualify, electing officers if the meeting is of the directors, doing any other or further acts to perfect the organization of the corporation, and transacting such other business as may come before the meeting."

18 New York Business Corporation Law Sec. 404(a). "After the corporate existence has begun, an organization meeting of the incorporator or incorporators shall be held … for the purpose of adopting by-laws, electing directors to hold office until the first annual meeting of shareholders."

19 Delaware General Corporation Law § 107.

20 If shareowners owned corporations in proportion to the number of shares they own, the proportion of ownership would change every time shares are sold and bought in the market.

21 Delaware General Corporation Law § 152. Shares issued in an IPO are issued for cash. See Chapter 6.

22 Delaware General Corporation Law § 158. Stock certificates; uncertificated shares. "The shares of a corporation shall be represented by certificates, provided that the board of directors of the corporation may provide by resolution or resolutions that some or all of any or all classes or series of its stock shall be uncertificated shares."

23 Delaware General Corporation Law §151.

24 Delaware General Corporation Law § 152.

25 New York Business Corporation Law Sec. 504(a).

26 Delaware General Corporation Law § 122(i)(2).

27 New York Business Corporation Law Sec. 202(a)(2).

28 Delaware General Corporation Law § 121(a).

29 New York Business Corporation Law Sec. 202(a)(16).

30 Delaware General Corporation Law § 122(4).

31 New York Business Corporation Law Sec. 202.

32 Rhode Island Hospital Trust Co. v. Doughton, 270 U.S. 69, 81, 46 S.Ct. 256 70, L.Ed. 475 (1926).

33 Rhode Island Hospital Trust Co. v. Doughton, 270 U.S. 69, 81, 46 S.Ct. 256 70, L.Ed. 475 (1926).

34 Miller v. McColgan, 17 Cal.2d 432 (CA, 1941).

35 Delaware General Corporation Law § 170.

Bibliography

Cases

Miller v. McColgan, 17 Cal.2d 432 (CA, 1941).
Rhode Island Hospital Trust Co. v. Doughton, 270 U.S. 69, 81, 46 S.Ct. 256 70, L.Ed. 475 (1926).

Authors and Statutes

Berle, A. A., & Means, G. C. (1991). *The modern corporation and private property* (2nd ed.). Routledge.
Booth, R. A. (2001). Who owns a corporation and who cares? *Chicago-Kent Law Review, 77*(1), 147–178. Retrieved from https://scholarship.kentlaw.iit.edu/cklawreview/vol77/iss1/8
Delaware General Corporation Law. https://delcode.delaware.gov/title8/title8.pdf
Friedman, M. (1970, Sept. 13). The social responsibility of business is to increase its profits. *N.Y. Times Magazine*, p. 2.
Huber, W. D. (2017). The saga of Huber vs. the American Accounting Association: Forensic accounting and the law. *Journal of Forensic & Investigative Accounting, 9*(2), 870–879. Retrieved from https://papers.ssrn.com/sol3/papers.cfm?abstract_id=2970636
Huber, W. D. (2020). *Corporate law and the theory of the firm: Reconstructing corporations, shareholders, directors, owners, and investors.* Routledge.
Levitt, A. Jr. (2008, July 1). How to boost shareholder democracy. *Wall Street Journal, l*, A17.
Levy, J. (2014). Accounting for profit and the history of capital. *Critical Historical Studies, 1*(2), 171–214. Retrieved from http://www.jstor.org/stable/10.1086/677977
Perrow, C. (2002). *Organizing America: Wealth, power, and the origins of corporate capitalism.* Princeton University Press.
New York Business Corporation Law. https://newyork.public.law/laws/n.y._business_corporation_law

Part III

Accounting and Securities Laws

While corporate law and the creation of corporations by registration played a major part in the decline and fall of *bourgeois* capitalists and capitalism by excluding owners of shares from owning the means of production, accounting, or more specifically corporate financial reporting and generally accepted accounting principles (GAAP) along with securities laws not only served as a catalyst to the complete extinction of capitalists and capitalism, but at the same time operated to perpetuate the false narrative that *bourgeois* capitalists and capitalism are alive and well.

Corporate financial reporting and GAAP are the subject of Chapter 6 while securities laws are covered in Chapter 7. Securities laws are included with accounting because securities laws require corporations whose shares are traded in the public to comply with GAAP.

While double-entry bookkeeping facilitated capitalism and the capitalist spirit, double-entry bookkeeping, what many people equate with accounting, is not the same as the financial reporting aspect of accounting. The financial reporting aspect of accounting, on the other hand, had a significant impact on the extinction of capitalists and capitalism.

Double-entry bookkeeping existed long before capitalism and corporations whose shares are traded in the pubic, and long before financial reports were issued to the public. Double-entry bookkeeping is concerned with how transactions are recorded and is still used today, albeit in a much more sophisticated manner. Financial reporting is concerned with how the financial position of the corporation is reported to the public.

Double-entry accounting and the introduction of the "capital account"—assets minus liabilities equals equity—allowed the owners of the business to separate business affairs from personal affairs and thus to calculate profits in a rational manner. Double-entry accounting and the capital account were assimilated by *bourgeois* capitalists beginning with the Industrial Revolution. Such accounting was well-suited for both merchants and the new *bourgeois* capitalist as the owners of the business. There were no "generally accepted accounting principles" to comply with and no financial reports to issue to the public.

DOI: 10.4324/9781003240969-8

Enter corporations whose shares are traded in the public. Now, we must contend with GAAP and the corporate financial accounting reporting requirements imposed by securities laws. Corporate financial accounting reporting requirements imposed by GAAP and securities laws have never been systematically integrated with capitalist and capitalism, and for good reason. They cannot be.

As we begin our study of accounting and securities laws let those who have accounting-phobia relax. Just as the technical aspects of double-entry accounting were not part of the study of capitalism, the actual GAAP are not part of the chapter on accounting, and there is no quiz at the conclusion of the chapter.

6 Accounting and Generally Accepted Accounting Principles

Introduction

Accounting is responsible in large part for the rise of *bourgeois* capitalists and capitalism while at the same time is responsible in an equally large part for their demise.

On the one hand, accounting—the double-entry bookkeeping part of accounting—had a major influence on the development of *bourgeois* capitalists and capitalism through the creation of the capital account and the separation of business assets from personal assets. Invented centuries prior to capitalism and *bourgeois* capitalists, double-entry bookkeeping was imported by *bourgeois* capitalists from mercantilists thus enabling the spirit of capitalism to prevail.

On the other hand, accounting—the financial reporting part of accounting—was a major factor in the extinction of *bourgeois* capitalists and capitalism.

As corporations proliferated and their shares began to be widely dispersed and traded in the public, it was imperative that standards be developed for how to measure transactions and how to report results of operations. Those standards, known as "generally accepted accounting principles" or GAAP, played a significant role in the extinction of *bourgeois* capitalists and capitalism.

Readers who have an apprehension about accounting may rest assured that there are no debits and credits in this chapter. This chapter is not concerned with double-entry bookkeeping, which was reviewed in Chapter 3. Rather, it discusses the development and application of GAAP that corporations whose shares are traded in the public must comply with when reporting their financial statements. This chapter considers how GAAP were developed and contributed to the extinction of *bourgeois* capitalists and capitalism.

Accounting considerations are broad and encompass securities laws. Accounting is inherently related to securities and securities laws, which are discussed in the next chapter.

DOI: 10.4324/9781003240969-9

While accountants (practicing or academics) will find the discussion of accounting in this chapter familiar and may be tempted so skip it, I encourage them to read it first, in order to have it fresh in their minds when they read the chapters that follow since this chapter considers how GAAP contributed to the extinction of *bourgeois* capitalists and capitalism and second, financial reporting is presented here from a different perspective than what is taught in textbooks.

I begin by considering corporate financial reporting as required by GAAP and the various financial statements corporations are required to report. Next, I examine the concept of GAAP, their history and purpose, followed by a review of the Financial Accounting Standards Board (FASB), the U.S., accounting standard-setting body, and its *FASB Conceptual Framework*.

Capitalism, Accounting, Corporations, and Financial Reporting

Accounting itself is not new. Some form of accounting was used in Ancient Egypt, Greece, and Rome among others (see, e.g., Ezzamel, 2012; Schroeder et al., 2005). However, sometime around the thirteenth century or earlier (Pacioli et al., 1914; Sangster, 2016), a new method of accounting was invented called double-entry accounting, or double-entry bookkeeping, that eventually changed the world which, along with the capital account that was an integral and inseparable part of double-entry accounting, paved the way for capitalists and capitalism as discussed in Chapter 3. Double-entry accounting was used by bankers, mercantilist, and *bourgeois* capitalists for several centuries to varying degrees. Nothing about accounting up to that time was concerned with financial statements and reporting. Accounting information was only prepared by and for the business owners. Then, beginning in the nineteenth century, things began to change.

Corporations and Financial Reporting

The Balance Sheet

The structure of the balance sheet, also known as the statement of financial position, per U.S. GAAP[1] is assets (the left side of the balance sheet, or sometimes the top) equals liabilities plus equity (the right side of the balance sheet or sometimes the bottom) or what is known as the basic accounting equation: A = L + E.

What constitutes assets and liabilities (debt) and how they are measured or valued is currently defined by the FASB, discussed below.[2] Simple arithmetic then shows that assets minus liabilities equals equity, or A – L = E. But equity is simply the net assets. (In other countries, the balance sheet is structured as A – L = E.)

The asset section of the balance sheet is divided between current assets and long-term assets. The assets are the property of the corporation, consisting of its financial and productive capital. The long-term assets include property and plant (land)[3] and equipment (the productive capital);[4] i.e., the property, plant, and equipment are the resources of production the corporation uses to produce commodities. The current assets include cash (and what is called "cash equivalents" such as Treasury bills), i.e., its financial capital, and other items that will be or can be converted into cash very quickly. The assets are therefore the corporation's actual capital structure contrary to what is taught in every introductory finance textbook.

Prior to the beginning of operations the cash received from shareowners in an IPO (see Chapter 7) comprises the financial capital of the corporation. At that time, total assets equals net assets which is its equity because there is no debt. The cash the corporation owns equals the equity of the corporation. The corporation's financial capital is not contributed by the corporation itself but from purchasers of shares. There is obviously no profit yet.

Immediately after receiving cash in an IPO the corporation uses part of its financial capital to acquire capital resources of production. The balance sheet still balances. The assets are still owned by the corporation, not the shareowners, as seen in Chapter 5. Total assets equals net assets which is equity. The equity is still owned by the corporation, not the shareowners.[5] But neither the financial capital alone nor the productive capital alone equals equity.

The liabilities, or debt, are self-explanatory. Property law and corporate statutory law mandate that it is the corporation that owns the assets, not the shareowners,[6] and it is the corporation that is responsible for the liabilities; i.e., shareowners have no legal liability for payment of corporate debts[7] (see Chapter 5).

The equity section is divided into stock and retained earnings. Stock is divided into common stock and preferred stock. But common stock is frequently referred to as "capital stock."[8] Furthermore, not only is common stock frequently referred to as capital stock, the entire right side of the balance sheet is erroneously referred to as its "capital structure."

Financial leverage is related to what is erroneously referred to as the corporation's capital structure and is measured by, among other things, the debt-to-equity ratio. The debt-to-equity equity ratio is calculated as (corporate debt ÷ corporate equity).[9] But calculation of the ratio is extremely troubling, particularly in the context of capitalists and capitalism. The denominator in the debt-to-equity ratio obviously is equity, but the question that has never been asked is, whose equity? If equity is the "stockholders' equity" as reported on the financial statements, then the calculation is comparing debt that is legally owed by the corporation to equity that is not owned by the corporation.

There can be no justification for comparing debt that is legally owed by the corporation to equity that is not legally owned by the corporation. Or, turned around, there can be no justification for comparing equity that is not legally owned by shareowners against debt that is legally owed by the corporation. There is thus a tacit admission in the calculation of the ratio that is universally ignored—equity must be owned by the corporation, not by the shareowners.

The categories of the balance sheet are misleading. Every introductory, intermediate, and advance accounting textbook; every scholarly paper in accounting, finance, economics, and law; and every judicial opinion refers to the equity of the corporation as "stockholders' equity." To refer to equity as stockholders' equity is a perversion of both property law and corporate law. If the corporation owns the total assets, then it owns the net assets which is equity. As I explained in Chapter 5 and in *Corporate Law and the Theory of the Firm: Reconstructing Corporations, Shareholders, Directors, Owners, and Investors*, to transform corporate ownership of total assets into shareowner ownership of net assets, and therefore equity, is worthy of anything coming out of Wizarding World! It is the corporation that owns the equity, not the stockowners.

The capital account as it was originally conceived reports the money invested in the firm by the owner(s) plus profit, i.e., its financial capital. But shareowners do not own either the assets of the corporation or the corporation. Thus, the capital account does not represent, and cannot report, the equity of shareowners. Nor does it represent, or report, the capital of the corporation which is the left side of the balance sheet, the financial capital plus productive capital. What is referred to as the corporation's capital, i.e., the capital account, is nothing more than the corporation's equity. To call the equity of the corporation its capital is misleading.

As previously noted, the "capital account" reports equity, not capital. But now we encounter conceptual as well as terminological problems. Both the entire right side of the balance sheet and the equity are referred to as the firm's capital, even though neither are related to either financial capital or physical capital. But now what happens when we consider assets minus liabilities equals corporate equity? The balance sheet still balances, but the firm's capital (right-hand side of the balance sheet) has been shattered by simple arithmetic—liabilities plus equity is capital, but subtracting liabilities still leaves capital. A further twist is seen in that if the firm's assets are entirely physical capital, then subtracting part of the firm's capital (liabilities) from the total assets (physical capital) still leaves capital (equity). All that is really being said is capital equals capital.

There are those who attempt to escape these contradictory usages of "capital," and equations that have no basis in fact or law by claiming capital means one thing in one context, but something else in another context. And that is the fundamental problem. Charles Lutwidge Dodgson, logistician that he was, had his character Humpty Dumpty tell Alice, "When I use a word it means just what I choose it to mean—neither more nor less."[10] Using "capital" to mean different things, especially within the narrow confines of financial statements, is nothing more than the Humpty Dumpty approach and explains why the mirage that capitalists and capitalism still exist continues to permeate the social structure.

The concept of capitalism was built on the equity (capital account) of individual owners and partners and transferred into the equity (capital account) of the corporation without questioning whether the capital account of individuals can be equated to the capital account of corporations. The FASB in fact emphasizes that the view that the reporting entity is not separate from its equity investors "has its roots in the days when most businesses were sole proprietorships and partnerships that were managed by their owners" (FASB, 2010, ¶BC1.8).

The capital account was injected into corporations almost by reflex; a label subsequently applied to corporations with no thought of what it meant or how, or even if, the capital account can apply to corporations. Hundreds of years later, there has been no improvement in the capital account. That is, there is still no correspondence between the "capital account" and either financial capital (money, cash) or physical capital as a means of production. Nor is there any relationship between "capital stock" or financial capital or physical capital. The "capital account" shows equity, not capital.

The Income Statement

The structure of the income statement, also known as the profit and loss statement or statement of operations, is revenue minus expenses equals net income (i.e., profit, or net earnings), R – E = NI. What constitutes revenue and expenses and how they are measured is defined by the FASB. But, as taught in every introductory accounting course, as a result of accrual accounting and the matching principle, revenue and expenses are not related to cash flows and therefore net income is not related to cash. In other words, profit is a definition. As Justice Edwards noted in his ruling in *United Steel Workers of America v. United States Steel Corporation*,[11] "with a different definition of profit [the] outcome of an accounting analysis could be made to be nonprofitability." Justice Edwards clearly recognized that profit is merely a "calculative practice open to interpretation" (see Levy, 2014).

Profit is much more than just the revenue generated from selling commodities minus the expenses of producing commodities as it was when capitalism began its historic journey. There is profit that has nothing to do with the production and sale of commodities, nothing to do with appropriating surplus value or exploiting wage-labor. Much of the profit reported on the income statement of a producer of commodities is generated by fictitious capital.

Furthermore, the corporation's profit as reported on its income statement is added to its retained earnings and becomes part of its equity. But in accordance with current GAAP, there is some profit that bypasses the income statement and is incorporated directly into the corporation's equity referred to as "other comprehensive income" (OCI) such as gains or losses on investments available for sale.[12] Thus, there is some OCI that does not result from transactions in the market and has nothing to do with the production and sale of commodities, accumulating capital, or appropriating surplus value.

Current GAAP requires that earnings per share ("EPS") be reported. EPS is simply net income divided by the number of shares outstanding. But there is more to earnings per share than the percentage of net income attributable to a share of stock owned by shareowners. Dilutive EPS is the earnings per share that includes items that could be turned into shares such as warrants and options, but are not shares and are therefore not owned by shareowners.

Statement of Cash Flows

The structure of the statement of cash flows reports the cash flows in and out of the corporation according to operating activities, investing activities, and financing activities. Operating activities show the increase or decrease in cash from daily operations. Financing activities report cash received from issuing stock (or bonds) or paid by the corporations for stock repurchases (or for retiring bonds). Investing activities report the corporation's investment in resources of production: long-term assets (capital) and land. Investing activities correspond to the "I" in the GDP equation C + I + G (where C is consumer goods, I is investment by businesses in productive capital, and G is government expenditures).

The importance of the statement of cash flows is that it reports how the corporation obtained its financial capital—partly from operations and partly from issuing stock (and bonds) to the public. It also shows how it used its financial capital to acquire productive capital.

Statement of Retained Earnings

The statement of retained earnings reports how the present balance of retained earnings changed as a result of additions for net income (or subtractions for net loss) or the payment of dividends, not how the balance changed due to changes in cash. Retained earnings does not equal cash (except by coincidence).

Statement of Stockholders' Equity

The statement of stockholders' equity, or statement of changes in stockholders' equity, which is not the equity of shareowners but is referred to as such by the FASB, reports how the corporation's equity (not the stockowners' equity) changed by additions to retained earnings, issuing new stock, or repurchasing outstanding stock. Corporate equity does not equal cash (except by coincidence).

Generally Accepted Accounting Principles

As discussed in Chapter 3, the spirit of capitalism is essentially the rational pursuit of profit by *bourgeois* capitalists who are the owners of physical capital, the means of production and who accumulate the surplus value of wage-labor (profit) in an M → C → M → C cycle.

While a corporation may accumulate profit, unlike a *bourgeois* capitalist, it is merely accumulating a definition, the result of an equation, which has no meaning. Since profit is not money Marx's *bourgeois* capitalist M → C → M → C cycle has been collapsed. And, since profit is not money it is not financial capital. Therefore, profit cannot be used to acquire commodities (productive capital) or to produce additional commodities.

Dividends may, in the discretion of the directors, be paid out of earnings. The amount of dividends received by a shareowner has no relationship to the amount the shareowner paid for the shares of stock she owns but on the number of shares she owns which is inconsistent with capitalism especially if she purchases the shares in the market rather than in an IPO since none of the money goes to the corporation when bought and sold in the market.

Marx considered profit to be "appropriated value," the surplus value created by labor and accumulated by *bourgeois* capitalists, the result of the exploitation of labor by *bourgeois* capitalists. (Marx may have preferred the terms "Statement of the Exploitation of Labor," rather than "Profit and Loss Statement," and "Statement of the Accumulated Exploitation of Labor" instead of "Statement of Retained Earnings.") But now we have a problem.

According to GAAP, profit is a definition. That means surplus value is created by definition, which makes exploitation of wage labor by *bourgeois* capitalists impossible. It is impossible to appropriate a definition. It is impossible to exploit surplus value created by labor when value itself is a definition. Profit equals revenue minus expenses, but what corporations are required, or allowed, to report as revenue and expenses changes according to changes in the definitions of revenue and expenses as pronounced by the FASB in the U.S. (or another standard-setting body such as IFRS in other countries). Profit as defined in the U.S. differs from profit as defined in Europe. This is inconsistent with capitalism.

It is, as the seventeenth century French philosopher Blaise Pascal is reported to have said, "There are truths on this side of the Pyrenees that are falsehoods on the other."[13] To underscore the differences in truth and importance (and ridiculousness) of definitions of profit, consider—"net income does not exist as a well-defined economic construct" (Scott, 2011, p. 54).

Furthermore, profit depends on definitions of profit in particular periods of time according to what accounting principles are "generally accepted" at the time. Given two identical years of production—for example, quantities of inputs, production functions, etc.,—profit changes from one year to the next merely as a result of changes in the definition of profit, which again is inconsistent with capitalism.

Accounting Principles

We are not concerned here with particular GAAP, e.g., how to value particular accounts or transactions, or when revenue and expenses must or may be recognized and when they may not be recognized. But when we say accounting principles, we really mean accounting standards. The FASB is actually the accounting standard-setter, not the accounting principles-setter. (In an odd twist of language, the standards adopted by the FASB are called principles, and the reporting system is referred to as rule based, whereas the system of standards adopted by the IASB are referred to as principles based.)

The American public did not invest large sums of money in corporations until the 1920s. Prior to the early 1930s, financial reporting was less regulated (Wolk et al., 2016). The crash of 1929 caused investors in shares to demand better financial reporting. Committees were formed such as the Trueblood Committee (1973), the Wheat Committee (1972), and the Committee on Accounting Procedures (1936) to study, adopt, or revise accounting standards (Wolk et al., 2016). The Committee on Accounting Procedures set accounting standards from 1936 to 1959. The Accounting Principles Board set accounting standards from 1959 to 1973 (Wolk et al., 2016).

Profit was not a definition in the days of feudalism, mercantilism, or during the time capitalism was in its developmental stage. While certainly profit was dependent on supply and demand as determined by market forces—the price of commodities minus the cost of producing the commodities, both determined by prices in the market—there were no standards and no standard-setting body to dictate when an enterprise may or may not recognize revenue, expenses, or profit. Recognition came at the time of the transactions.

Corporations are required by securities laws (see Chapter 7) to issue financial statements annually prepared in accordance with GAAP audited by an independent public accountant (Certified Public Accountant, CPA in the U.S.) who must issue an opinion stating whether or not the corporation's financial statements are prepared in conformity to GAAP. Failure to conform to GAAP may result in civil damages, fines, and even imprisonment. They must also submit audited financial statements to the SEC when registering the securities before they can issue securities to the public in an IPO.

In 2009 the FASB released the *FASB Accounting Standards Codification*™ (*Codification*). The *Codification* is the only source of authoritative U.S. GAAP and organizes thousands of GAAP pronouncements into 90 accounting topics but, importantly, "the Codification does not change GAAP, it introduces a new structure ..." (FASB Codification, n.d.).[14]

The *Codification* is an assemblage, a compilation, of the GAAP that had been used for decades, in some cases centuries, with differences in particular standards as revised from time to time. For example, over the years accounting standards for reporting pensions, derivatives, stock options, foreign currency translation, and leases have been revised several times. Those standards vary with how and where those items are reported, and methods of valuation for reporting those particular items on the financial statements. The fundamental structure of the financial statements has not changed in centuries.

The *Codification* is "the source of authoritative generally accepted accounting principles (GAAP) recognized by the FASB" and thus of the SEC.[15] The *Codification* "contains the authoritative standards that are applicable to public nongovernmental entities."[16] Relevant here is the following:

> A full set of financial statements for a period *shall* show all of the following:
>
> a Financial position at the end of the period,
> b Earnings (net income) for the period,
> c Cash flows during the period[17]
>
> (emphasis added)

These are, of course, the most basic financial statements issued by corporations whose shares are traded in the public: the Balance Sheet, the Income Statement, and the Statement of Cash Flows (the particular names of the statements vary). The most incriminating standard, however, is

> A full set of financial statements for a period *shall* show all of the following … e. *Investments by and distributions to owners during the period.*
>
> (emphases added)[18]

The purpose of financial reporting is no longer about providing rationally calculated profit calculations for the owners, but about providing information that shareowners and potential shareowners use to determine the market price of the stock.

By law, corporations must issue financial statements that disclose "investments by and distributions to owners during the period" even though there is absolutely no legal justification for considering shareowners as owners of the corporation, and is in fact contrary to property law and corporate law (Huber, 2020a). The FASB, and consequently the SEC, continue to maintain the false narrative that shareowners own corporations and thus capitalism still exits even after corporate law and securities laws killed it.

Accounting standards were pronounced by different bodies during different periods in history,[19] even if they were imposed rather than generally accepted. Since 1973, the FASB develops the accounting standards that all corporations that issue securities to the public in the U.S. must comply with. The FASB was designated the only private accounting standard setting body recognized by the Securities and Exchange Commission.[20]

The standards themselves underwent many revisions over time, the particulars of which are not relevant to this book. What is relevant is that although particular standards changed over time, the fundamental reporting requirements remained unchanged. Where the "capital account" of the merchant and *bourgeois* capitalist reflected the equity of the ownership of the business, and the profits accruing to the owner, it is now falsely attributed to the shareowners as "Investments by and distributions to owners during the period" thus denoting ownership by *bourgeois* capitalists, an impossibility.

Accounting Theory

GAAP is related to accounting theory but not identical to accounting theory. Accounting numbers (i.e., financial statements) have important social consequences, therefore, the choice of different values falls within the domain of accounting theory (Wolk et al., 2016).

Accounting theory embraces the assumptions, definitions, principles, and concepts that underlie accounting rule-making by an authoritative body, and the reporting of financial information by corporations (Wolk et al., 2016). GAAP, on the other hand, may or may not be based on accounting theory. GAAP determines how assets and liabilities are valued, when revenue and expenses must be (or may be) recognized, and what and how financial information is reported. GAAP may be adopted and enforced for political reasons, rather than based on accounting theory (Wolk et al., 2016).

Prior to the nineteenth century, there was no GAAP or accounting theory because it was not necessary for *bourgeois* capitalists to use GAAP or accounting theory to determine their profit. As a result of the panic of 1837, many investors suffered heavy losses. The New York Stock Exchange began to demand that companies disclose to the public more information about their finances as a condition of offering stock.[21]

There are two approaches to accounting theory—normative accounting theory and positive accounting theory. Normative accounting theory "tells accounting policy makers what should be done based on a theoretical principle" while positive accounting theory "examines real life occurrences and seeks to understand and then predict how actual companies address the accounting treatment of those transactions."[22]

Of course, accounting theory presents us with a fundamental question—how is capitalism related to accounting theory? The answers is, it isn't. Accounting theory, regardless whether it is normative or positive, as well as GAAP, stands in stark contrast to capitalism where profit is owned by the *bourgeois* capitalists and is not a definition. Accounting theory, and GAAP, are directed solely at corporations whose shares are traded in the public.

The Financial Accounting Standards Board

The FASB is the accounting standard-setting body in the U.S. Other countries use accounting standards determined by other standard-setting bodies such as the International Accounting Standards Board.[23] Thus, the definitions, recognition, and reporting of revenue and expenses and therefore profit as wells as the valuation and reporting of assets and liabilities differ from country to country.

History and Purpose

The Securities and Exchange Commission was given exclusive authority by Congress to make, amend, and rescind rules and regulations defining accounting including "the items or details to be shown in the balance sheet and earning statement, and the methods to be followed in the preparation of accounts, in the appraisal or valuation of assets and liabilities, in the determination of depreciation and depletion, in the differentiation of recurring and non-recurring income, in the differentiation of investment and operating income..."[24]

The FASB was established in 1973 as an "independent, private-sector, not-for-profit organization...that establishes financial accounting and reporting standards..." The FASB is currently the only private standard-setting body recognized by the Securities and Exchange Commission (Huber, 2016).

The FASB is comprised of seven full-time members plus staff. The mission of the FASB is to develop and issue financial accounting standards through a transparent and inclusive process to establish and improve financial accounting and reporting standards for corporations and others that issue financial statements to the public in order to provide useful information to investors and other users of financial reports.[25]

"The FASB is committed to following an open, orderly process for setting standards" which is intended "to permit timely, thorough, and open study of financial accounting and reporting issues and to encourage broad public participation in the standards-setting process by creating channels for the communication of all points of view and expressions of opinion at all stages of the process."[26] In order to issue a new or revised standard, a majority of the members of the FASB must approve the issuance of the standard.[27] (For comparative purposes, the International Accounting Standards Board (IASB) goes through a similar process when adopting its standards.)

The Financial Accounting Standards Board Conceptual Framework

Shortly after the FASB was created in 1973, it began developing a conceptual framework for accounting that in essence condensed the purpose of GAAP embodied in corporate financial reports that had been much debated over the previous decades.

> …the objective of financial reporting is to provide financial information about the reporting entity that is useful to present and potential investors, lenders, and other creditors in making decisions in their capacity as capital providers.
>
> (FASB, 2018, BC1.26)

The *FASB's Statement of Financial Accounting Concepts (Concepts Statement)* is part of the FASB's *Conceptual Framework*. The FASB issued its first *Conceptual Framework* in 1978 and has gone through several revisions since then. For convenience, all versions are referred to simply as the *Conceptual Framework*, with appropriate dates.

From the corporate perspective, "Concepts Statements are intended to set forth objectives and fundamental concepts that will be the basis for development of financial accounting and reporting guidance. The objectives identify the goals and purposes of financial reporting" (FASB, 2010, p. 5). The objectives of the *Conceptual Framework* are to identify the goals and purposes of financial reporting and therefore the *Conceptual Framework* applies to corporations that issue shares to the public. The *Conceptual Framework* is not itself a set of standards. However, it reveals much about the relationship between accounting and capitalism.

In the latest iteration, prepared jointly with the IASB, the FASB announced that the *Conceptual Framework* was

> intended to provid[e] structure and direction to financial accounting and reporting to facilitate the provision of unbiased financial and related information. *That information helps capital and other markets to function efficiently in allocating scarce resources in the economy and society.*
>
> (FASB, 2018, emphasis added)

The *Conceptual Framework* further states, "Well-developed *securities markets tend to allocate scarce resources to enterprises* that use them efficiently and away from inefficient enterprises" (FASB, 1978, ¶13, emphasis added).

There is no mention of capitalists or capitalism; only that financial and related information helps capital and other markets to function efficiently in allocating scarce resources in the economy and society, and well-developed securities markets tend to allocate scarce resources to enterprises that use them efficiently and away from inefficient enterprises. That is false. Securities markets, even well-developed ones, do not tend to allocate any resources toward any enterprise, efficient or not.

Securities markets are not markets for obtaining or transferring resources of production. Securities markets are not used to allocate scarce resources of production. Enterprises do not receive or acquire resources of production from purchasers of securities. In fact, the *Conceptual Framework* actually does acknowledge that by stating "Numerous, perhaps most, transactions in those markets are transfers from one investor or creditor to another with no part of the exchange price going to the issuing enterprise" (FASB, 1978, ¶13). That is, the exchange price in the market is the cash exchanged among buyers and sellers in the market for the security with no cash going to the enterprise.

We are forced to ask, who makes reasoned choices among alternative uses of scarce resources? To answer that question we must first acknowledge what are scarce resources. Scarce resources are land, labor, and productive capital, keeping in mind that cash is not a scarce resource. Who then decides how to use land, labor, and capital?

Purchasers of securities do not and cannot allocate resources of production of an enterprise whose shares are traded in the public because they do not own the resources of production. They are prohibited by corporate statutory law from making such decisions. They can only "allocate" cash to the firm when they purchase stock in an IPO. It is the enterprise, or more specifically, the managers and directors of the firm, that decides how to (re)allocate the land, labor, and capital on behalf of the corporation (FASB, 1978, ¶12).

As discussed in the *FASB Conceptual Framework—A Case of the Emperor's New Clothes* (Huber, 2020b), the *FASB Conceptual Framework* frequently uses "capital" and "cash" interchangeably, with no overt explanation as to why it uses the terms interchangeably. There is an implicit assumption that the reader understands, and agrees with, the interchangeability.

The *FASB Conceptual Framework* sometimes uses "capital" when it means "cash." For example, "...the objective of financial reporting is to provide financial information about the reporting entity that is useful to present and potential investors, lenders, and other creditors in making decisions in their capacity as *capital providers*" (FASB, 2018, BC1.26, emphasis added). The "capital" that capital providers provide is cash which is provided when investors in shares purchase stock from the corporation in an IPO, which the *FASB* acknowledges elsewhere:

> Business enterprises *raise capital for production* and marketing activities not only from financial institutions and small groups of individuals but *also from the public through issuing equity* and debt securities that are widely traded in highly developed securities markets.
>
> (FASB, 1978, ¶ 13, emphasis added)

Obviously raising financial capital from the public for production activities through "issuing equity" can mean nothing other than raising cash in an IPO pursuant to the '33 Act. Financial capital can be obtained in no other way than from the public in an IPO when beginning operations.

The FASB correctly links financial capital to individual savings: "Production and marketing of goods and services often involve long, continuous, or intricate processes that *require large amounts of capital, which in turn require substantial savings in the economy*" (FASB, 1978, ¶11, emphasis added), again demonstrating that large amounts of capital come from substantial savings by individuals in the economy (see Chapter 2).

At other times the *FASB Conceptual Framework* distinguishes "capital" from "cash." For example, *Statement of Financial Accounting Concepts No. 1, Objectives of Financial Reporting by Business Enterprises*, a previous iteration of the *Conceptual Framework*, states, "saving and investing in *productive resources (capital formation)* are generally considered to be prerequisite to increasing the standard of living in an economy" (FASB, 1978, ¶33, emphasis added).[28] Here, capital formation refers to investing in capital resources of production, not to acquiring cash, as reported in the Investing Activities section of the Statement of Cash Flows, the "I" of C + I + G. The FASB thus adds to the confusion and contradictory use of the term "capital."

So now we are presented with a question. If the Securities Act of 1933 and the Securities Exchange Act of 1934 are both concerned with "capital formation" (acquiring financial capital) in the securities market, exactly what kind of capital can be formed in the securities market? It can mean nothing other than financial capital, i.e., cash. And if the FASB is concerned with the production of goods that require large amounts of financial capital which in turn require substantial savings, how are large amounts of capital linked to substantial savings? The substantial savings is the cash provided to corporations by purchasers of securities, i.e., the "capital formation," when corporations issue shares in an IPO which is then used to invest in productive capital resources. There is no alternative reasonable explanation.

The FASB again links savings to financial capital: "Business enterprises *raise capital for production … from the public through issuing equity* … securities that are widely traded in highly developed securities markets" and "production … involves … processes that require large amounts of capital, which in turn require substantial savings in the economy." Here, capital is cash. In the same document the FASB recognizes "saving and *investing in productive resources* (capital formation) are generally considered to be prerequisite to increasing the standard of living in an economy." The FASB is recognizing first that financial capital used to acquire resources for production is raised in securities markets which can only mean the cash that is raised in an IPO, and second that cash is not itself a productive resource. Thus, productive resources are not actually raised in securities markets. Rather, cash is raised in securities markets which is then used by corporations to acquire productive resources, the capital assets on the left side of the firm's balance sheet. Thus, capital formation refers to raising financial capital, cash, which comes from savings, which is then used to acquire capital assets (productive capital).

The securities market, also called the capital market (Sharpe, 1964), is the forum where financial capital (cash), not productive capital (capital assets), is raised by corporations in an IPO. Corporations do not issue capital assets for cash. They issue financial assets (stock) for cash in an IPO. Corporations might sell capital assets for cash which appears on the Statement of Cash Flows as an Investing Activity, but shares of stock are not and do not represent capital assets. Capital assets are only physical assets that are used in production. Yet, a Nobel Prize winning theory has evolved which considers stock to be capital assets.

Chapter Summary

This chapter examined the financial reporting aspect of accounting and its relationship to corporations, capitalists, and capitalism.

Corporations are required by securities laws to issue financial statements that comply with GAAP. GAAP determines how assets, liabilities, and equity are valued and reported. GAAP also defines revenue and expenses, and determines when revenue and expenses can, or must be, recognized.

We saw that the "capital account" was invented for use by individuals and partnership to record their initial investment in their firms which allowed owners of the firm to separate their business assets from their personal assets. We further saw the subsequent misuse and misinterpretation of the capital account (equity) of *bourgeois* capitalists by assimilating it into corporations as "shareholders' equity."

The development of double-entry bookkeeping introduced the capital account into the accounting system which allowed the separation of the owner's personal assets from the business assets and the rational pursuit of profit. Yet, as the capital account is not an account of either financial capital or physical capital, it does not record anything actually related to capital. There is no relationship between the "capital account" and either financial capital (money) or physical capital as a means of production. The "capital account" shows equity, not capital.

The role and function of accounting is no longer to account for money contributed to the firm by the *bourgeois* capitalist as the owner of the firm, or to account for the owner's profits, but to account for net income as defined by the FASB, along with earnings per share, dividends, and other required disclosures as determined by the FASB and securities laws.

The role and function of accounting is no longer to calculate profit for the owners of the firm since shareowners do not own a corporation. Nor is it to calculate profit to capital through the $M \rightarrow C \rightarrow M$ cycle since profit is not money.

Notes

1 Other countries use different generally accept accounting principles, but they are substantially similar.
2 See *Financial Accounting Standards Board. Codification*, https://asc.fasb.org/.
3 The factory buildings are a part of the land.

4 There are also other types of assets such as intangible assets which is beyond the scope of this book. Basically, intangible assets include assets that are considered part of productive capital such as computer programs.
5 Equity is not actually owned. It is the net value of the property that is owned. You may have equity in your house, for example. But it is the house that you own while the equity is the net value of the house (market value minus mortgage). Owning equity is used here simply for convenience in order to emphasize it is the corporation's equity and not the shareowners'.
6 Delaware General Corporation Law § 122(4).
7 See, e.g., Delaware General Corporation Law § 282.
8 See, e.g., https://www.sec.gov/Archives/edgar/data/1652044/000119312515336577/d82837dex991.htm.
9 Either long-term debt or total debt may also be used in the numerator.
10 Lewis Carroll, author of *Through the Looking Glass* in which the character Humpty Dumpty appears, is the pen name of Charles Lutwidge Dodgson. Dodgson wrote in mathematical logic, among other mathematical disciplines under his own name. https://en.wikipedia.org/wiki/Lewis_Carroll.
11 *United Steel Workers of America v. United States Steel Corporation*, 631 F. 2d 1264 (6th Cir. 1980).
12 *No Conceptual Basis for Other Comprehensive Income, FASB Says,* https://tax.thomsonreuters.com/news/no-conceptual-basis-for-other-comprehensive-income-fasb-says/.
13 Blaise Pascal. http://www.knowyourquotes.com/There-Are-Truths-On-This-Side-Of-The-Pyrenees-Which-Are-Falsehoods-On-The-Other-Blaise-Pascal.html.
14 Although made by FASB, GAAP are under the jurisdiction of the Securities and Exchange Commission who may override FASB pronouncements.
15 Codification, §105-10-05-1.
16 Codification, §105-10-05-5.
17 Codification, §205-10-45-1.
18 Codification, §205-10-45-1.
19 For example, prior to 1973, the AICPA's Accounting Principles Board issued accounting standards.
20 See Huber (2016) for an explanation of the *SEC's Ultra Vires Recognition of the FASB as a Standard-Setting Body.*
21 New York Stock Exchange. https://www.britannica.com/topic/New-York-Stock-Exchange.
22 *Differences Between Positive and Normative Accounting.* https://www.nasdaq.com/articles/differences-between-positive-and-normative-accounting-2015-11-01.
23 Oddly, while the FASB determines accounting standards referred to as generally accepted accounting *principles*, it is called "rule-based" accounting, while international standards are called "principles based" accounting.
24 15 U.S.C. §77s(a).
25 ABOUT THE FASB, https://www.fasb.org/facts/.
26 Rules of Procedure, Due Process. https://www.fasb.org/cs/ContentServer?c=Document_C&cid=1176162391050&d=&pagename=FASB%2FDocument_C%2FDocumentPage.
27 ABOUT THE FASB, https://www.fasb.org/facts/.
28 The Securities Exchange Act of 1934 also uses the term "capital" to mean "cash." ("CONSIDERATION OF PROMOTION OF EFFICIENCY, COMPETITION, AND CAPITAL FORMATION.—Whenever pursuant to this title the Commission is engaged in rulemaking, or in the review of a rule of a

self-regulatory organization, and is required to consider or determine whether an action is necessary or appropriate in the public interest, the Commission shall also consider, in addition to the protection of investors, whether the action will promote efficiency, competition, and capital formation" (15 U.S.C. §78(f)).

Bibliography

Ezzamel, M. (2012). *Accounting and order.* Routledge.

Financial Accounting Standards Board (FASB). (n.d.). *FASB accounting standards codification.* Retrieved from https://asc.fasb.org/help&cid=1175804733759

Financial Accounting Standards Board (FASB). (1978). *Statement of financial accounting concepts no. 1, objectives of financial reporting by business enterprises.* FASB.

Financial Accounting Standards Board (FASB). (2010). *Statement of financial accounting concepts no. 8, conceptual framework for financial reporting.* FASB.

Financial Accounting Standards Board (FASB). (2018). *Statement of financial accounting concepts no. 8, conceptual framework for financial reporting.* FASB.

Huber, W. D. (2016). The SEC's ultra vires recognition of the FASB as a standard-setting body. *Richmond Journal of Law & the Public Interest, 19*(2), 120–152. Retrieved from https://papers.ssrn.com/sol3/papers.cfm?abstract_id=2662634

Huber, W. D. (2020a). *Corporate law and the theory of the firm: Reconstructing corporations, shareholders, directors, owners, and investors.* Routledge.

Huber, W. D. (2020b). The FASB conceptual framework – A case of the emperor's new clothes. *Journal of Accounting, Ethics & Public Policy, 21*(1), 77–114.

Levy, J. (2014). Accounting for profit and the history of capital. *Critical Historical Studies, 1*(2), 171–214. Retrieved from http://www.jstor.org/stable/10.1086/677977

Pacioli, L., Geijsbeek, J. B., Manzoni, D., Pietra, A., Mainardi, M., Christoffels, J. Y., Stevin, S., & Dafforne, R. (1914). *Ancient double-entry bookkeeping: Lucas [sic] Pacioli's treatise (A.D. 1494–the earliest known writer on bookkeeping).* J.B. Geijsbeek.

Sangster, A. (2016). The genesis of double entry bookkeeping. *The Accounting Review, 91*(1), 299–315. https://doi.org/10.2308/accr-51115

Schroeder, R. G., Clark, M. W., & Cathey, J. M. (2005). *Financial accounting theory and analysis: Text readings and cases* (8th ed.). Wiley.

Scott, W. R. (2011). *Financial accounting theory* (6th ed.). Pearson.

Sharpe, W.F. (1964). Capital asset prices: A theory of market equilibrium under conditions of risk. *The Journal of Finance, 19*(3), 425–442. https://doi.org/10.1111/j.1540-6261.1964.tb02865.x.

Wolk, H. I., Dodd, J. L., & Rozycki, J. J. (2016). *Accounting theory: Conceptual issues in a political and economic environment* (9th ed.). SAGE Publications.

7 Securities Laws

Introduction

At the height of the Great Depression, in an action that I like to call, "The horses escaped! Quick! Close the barn door!," the U.S. Congress enacted the Securities Act of 1933 ('33 Act) to regulate the issuance of securities to the public in an initial public offering (IPO). It also enacted the Securities Exchange Act of 1934 ('34 Act), which established the Securities and Exchange Commission (SEC, or Commission), to regulate the trading of securities subsequent to their initial issue.

The securities laws govern the way corporations are allowed to raise financial capital from the public and the information that corporations must report to the SEC, the shareowners, and the public. Other countries adopted their own versions of securities laws, but were quite similar in all essential aspects.

The Securities Act of 1933 and the Securities Exchange Act of 1934 require corporations that issue securities to the public to issue financial statements audited by an independent accounting firm that comply with generally accepted accounting principles. Failure to comply with generally accepted accounting principles can result in fines to the corporation, and fines and imprisonment for directors and officers.

The securities laws were, for *bourgeois* capitalists and capitalism, the equivalent of the Chicxulub event for the extinction of dinosaurs,[1] their fate irrevocably sealed while ushering in the era of what has been referred to as "financial capitalism" (see Chapter 3). But even though the securities laws were cataclysmic to *bourgeois* capitalists and capitalism, the importance of the consequences of those laws to *bourgeois* capitalists and capitalism went virtually unnoticed by accountants, politicians, economists, sociologists, and lawyers, not to mention the public. More amazing than the demise of *bourgeois* capitalists and capitalism is that *bourgeois* capitalists and capitalism continued to be denounced or praised as if they still existed, and the debate on the virtues or depravity of capitalism carried on as if capitalism were still viable as an economic system.

DOI: 10.4324/9781003240969-10

Both the '33 Act and '34 Act are concerned with "capital formation." But "capital formation" refers only to how corporations raise financial capital by issuing securities (here, stock) to the public in an IPO. Securities laws are not concerned with the formation of capital as the resource of production or the allocation of the resources of production.

The securities market, also called the capital market, is the forum where financial capital, not productive capital, is obtained by corporations when they issue shares to the public as reflected in the Statement of Cash Flows. Sharpe (1964) and many others refer to the stocks traded on an exchange as "capital assets" although capital assets are physical assets of production. The securities laws and state corporate statutory laws do not refer to securities traded on an exchange as capital assets.[2] The Uniform Commercial Code in fact categorizes shares of stock as financial assets, not capital assets.[3]

This chapter examines the Securities Act of 1933 and the Securities Exchange Act of 1934 and explains how the securities laws contributed to the extinction of *bourgeois* capitalists and capitalism.

This chapter first reviews the purpose and relevant provisions of the Securities Act of 1933. Next, the purposes of the Securities Exchange Act of 1934 are considered. Third, the role of securities laws in establishing corporate financial reporting standards is examined. Fourth, the relationship between capital, capital markets, securities laws, and capitalism is described, along with the impact of securities laws on *bourgeois* capitalists and capitalism and how the securities laws contributed to the extinction of *bourgeois* capitalists and capitalism.

It is widely believed that these two securities laws were enacted to protect the public interest. But as I explained in *The Myth of Protecting the Public Interest: The Case of the Missing Mandate in Federal Securities Law* that is false. Nor are the purposes of securities laws to protect *bourgeois* capitalists or capitalism (although the intent of both was to improve and correct weaknesses in a system considered to be capitalism) and to curb abuses by corporations whose shares were traded in the public that was the initial cause of the Great Depression. Securities laws were, in fact, designed to protect the securities market. But, as dictated by the law of unintended consequences while securities laws did enhance protections of the securities market, they had quite the opposite effect on capitalism.

Securities Act of 1933

Recall that in the U.S., the creation and governance of corporations falls entirely under the jurisdiction of each state, including the issuing of shares, as a result of the Tenth Amendment of the Constitution.[4] There are thousands of corporations whose shares are owned by one, or a few, individual *bourgeois* capitalists who merely choose to operate using a corporate form.[5] However, once a corporation begins to issue shares to the public, the corporation must comply with federal securities laws, which can be time-consuming and expensive. Most important, the corporation loses its "alter ego" status. There is then no longer an owner; no longer a *bourgeois* capitalist.[6]

Purpose of the Securities Act of 1933

When a *bourgeois* capitalist establishes her enterprise, she raises financial capital first by contributing money from her own savings (e.g., a savings account, or investment in bonds) to the enterprise and then by borrowing from family and friends which she then uses to acquire productive capital. It is no different if she chooses to operate as a corporation with the exception that instead of contributing her money directly to the enterprise she, as the sole director of the corporation, issues stock to herself. Her ownership of the stock of the corporation is now, by definition, another form of savings and the stock she now owns is a financial asset.

The money the corporation receives from issuing stock is now the financial capital of the corporation which is then used to acquire productive capital (assuming the enterprise is a producer of commodities). Legally, as seen in Chapter 5, instead of owning the enterprise, she now owns the shares issued by the enterprise that owns both the financial capital and productive capital.

The Securities Act of 1933 was enacted to regulate the initial issue of securities (initial public offering, or IPO). In an IPO, stock is issued to the public by corporations through an underwriter in order to obtain financial capital.[7] There is no trading of securities in an IPO. Underwriters arrange for the distribution of the stock to the public. The market for initial issues is referred to as the primary market, while the subsequent trading of securities is referred to as the secondary market.

Congress declared the purpose of the '33 Act is to

> provide full and fair disclosure of the character of securities sold in interstate and foreign commerce and through the mails, and to prevent frauds in the sale thereof, and for other purposes.[8]

The purpose of the '33 Act must be considered in conjunction with the purposes of the '34 Act as explained in the next section. Here, we will first consider the purpose of the '33 Act by itself.

The purpose of the '33 Act certainly is reasonable for purposes of purchasing securities in an IPO given the widespread fraud that went on in the issuance and subsequent trading of securities that contributed to the Great Depression. Fraud in issuing stock still goes on, but to a lesser extent due to the securities laws. However, as will become clear, the securities laws are anathema to *bourgeois* capitalists and capitalism.

"Full and fair disclosure" refers to the information disclosed in the corporation's financial statements and accompanying notes to the statements that allow present and potential shareowners to make decisions on risk and the prices of shares. But what is "full and fair" is, like beauty, in the eye of the beholder, or in this case, in the eye of the Financial Accounting Standards Board and the Securities and Exchange Commission.

The '33 Act requires issuers of securities to register and obtain approval[9] from the Securities and Exchange Commission prior to issuing securities to the public.[10] It can be seen that the language throughout the '33 Act (and also in the '34 Act) admits to the presence of two factors—the public interest and the interests of investors in shares, but both are subjugated to the primary purpose of protecting the securities market, i.e., the efficiency of the market system, competition within the market, and capital formation in the market. The requirement to register and obtain approval from the SEC is not primarily intended to protect the public interest. According to the Supreme Court in *A.C. Frost & Co. v. Coeur D'Alene Mines Corp.*,[11] "[t]he magnitude of the federal interest in *protecting the integrity and efficiency of the national securities market* cannot be overstated" (emphasis added).[12] It is clear that the integrity and efficiency of the national securities market has nothing to do with *bourgeois* capitalists or capitalism.

To underscore the importance of the requirements of the '33 Act and its destructive effect on capitalism, it is essential to understand the relevant sections of the Act which are set forth below.

> Unless a registration statement is in effect as to a security, it shall be unlawful for any person, directly or indirectly—(1) to make use of any means or instruments of transportation or communication in interstate commerce or of the mails to sell such security through the use or medium of any prospectus or otherwise; or (2) to carry or cause to be carried through the mails or in interstate commerce, by any means or instruments of transportation, any such security for the purpose of sale or for delivery after sale.[13]
>
> It shall be unlawful for any person, directly or indirectly, to make use of any means or instruments of transportation or communication in interstate commerce or of the mails to offer to sell or offer to buy through the use or medium of any prospectus or otherwise any security, unless a registration statement has been filed as to such security, or while the registration statement is the subject of a refusal order or stop order or (prior to the effective date of the registration statement) any public proceeding or examination...[14]

How does an issuer register the security?

> Any security may be registered with the Commission under the terms and conditions hereinafter provided, by filing a registration statement

> in triplicate, at least one of which shall be signed by each issuer, its principal executive officer or officers, its principal financial officer, its comptroller or principal accounting officer, and the majority of its board of directors or persons performing similar functions...[15]

What does unlawful mean?

> Any person who willfully violates any of the provisions of this title, or the rules and regulations promulgated by the Commission under authority thereof, or any person who willfully, in a registration statement filed under this title, makes any untrue statement of a material fact or omits to state any material fact required to be stated therein or necessary to make the statements therein not misleading, shall upon conviction be fined not more than $10,000 or imprisoned not more than five years, or both.[16]

Capital and the Securities Act of 1933

In order for an enterprise to expand, it must obtain financial capital from more than just the savings of the owner and his friends and relatives. It must obtain financial capital from the public. Providing for the full and fair disclosure of the character of securities is the all-embracing purpose of the '33 Act. Within that purpose is concern for "capital formation," which is how corporations obtain financial capital from the public. Equally important as the purpose of the Act is what is not the purpose of the Act. The purpose of the Act is not to regulate the actual capital formation—the capital assets of production.

The '33 Act is concerned solely with how corporations obtain financial capital by issuing securities to the public and what corporations do with the cash they receive when they issue stock to the public in an IPO.

> CONSIDERATION OF PROMOTION OF EFFICIENCY, COMPETITION, AND CAPITAL FORMATION.—Whenever pursuant to this title the Commission is engaged in rulemaking, or in the review of a rule of a self-regulatory organization, and is required to consider or determine whether an action is necessary or appropriate in the public interest, the Commission shall also consider, in addition to the protection of investors, whether the action will promote efficiency, competition, and *capital formation*
>
> (emphasis added)[17]

Capital formation refers only to the obtaining of financial capital in an IPO, not with the formation of physical capital. To see this, consider

> (a) REQUIREMENTS ON INTERMEDIARIES.—A person acting as an intermediary in a transaction involving the offer or sale of securities for the account of others pursuant to section 4(6) shall—

(7) ensure that all *offering proceeds are only provided to the issuer when the aggregate capital raised from all investors* is equal to or greater than a target offering amount, and allow all investors to cancel their commitments to invest, as the Commission shall, by rule, determine appropriate...

(emphasis added)[18]

The term "capital" is used 17 times in the '33 Act. While the '33 Act contains a list of 19 definitions used on the Act, capital is not one of them. To make matters worse, the securities laws use the term "capital" inconsistently.

TAKING EFFECT OF REGISTRATION STATEMENTS AND AMENDMENTS THERETO

SEC. 8. 77h(a). Except as hereinafter provided, the effective date of a registration statement shall be the twentieth day after the filing thereof or such earlier date as the Commission may determine, having due regard to the adequacy of the information respecting the issuer theretofore available to the public, to the facility with which the nature of the securities to be registered, their relationship to the *capital structure of the issuer* and the rights of holders thereof can be understood, and to the public interest and the protection of investors.

Section 77s(b)(2)(D) refers to "investment capital" in annual reports. Section 77z–2 (i)(1)(A) refers to "capital expenditures, capital structure, and other financial items;" while 77z–3(9) refers to the "capitalization of the issuer, including the authorized and outstanding amounts of its capital stock."

By "capital structure" is meant debt plus equity, but "capitalization of the issuer" means only the common (and preferred) stock.

Capitalists and the Securities Act of 1933

The Securities Act of 1933 obviously has much to say about financial capital. It has nothing to say about capitalists or capitalism. A corporation that obtains financial capital by issuing shares to the public has no relationship to *bourgeois* capitalists. A *bourgeois* capitalist does not obtain financial capital by issuing shares to the public. Once a *bourgeois* capitalist issues shares to the public, she ceases to be a *bourgeois* capitalist:

The stock-company business, which *represents the abolition of capitalist private industry* on the basis of the capitalist system itself *and*

> *destroys private industry* as it expands and invades new spheres of production...
>
> (*Capital*, Vol. III, p. 317, emphases added)

> To be a capitalist, is to have not only a *purely personal*, but a social status in production.
>
> (*Manifesto*, p. 23, emphases added)

Securities Exchange Act of 1934

The '34 Act does not address financial capital formation other than specifying the requirements for the registration statement for an IPO under the '33 Act. The '34 Act only governs the trading of securities in the market after the initial issue, not the actual initial issuance of the securities. Although the '34 Act does refer to "capital formation," trading securities in the market does not provide financial capital to the corporation and therefore cannot actually address capital formation. As with the '33 Act, the '34 Act is not concerned with the capital resources of production or the allocation of resources of production.

Purpose of the Securities Exchange Act of 1934

There are several purposes identified in the Securities Exchange Act of 1934 which was enacted to regulate securities exchanges and the subsequent trading of securities in the market. The purposes of the '34 Act are an extension of the purpose of the '33 Act. These purposes must be considered within the context of the Great Depression and its deleterious effects on interstate commerce, the national credit, federal taxes, and the national banking system.

> For the reasons hereinafter enumerated, *transactions in securities* as commonly conducted upon securities exchanges and over-the-counter markets are effected with *a national public interest* which makes it necessary to provide for regulation and control of such transactions and of practices and matters related thereto, including transactions by officers, directors, and principal security holders...*in order to protect interstate commerce, the national credit, the Federal taxing power, to protect and make more effective the national banking system and Federal Reserve System, and to insure the maintenance of fair and honest markets in such transactions...*
>
> (emphasis added)[19]

We must again consider "unlawful."

> It shall be unlawful for any member, broker, or dealer to effect any transaction in any security ... on a national securities exchange unless a registration is effective as to such security ...[20]

Corporations are required to file reports, but what reports? What are the contents of the reports?

> A security may be registered on a national securities exchange by the issuer filing an application with the exchange (and filing with the Commission such duplicate originals thereof as the Commission may require), which application shall contain—(1) Such information, in such detail...as the Commission may by rules and regulations require, as necessary or appropriate in the public interest or for the protection of investors, in respect of the following...(J) *balance sheets* for not more than the three preceding fiscal years, certified if required by the rules and regulations of the Commission by a registered public accounting firm; (K) *profit and loss statements* for not more than the three preceding fiscal years, certified if required by the rules and regulations of the Commission by a registered public accounting firm ... (2) such annual reports (and such copies thereof), certified if required by the rules and regulations of the Commission by independent public accountants, and such quarterly reports (and such copies thereof), as the Commission may prescribe.
>
> (emphases added)[21]

> The Commission may prescribe, in regard to reports made pursuant to this title, the form or forms in which the required information shall be set forth, the items or details to be shown in the *balance sheet* and the *earnings statement*, and the methods to be followed in the preparation of reports, in the appraisal or valuation of assets and liabilities, in the determination of depreciation and depletion, in the differentiation of recurring and nonrecurring income, in the differentiation of investment and operating income ...
>
> (emphases added)[22]

> Every issuer which has a class of securities registered pursuant to section 12 of this title and every issuer which is required to file reports pursuant to section 15(d) of this title shall—(A) make and keep books, records, and accounts, which, in reasonable detail, accurately and fairly reflect the transactions and dispositions of the assets of the issuer; (B) devise and maintain a system of internal accounting controls sufficient to provide reasonable assurances that...(i) transactions are executed in accordance with management's general or specific authorization; (ii) transactions are recorded as necessary (I) to permit preparation of financial statements *in conformity with generally accepted accounting principles* or any other criteria applicable to such statements, and (II) to maintain accountability for assets...
>
> (emphasis added)[23]

The question arises, why are such reports necessary? Obviously, financial reports that conform to GAAP are not required for *bourgeois* capitalists. Such reports are for shareowners and the public.

Capital and the Securities Exchange Act of 1934

The '34 Act uses the term "capital" 57 times, but again there is no definition of capital. It's as if the term "capital" were self-evident. To make matters worse, the '34 Act uses the term "capital" inconsistently.

The '34 Act refers to "capital formation," "capital expenditures," "capital resources," "capital adequacy," "capital requirements," "capital structure," and "venture capital funds." "Capital" alone, i.e., with no preceding adjective or following noun, is also used: "A futures commission merchant, introducing broker, broker, or dealer shall maintain sufficient capital to comply with the stricter of any applicable capital requirements..."[24]

"Capital adequacy" and "capital requirements," on the other hand, refer to the dollar amount of shares issued by the corporation, along with other components of equity such as preferred stock, while the erroneous term "capital structure" refers to the ratio of corporate debt to corporate equity (the debt/equity ratio) as is taught in every introductory finance course. That is, as discussed in chapter 6, the right-hand side of the balance sheet, which includes debt and equity, is deemed by some to be the capital corporation's structure, thus exhibiting the confusion in the application of the term "capital."

However, while "capital requirements" refers to the equity section of the balance sheet, the equity section of the balance sheet is not related to the cash of the corporation; i.e., "capital requirements" refers to adequate equity, not adequate cash. "Capital requirements" could not refer to adequate equity if "capital" includes everything on the right side of the balance sheet—debt plus equity—since that would mean that a debt/equity ratio of 99 would satisfy capital requirements. That is untenable and therefore, we can conclude confidently that "capital requirements" refers to equity only. But that, then, is itself a problem since equity does not equal cash. To understand the validity of that proposition, consider that Levy (2014) notes, "Global banks howl against new regulations that would increase *their equity (their capital)*" (p. 213, emphasis added). This raises two issues.

One issue is banks' complaints against such regulations show that capital is not the right side of the balance sheet. It would be strange indeed, not to mention illogical, to consider the capital of a bank to be the equity of the bank, but to consider the capital of non-bank corporations to be the entire right side of the balance sheet. The second issue is, either the entire right side of the balance sheet of a bank is its capital, in which case regulators' concerns of a bank's financial structure is baseless, or the entire right side of the balance sheet of a non-bank corporation is not its capital. It cannot be both ways except in Alice's Wonderland where the meaning of words changes with the whim of the speaker.

"Capital expenditures" does refer to cash since capital expenditure requires the use of cash to acquire the physical capital to be used in production (Investment Activities in the Statement of Cash Flows).

By definition, the trading of securities on an exchange cannot be concerned with any type of capital since trading securities on an exchange does not provide either financial capital or productive capital to corporations.

An initial issue of stock is not trading on an exchange since it does not involve the exchange of shares between a current owner of the shares who is selling the shares and a purchaser of the shares. Initial issues of shares are accomplished through an underwriter. An underwriter is defined as "any person who has purchased from an issuer with a view to, or offers or sells for an issuer in connection with, the distribution of any security, or participates or has a direct or indirect participation in any such undertaking, or participates or has a participation in the direct or indirect underwriting of any such undertaking..."[25]

The '34 Act makes it clear that capital formation refers to access to capital and the financial capital obtained by issuing securities to the public.

> OFFICE OF THE ADVOCATE FOR SMALL BUSINESS CAPITAL FORMATION.—(1) OFFICE ESTABLISHED.—There is established within the Commission the Office of the Advocate for Small Business Capital Formation (hereafter in this subsection referred to as the "Office")...The Advocate for Small Business Capital Formation shall... identify problems that small businesses have with securing *access to capital*...
>
> (emphasis added)[26]

The access to capital to which small businesses may have a problem securing is obviously nothing other than financial capital. The '34 Act is not concerned with capital formation itself which is the domain of the '33 Act. The '34 Act merely establishes the Office of the Advocate for Small Business Capital Formation within the Securities and Exchange Commission since it is the '34 Act that created the Commission and defined its powers.

Capitalists and the Securities Exchange Act of 1934

The exclusion of capitalists from the '34 Act is even more evident than under the '33 Act since there is absolutely no relationship between corporations, financial capital, and *bourgeois* capitalists within the trading of securities in the market. By definition trading securities in the market excludes any consideration of either corporations or *bourgeois* capitalists obtaining financial capital in the market.

Accounting and Securities Laws

> An essential element of capitalism is corporate reporting. Today's capitalism is supported by financial reporting.
>
> (Eccles & Spiesshofer, 2015, p. 1)[27]

Corporate financial reporting is not an essential element of capitalism, and capitalism is not supported by financial reporting. In fact, corporate financial reporting destroyed capitalism. (Corporate financial reporting and its role in the destruction of capitalism was dealt with in Chapter 6.)

Prior to the enactment of the securities laws, corporations were pretty much free to use any financial accounting reporting standards they chose because there was no government agency to enforce any particular accounting standard. With the creation of the Securities and Exchange Commission to enforce financial accounting standards under penalty of fines and imprisonment all corporations were required to report their financial statements in compliance with the standards set by the Commission or the body the Commission designated which changed from time to time.

Securities laws require corporations to issue on an annual basis financial statements that comply with GAAP, and to include financial statements that comply with GAAP when filing a registration statement with the SEC. Congress conferred on the Securities and Exchange Commission the sole authority to determine financial accounting reporting standards with which issuers of securities must comply, again, under penalty of fines and/ or imprisonment.

> *The Commission shall have authority from time to time to make, amend, and rescind such rules and regulations* as may be necessary to carry out the provisions of this title, including rules and regulations governing registration statements and prospectuses for various classes of securities and issuers, and *defining accounting, technical and trade terms used in this title.* Among other things, the Commission shall have authority, for the purposes of this title, *to prescribe the form or forms in which required information shall be set forth, the items or details to be shown in the balance sheet and earning statement, and the methods to be followed in the preparation of accounts*, in the appraisal or valuation of assets and liabilities, in the determination of depreciation and depletion, in the differentiation of recurring and nonrecurring income, in the differentiation of investment and operating income …
>
> (emphases added)[28]

As discussed in Chapter 6, from its inception the SEC has "outsourced" the development of accounting standards, unofficially at first (Chatov, 1975) then officially in 2002. In 2002 Congress amended the '34 Act granting the SEC the authority to recognize private bodies as accounting standard-setters.[29]

> (b)(1) IN GENERAL. In carrying out its authority under subsection (a) and under section 13(b) of the Securities Exchange Act of 1934, the Commission may recognize, as *"generally accepted" for purposes of the securities laws, any accounting principles established by a standard setting body*

(A) that

(i) is organized as a private entity;...

(iv) has adopted procedures to ensure prompt consideration, by majority vote of its members, of changes to accounting principles necessary to reflect emerging accounting issues and changing business practices; and

(v) considers, in adopting accounting principles, the need to keep standards current in order to reflect changes in the business environment, the extent to which international convergence on high quality accounting standards is necessary or appropriate in the public interest and for the protection of investors; and

(B) that the Commission determines has the capacity to assist the Commission in fulfilling the requirements of subsection (a) and section 13(b) of the Securities Exchange Act of 1934, because, at a minimum, the standard setting body is capable of improving the accuracy and effectiveness of financial reporting and the protection of investors under the securities laws.

(emphases added)[30]

However, the SEC retains the authority to overrule any rule-making body and has occasionally done so.

Capital Assets, Capital Markets, Capitalism, and Securities Laws

As previously noted, there is much confusion, both careless and intentional, between what is called capital, what is called capital markets, and what is called capitalism. The confusion is compounded exponentially with "capital market theory" or "portfolio theory" and the associated efficient market hypothesis, both of which were enabled and invigorated by the introduction of securities laws into the relationship between corporations and owners of shares and GAAP.

Capital Assets and Securities Laws

Recalling that the definition of savings is any consumer income that is not spent on consumer goods is savings, since an individual's ownership of stock is just a form of savings, to call the stock owned by an individual a capital asset makes no sense. One may as well call a bond a capital asset, or a savings account a capital asset. These are all just forms of savings, and individuals seek to receive the highest returns from their chosen means of savings. Merely transferring the preferred method of savings from bonds or savings accounts to stock does not transform stock into capital assets.

Merely calling the ownership of stock the ownership of capital assets begs the questions—what is the capital that is owned and whose capital is it? The questions of what is the capital asset and who owns the capital asset must be answered before it can legitimately be determined whether it is actually a capital asset. The assumption that owning stock is owning capital assets has never been proven.

Particularly noteworthy in this regard is the fact that neither the Securities Act of 1933 or the Securities Exchange Act of 1934 uses the term "capital asset" in reference to securities issued by a corporation or traded in the market, a point to be remembered when we again consider the Financial Asset Pricing Model. Neither the '33 Act nor the '34 Act provides any justification for referring to shares of stock as capital assets. Nothing in either act can explain why an ownership of stock is ownership of a capital asset.

Capital Markets, Portfolio Theory, and Securities Laws

The only market that can legitimately be called a capital market, other than the market where productive capital is bought and sold, is the market in which the initial public offering occurs through an underwriter that raises financial capital for the corporation, i.e., the primary market. Nevertheless, what is called capital market theory has been the foundation of finance and accounting research, as well as economics and legal research, for well over half a century.

Fifty years ago, for example, Jensen (1972) reviewed "the foundations and current state of mean-variance capital market theory" which relies on "the mean-variance portfolio model of Markowitz (1959), deals with the determination of the prices of capital assets under conditions of uncertainty," which in turn builds on the "Sharpe-Lintner capital asset pricing model," which in turn builds on "the work of Irving Fisher on the theory of interest" (p. 357). And it only gets worse from there since capital market and portfolio theory and research have come to be the predominant and pre-eminent method of accounting and finance research (Huber, 2016b, 2017). But capital market and portfolio theory could not have risen to such a status in accounting and finance research without the introduction of securities laws. It is the securities laws that dictate the information corporations are required to disclose in their financial statements issued to the public (Cunningham, 1994).

Financial Asset Pricing Model

Known as the "capital asset pricing model" or CAPM, the CAPM attempts to relate the expected return on stock, which is referred to as a capital asset, to risk.[31] However, even those whose works are among the most well known do not bother to define a capital asset or explain what a capital asset is, even in Nobel Prize winning lectures such as that of Sharpe, who was awarded the Nobel Prize for his work on developing the CAPM,[32] although many other contributed to it.

Sharpe (1964) addresses the problem of attempting to predict the behavior of capital markets while at the same time incorporating risk. He surmises that a typical classroom explanation of the determination of capital asset prices begins with a description that the interaction of individual preferences and physical relationships that determine an equilibrium pure interest rate which in turn determine a market risk-premium which then determine the prices of assets. Yet, for all that, we do not know what is a capital asset. Nothing is defined or explained.

We must infer that what Sharpe (and others) refer to as a capital asset is in fact shares of stock:

> in equilibrium there is a linear relationship between *the expected returns on securities* and their covariances with the market portfolio. Usually the relationship is expressed in terms of a security's beta, a scaled measure obtained by dividing a security's covariance with the market portfolio by the variance of the market portfolio.
>
> (1990, emphasis added, p. 318)

Still, that only tells us that Sharpe considered shares of stock to be capital assets. Neither he nor anyone else explains why a share of stock is a capital asset.

The problem is, individuals simply cannot own capital. They own wealth—real estate, bonds, gold, jewelry, art, and shares of stock. They cannot own capital unless the capital they own is that which is used in a business that is separate from their personal wealth (see chapter 3). Obviously, individuals seek the highest return from any savings—savings accounts, bonds, or shares of stock.

What is (erroneously) referred to as the Capital Asset Pricing Model is a rather simple equation that is used to estimate the price of what he calls a capital asset, i.e., a security traded, in the market (not in an IPO):

$$E_r = R_f + \beta(R_m - R_f)$$

where E_r is the expected return on a security, R_f is the risk-free rate of return (U.S. Treasury Bills), β (simply referred to as "beta") is the risk of the security as measured by its correlation with the market risk premium, R_m is the market rate of return, and $R_m - R_f$ is the market risk premium which is based on the risk of changes in the return and thus the market prices of the securities. The risk is a function of shareholders' investment in the securities, not their investment in the corporation. Since the return is on the financial asset, not the capital asset, the correct term of the model is the Financial Asset Pricing Model (FAPM).

The model only applies to securities traded in the market, not to securities issued in an IPO. The model is used to evaluate the equilibrium prices of securities and how securities' prices relate to each other and to the market factoring in risk. Thus, it has no relationship to corporations and, therefore, it has no direct relationship to corporations issuing securities to raise financial capital.

Recall that financial capital is money to be used to acquire capital resources of production. It is not stock. Financial capital is acquired when shares are issued in an IPO and used to acquire physical capital (capital assets). Capital assets are physical assets used in production. If, as the model alleges, the securities traded in the market are capital assets, what is it that purchasers of the securities own? If the purchaser is an individual, the securities form part of her portfolio and are a part of her total assets along with bonds, real property, art, or jewelry. Securities are, by legal definition, personal property and financial assets. Capital assets are assets used in production. Individuals do not invest in or own capital assets because they don't produce anything. Individuals consume and save by investing in financial assets such as bonds and stock among others. While enterprises seek to maximize profit, individuals seek to maximize utility and wealth.

Efficient Market Hypothesis

The efficient market hypothesis, or EMH, attempts to explain how quickly information affects security prices and returns and is therefore related to the FAPM. There are three variations to the EMH. The weak form states that securities prices merely reflect the historical prices. Then semi-strong concerns whether securities prices efficiently adjust to public information. The strong questions whether investors have monopolistic access to non-public information (Fama, 1970).

Cunningham (1994) refers to the EMH as the ECMH ("efficient capital market hypothesis") which he said was "heralded by numerous corporate and securities law scholars as an accurate account of public capital market behavior," notwithstanding the failure of the EMH to account for the crash of October 1987. But this is not the time or place to discuss the validity of the EMH. The point is, the function of the EMH is "price discovery" where the price of a security is a function of its expected return which is in turn a function of a risk premium.

Cunningham links the EMH to the mandatory disclosure rules for corporate financial reports incorporated in the '34 Act. But he suggests that the EMH "overlooked a key connection between the process of price discovery and the role of the mandatory disclosure system," the particulars of which are unimportant for the purposes of this book. The relevance of the EMH and Cunningham's linking it to the '34 Act is the relationship between the '34 Act to the behavior of the prices of securities in the "capital market" thus is not related to capital or capitalism.

Capital Assets, Capital Markets, Capitalism, and Securities Laws

Markets for financial capital existed long before securities laws. The market for corporations to raise financial capital was one of the reasons for enacting the securities laws as stated in the purpose of the '33 Act. But capital market theory, portfolio theory, the financial asset pricing model, and the efficient market hypothesis are all a function of the prices of securities and securities returns after they have been issued.

Some readers may be puzzled and may ask, "what does all this have to do with capitalism?" Other readers may say, "So? That is what capitalism is all about," or "Well, we use the terms 'capital' and 'capitalism' in a different sense."

My response to the question is, nothing. While the particulars of capital market and portfolio theory are way beyond the scope of the purpose of this book, the fact that they exist is not. What makes them relevant to the scope of this book is not that they are related to capitalism, but that they are not related to capitalism. Yet, they assuredly rest on the assumptions not only that capitalism exists, but that the market is itself capitalism (see, e.g., Levitt, 2008, and Eccles & Spiesshofer, 2015).

To those who may say, "So? That is what capitalism is all about," I say, "Thank you. Thank you for proving my point" that people use the term "capitalism" without understanding what capitalism is. To those who may say, "we use the terms 'capital' and 'capitalism' in a different sense," I again say, "Thank you. Thank you for proving my point" that people change the definitions of words to mean what they want them to mean, rather than what they actually mean.

Trading in stock, i.e., financial assets, has nothing to do with financial capital since financial capital is owned by the corporation, and obviously nothing to do with productive capital. Yet, the market, and the transactions that take place in the market, is what is referred to as capitalism.

As Levitt (2008) declared, "The principle that shareholders own the companies in which they invest...is central to modern capitalism" (Levitt, 2008; see also Friedman, 1970). This is, of course, financial capitalism:

> What made securities central to financial capitalism was the growing importance of joint-stock companies...It was in the nineteenth century that joint-stock companies began go play a central role in economic activity...In financial capitalism the investment became center stage, with everything directed towards maximizing the returns obtained from the security.
>
> (pp. 235–236)

Yet, it cannot be financial capitalism because it is trading securities in the market, which has nothing to do with financial capital obtained by corporations in an IPO.

Chapter Summary

This chapter surveyed the U.S. securities laws, the Securities Act of 1933 and the Securities Exchange Act of 1934, and explained how they contributed to the extinction of *bourgeois* capitalists and capitalism.

How are the securities laws related to *bourgeois* capitalists or capitalism? Securities laws are not related to *bourgeois* capitalists or capitalism. The securities laws were, for *bourgeois* capitalists and capitalism, the equivalent of the Chicxulub event. Securities trading continues at an ever increasing pace, while *bourgeois* capitalists or capitalism have disappeared.

This is not to say that the regulations for issuing and trading securities were not necessary. They were. It is merely to say that coupled with creating corporations by registration for any legal purpose securities laws accelerated the downward spiral of *bourgeois* capitalists and capitalism into extinction and sealed the fate of *bourgeois* capitalists and capitalism.

The securities laws did make it more difficult, and expensive, for a corporation to issue securities as a result of the process of requiring a registration statement to be in effect with the Securities and Exchange Commission in order to issue securities.[33] At the same time, the securities laws greatly reduced risk for purchasers of securities.[34] However, the securities laws also facilitated the exponential growth of corporations whose shares are traded in the public both numerically and geographically.

Capital market theory (portfolio theory), financial asset pricing model, and the efficient market hypothesis are built on nothing more than fictitious capital, a foundation of sand. The entire securities market is in fact based completely on fictitious capital, the present value of an expected stream of future cash flows, and fictitious capital is not capitalism.

Notes

1 The prevailing theory of why the dinosaurs became extinct is an asteroid struck the Yucatán peninsula near the town of Chicxulub 65 million years ago causing the extinction of the dinosaurs.

2 The Internal Revenue Code taxes profits from the sale of stock as "capital gains" even though they are financial assets, not capital assets.

3 Uniform Commercial Code §8-102: "(9) 'Financial asset'...means: (i) a security." Uniform Commercial Code §8-103: "(15) 'Security'...means...a share, participation, or other interest in an issuer or in property or an enterprise of an issuer...(iii) which: (A) is, or is of a type, dealt in or traded on securities exchanges or securities markets." (See Huber, 2020.)

4 "The powers not delegated to the United States by the Constitution, nor prohibited by it to the States, are reserved to the States respectively, or to the people." U.S. Constitution Amendment X.

5 This assumes the enterprise is engaged in the production of commodities, and not an enterprise engaged in providing a service.

6 In most states, Delaware, for example, corporations can form other corporations as a subsidiary and own 100% of the shares. However, the corporation forming another corporation must have been formed by persons.

7 Securities as defined by the Act encompasses more than just stock. However, only stock is relevant here.
8 15 U.S.C. §77.
9 Approval means only that the registration statement fulfills all the conditions required by the securities laws. The SEC does not approve or disapprove any security.
10 15 U.S.C. § 77f.
11 A.C. Frost & Co. v. Coeur D'Alene Mines Corp., 312 U.S. 38 (1941).
12 Merrill Lynch, Pierce, Fenner & Smith Inc. v. Dabit, 547 U.S. 71 (2006).
13 15 U.S.C. § 77e(a).
14 15 U.S.C. § 77e(c).
15 15 U.S.C. § 77f(a).
16 15 U.S.C. § 77x.
17 15 U.S.C. 77b(b).
18 15 U.S.C. 77d–1, REQUIREMENTS WITH RESPECT TO CERTAIN SMALL TRANSACTIONS.
19 15 U.S.C. § 78(b).
20 15 U.S.C. § 78l(a).
21 15 U.S.C. § 78l(b).
22 15 U.S.C. § 78l(b)(1).
23 15 U.S.C. § 78l(b)(2).
24 15 U.S.C. § 78o–10(e)(3)(B)(ii).
25 15 U.S.C. § 77b(a)(11).
26 15 U.S.C. § 78d.
27 Birgit Spiesshofer is an attorney. Robert G. Eccles, formerly of Harvard Business School, is the Founding Chairman of the Sustainability Accounting Standards Board (SASB).
28 15 U.S.C. § 77s(a).
29 See *The SEC's Ultra Vires Recognition of the FASB as a Standard-setting Body* that argues the SEC's recognition of the FASB was an *ultra vires* act.
30 15 U.S.C. 77s(a).
31 The types of risk associated with stock returns are systematic and unsystematic.
32 William F. Sharpe, *Capital asset prices with and without negative holdings.* Nobel Lecture, December 7, 1990, https://www.nobelprize.org/uploads/2018/06/sharpe-lecture.pdf.
33 15 U.S.C. §77e.
34 Of course, the securities laws did not prevent subsequent financial statement frauds and market crashes.

Bibliography

Chatov, R. (1975). *Corporate financial reporting: Public or private control?* Free Press.

Cunningham, L. A. (1994). Capital market theory, mandatory disclosure, and price discovery. *Washington & Lee Law Review, 51*(3), 843–877. Retrieved from https://scholarlycommons.law.wlu.edu/cgi/viewcontent.cgi?referer=&httpsredir=1&article=1584&context=wlulr

Eccles, R. G., & Spiesshofer, B. (2015). *Integrated reporting for a re-imagined capitalism.* Harvard Business School Working Paper, No. 16-032. Retrieved from https://dash.harvard.edu/handle/1/22824053

Fama, E. F. (1970). Efficient capital markets: A review of theory and empirical work. *The Journal of Finance, 25*(2), 383–417. https://doi.org/10.2307/2325486

Fisher, I. (1906). *The nature of capital and income.* Macmillan.

Friedman, M. (1970). *The social responsibility of business is to increase its profits. N.Y. Times Magazine*, Sept. 13, p. 2.

Huber, W. D. (2015). The myth of protecting the public interest: The case of the missing mandate in federal securities laws. *Journal of Business & Securities Law, 16*(2), 401–423. Retrieved from https://papers.ssrn.com/sol3/papers.cfm?abstract_id=2605301

Huber, W. D. (2016a). The SEC's *ultra vires* recognition of the FASB as a standard-setting body. *Richmond Journal of Law & the Public Interest, 19*(2), 120–152. Retrieved from https://papers.ssrn.com/sol3/papers.cfm?abstract_id=2662634

Huber, W. D. (2016b). The research-publication complex and the construct shift in accounting research. *International Journal of Critical Accounting, 7*(1), 1–48. Retrieved from https://papers.ssrn.com/sol3/papers.cfm?abstract_id=2360378

Huber, W. D. (2017). On neo-colonialism and the colonization of accounting research. *International Journal of Critical Accounting, 9*(1), 18–41. Retrieved from https://papers.ssrn.com/sol3/papers.cfm?abstract_id=2548742

Huber, W. D. (2020). *Corporate law and the theory of the firm: Reconstructing corporations, shareholders, directors, owners, and investors*. Routledge.

Huber, W. D. (2021). *Economics, capitalism, and corporations: Contradictions of corporate law, economics, and the theory of the firm*. Routledge.

Jensen, M. C. (1972). Capital markets: Theory and evidence. *The Bell Journal of Economics and Management Science, 3*(2), 357–398. https://doi.org/10.2307/3003029

Levitt, A. Jr. (2008). How to boost shareholder democracy. *Wall Street Journal*, July 1, p. A17.

Levy, J. (2014). Accounting for profit and the history of capital. *Critical Historical Studies, 1*(2), 171–214. Retrieved from http://www.jstor.org/stable/10.1086/677977

Markowitz, H. (1959). *Portfolio selection: Efficient diversification of investments*. Yale University Press.

Michie, R. (2014). The rise of capitalism from ancient origins to 1948. In L. Neal & J. G. Williamson (Eds.), *The Cambridge history of capitalism* (Vol. 2, pp. 230–263). Cambridge University Press.

Sharpe, W. F. (1964). Capital asset prices: A theory of market equilibrium under conditions of risk. *The Journal of Finance, 19*(3), 425–442. https://doi.org/10.1111/j.1540-6261.1964.tb02865.x

Part IV
The Extinction of Capitalism

In Part IV, I weave the elements of capital, capitalists, and capitalism together with corporate law, accounting, and securities laws to prove that while capital still exists, capitalists and capitalism are extinct.

Chapter 8 explains how in an ironic application of the law of unintended consequences corporate law, accounting, and securities laws actually worked against their objectives to promote, protect, and sustain capitalists and capitalism by bringing about their extinction. There is no capitalism absent the ownership of capital resources of production by *bourgeois* capitalists.

In Chapter 9, I briefly discuss social systems and the new classes institutionalized by capitalism—*bourgeois* capitalists and free wage-labor. Free wage-labor did not of course choose to become free wage-labor, but were thrust into that class by *bourgeois* capitalists as they were replaced by machines.

DOI: 10.4324/9781003240969-11

8 Capitalism and the Law of Unintended Consequences

Introduction

So far we have looked at capital, capitalists, capitalism, corporations, corporate law and property law, generally accepted accounting principles, and securities laws. When put together unless you engage in changing the meanings of words to make them mean what you want them to mean, there is no reasonable conclusion that can be reached other than that *bourgeois* capitalists and capitalism are extinct.

Capitalism as an economic system has been extinct for nearly a century after being exterminated, although unintentionally, by politicians, lawyers, and economists, after having contracted a deadly illness the century before. Unfortunately, capitalism has never been given a decent burial. In fact, no burial at all. Not even a funeral. Its decayed carcass continues to be displayed in public as if it were still alive, propped up by rhetoric that has long since lost any real meaning or relevance, but which nevertheless continues to shape economic, political, and social relations.

This chapter brings together what we now know of capital, capitalists, capitalism, corporations, corporate law and property law, generally accepted accounting principles, and securities laws as seen in the previous chapters that show that, in an ironic case of the law of unintended consequences, the very things that were intended to promote, protect, and sustain capitalists and capitalism are the very things that caused their extinction: corporate law, securities laws, and generally accepted accounting principles.

A synopsis of the discussions provided in the previous chapters is provided below to provide the context for how they are related to the extinction of *bourgeois* capitalists and capitalism.

The Necessary Conditions for Capitalism—A Review

The necessary conditions for the existence of capitalism as outlined in the previous chapters are productive capital used in greater proportion than labor in the economy as a whole, *bourgeois* capitalists (persons who own capital as the means of production), a money-based economy, land, financial

DOI: 10.4324/9781003240969-12

intermediaries (principally banks), a legal system that supports and defends private property, free wage-labor, a free market, double-entry bookkeeping and the capital account, and a spirit of capitalism residing within *bourgeois* capitalists. The absence of any one of these renders capitalism non-existent. For example, a legal regime that does not support and defend private property does not permit the presence of capitalism. The absence of a money-based economy, e.g., bartering, does not permit the presence of capitalism. The absence of free wage-labor, e.g., the use of slaves instead of free wage-labor, does not permit the presence of capitalism. Obviously, the absence of capital does not permit the presence of capitalism.

So now let us see which necessary conditions still exist, and which do not.

The conditions that still exist are productive capital used in greater proportion than labor in the economy as a whole, a money-based economy, land, financial intermediaries (principally banks), a legal system that supports and defends private property, free wage-labor, a free market, double-entry bookkeeping and the capital account.

There are two necessary conditions, however, that do not exist—*bourgeois* capitalists that own the means of production, and a spirit of capitalism.

Corporations, Corporate Law, and the Extinction of Capitalism

Corporations (also known as joint-stock companies) pre-date capitalism by centuries. Originally chartered by the sovereign, corporate charters were awarded to a limited group of individuals for very limited purposes, often for international trade ventures.[1] The shareowners contributed money to the venture to build ships thereby reducing the risk by sharing the risk with other shareowners. Upon the successful completion of the venture, the corporation distributed the profits to the shareowners in proportion to their investment and the corporation was dissolved.

Eventually, corporate charters were granted that permitted the corporation to continue for multiple voyages without requiring dissolution. The profits were still distributed to the shareowners in proportion to their contribution but the corporation was not dissolved. Shares could also be traded in primitive exchanges.

When the English colonies became a separate nation in 1789, due to the limitations placed on the federal government by the U.S. Constitution corporate charters were awarded by individual state legislatures. The development of capitalism was well underway by that time and the momentum of the development of capitalism shifted from England to the U.S. Corporate charters were still awarded for specific, limited purposes, such as the building and operation of railroads.

Even as capitalism was reaching its peak, a harbinger of its extinction appeared in 1837 when Connecticut enacted legislation abolishing the awarding of charters by specific legislation, allowing corporations to be formed for any lawful purpose by the mere act of registering the corporation with the department (or secretary) of state. Subsequently, all other states followed the Connecticut model.

Corporate statutory law in countries following the Anglo-American model provides that corporations are the sole owners of their property (assets). Shareowners have no ownership rights in corporate assets, either financial capital or productive capital.

Furthermore, corporate statutory law does not confer on shareowners ownership rights in the corporation. Corporate statutory law in fact prohibits shareowners from exercising any ownership rights in the corporation. Owners of shares own only a proportion of the shares, not of the corporation.

Corporate statutory law vests all decisions regarding corporate operations and the allocation of capital resources of production in the board of directors. Shareowners' rights are essentially limited as explained in Chapter 5. Shareowners have no right to share in the profits of the corporation. They may only share in the profits of the corporation if the board of directors chooses to declare a dividend. Dividends are paid based on the number of shares owned, not on the amount contributed by the shareowner when shares are acquired in an IPO and obviously not based on the amount paid by purchasers of shares in the market subsequent to the IPO. Different shareowners may contribute different amounts depending on whether the corporation had multiple IPOs issued at different prices.

Allowing incorporation for any lawful purpose by mere registration removed any political influences that restricted corporate formation. The number of corporations soon expanded as did the public trading of shares on exchanges. For example, the New York Stock Exchange was formally created in 1817. However, "Greater commercial activity in the United States after the War of 1812 and speculation in railroad stocks in the 1830s increased demand for capital and stimulated trading at the exchange. After the Civil War [that ended in 1865] the exchange provided the capital for the accelerating industrialization of the United States."[2]

Importantly, as the number of joint-stock companies rises, the number of capitalists falls (Scott, 1979), resulting in the extinction of *bourgeois* capitalists and capitalism as Marx himself acknowledged: "*The stock-company business*, which *represents the abolition of capitalist private industry* on the basis of the capitalist system itself *and destroys private industry* as it expands and invades new spheres of production" (*Capital*, Vol. III, p. 317, emphasis added).

Accounting, GAAP, and the Extinction of Capitalism

One of the hallmarks as well as criticisms of capitalism and *bourgeois* capitalists is that they accumulate profit. But the profit on which Marx relied in formulating his thesis is money, not a definition, which is the basis of his

$M \rightarrow C \rightarrow M \rightarrow C$ cycle. However, with corporate statutory law, securities laws, and generally accepted accounting principles, Marx's thesis no longer has any validity. Profit is now a matter of definition. Definitions cannot be accumulated.

While obviously profit is accumulated by corporations as reflected in the corporation's retained earnings, Marx's $M \rightarrow C \rightarrow M \rightarrow C$ cycle has been rendered meaningless. The cycle would have to be $P \rightarrow C \rightarrow P \rightarrow C$, where P is profit, which makes no sense because capital cannot be acquired with profit because profit is not money. Nor can wage-labor be paid with profit. Furthermore, shareowners cannot accumulate profit because they do not own the corporation or its profit.

By changing profit to a mere definition, generally accepted accounting principles resulted in the extinction of *bourgeois* capitalists and capitalism.

Securities Laws and the Extinction of Capitalism

As previously noted, the U.S. securities laws of 1933 and 1934 were enacted at the height of the Great Depression. Other countries soon adopted similar securities laws. The securities laws were, for *bourgeois* capitalists and capitalism, the equivalent of the Chicxulub event for the extinction of dinosaurs, their fate irrevocably sealed. But even though the securities laws were cataclysmic to *bourgeois* capitalists and capitalism, the importance of the consequences of those laws to *bourgeois* capitalists and capitalism went virtually unnoticed by accountants, politicians, economists, sociologists, and lawyers, not to mention the public. More amazing than the demise of *bourgeois* capitalists and capitalism is that *bourgeois* capitalists continued to be denounced or praised as if they still existed, and the debate on the virtues or depravity of capitalism carried on as if capitalism were still viable as an economic system.

The Securities Act of 1933 ('33 Act) was enacted to regulate the initial issue of securities (initial public offering, or IPO, here concerned with stocks). The '33 Act is

> AN ACT To provide full and fair disclosure of the character of securities sold in interstate and foreign commerce and through the mails, and to prevent frauds in the sale thereof, and for other purposes.[3]

"Full and fair disclosure" of course refers to the information disclosed in the financial statements and notes that allow shareowners and potential shareowners to make decisions on risk, return, and the market prices of shares.

The Securities Exchange Act of 1934 ('34 Act) was enacted to regulate securities exchanges and the subsequent trading of securities in the market. The purposes of the '34 Act is an extension of the purpose of the '33 Act.

> For the reasons hereinafter enumerated, transactions in securities as commonly conducted upon securities exchanges and over-the-counter markets are effected with a national public interest which makes it necessary to provide for regulation and control of such transactions and of practices and matters related thereto, including transactions by officers, directors, and principal security holders ... *in order to protect interstate commerce, the national credit, the Federal taxing power, to protect and make more effective the national banking system and Federal Reserve System, and to insure the maintenance of fair and honest markets in such transactions ...*
>
> (emphasis added)[4]

Both acts are concerned with "capital formation." But "capital formation" refers only to how corporations raise financial capital by selling securities to the public in an IPO, not to raising financial capital by *bourgeois* capitalists. Corporations then use the financial capital obtained in an IPO to acquire productive capital. It is the corporation that owns the means of production, not *bourgeois* capitalists. Securities laws are not concerned with the formation of capital as the resource of production or the allocation of the resources of production.

The securities market, also called the capital market, is the forum where financial capital, not productive capital, is obtained by corporations when they issue shares to the public in an IPO as reflected in Investing Activities in the Statement of Cash Flows.

The securities laws enabled the growth of corporations whose shares are traded in the public, and as previously noted, as the number of joint-stock companies that issued shares to the public rose, the number of *bourgeois* capitalists fell, resulting in the extinction of *bourgeois* capitalists and capitalism.

The Extinction of Capitalism and the Law of Unintended Consequences

To conclude in a syllogistic-type argument, I will state the premises upon which the conclusion that *bourgeois* capitalists and capitalism are based:

- Capitalism requires *bourgeois* capitalists.
- *Bourgeois* capitalists embody a spirit of capitalism.
- In capitalism, *bourgeois* capitalists are the owners of the capital resources of production.
- *Bourgeois* capitalists accumulate profit (surplus value created by free wage-labor).
- Corporate law and property law prohibit the ownership of capital resources of production by anyone other than the corporation.

- Owners of share of corporations whose shares are traded in the public do not own the corporation.
- Owners of share of corporations whose shares are traded in the public do not own the capital resources of production of the corporation.
- Shareowners do not accumulate the profit of the corporation.
- Corporate law prohibits the management of the corporation by anyone other than the directors of the corporation and those whom they appoint.
- Corporate law prohibits the management of the capital resources of production by anyone other than the directors of the corporation and those whom they appoint.
- Corporations own the financial capital and productive capital.
- Corporations are fictitious persons.
- Fictitious persons cannot be capitalists.
- Fictitious persons cannot have a spirit of capitalism.
- Fictitious persons own both the financial capital and productive capital.
- Wage-labor is not employed by *bourgeois* capitalists.
- Wage-labor is employed by corporations.
- Wage-labor is employed by fictitious persons.
- Shareowners cannot appropriate surplus value of labor.
- Shareowners do not own the means of production.
- Shareowners cannot accumulate capital.
- Therefore, there are no *bourgeois* capitalists.
- Therefore, there is no capitalism.

Capitalists and capitalism are extinct. *Q.E.D.*

As further proof that *bourgeois* capitalists and capitalism are extinct consider that the current movement in both the U.S. and Europe to have greater diversity on boards of directors of corporations whose shares are traded in the public eliminates any possible argument that either corporations or shareowners are capitalists.[5]

Chapter Summary

This chapter has synthesized capital, capitalists, capitalism, corporations, corporate law and property law, generally accepted accounting principles, and securities laws thereby demonstrating that *bourgeois* capitalists and capitalism are extinct.

The irony is that the very things that were designed to promote, protect, and sustain what was believed to be capitalists and capitalism—corporate statutory law, securities laws, and GAAP—are the very things that destroyed them. Corporate law, accounting, and securities laws destroyed the *bourgeois* capitalist. Neither *bourgeois* capitalists nor capitalism can be resurrected.

Shareowners cannot be *bourgeois* capitalists because they own neither the corporation's capital nor the corporation itself. By corporate statutory law, the profit of the corporation is just that—the profit of the corporation, not the shareowners. The profit is not owned by the shareowners and it is not part of the shareowners' wealth. Thus, shareowners cannot accumulate profit. Furthermore, by corporate statutory law none of the corporation's initial financial capital was its own as the financial capital of the *bourgeois* capitalist was hers. The initial financial capital of the corporation was acquired in its entirety from outside the corporation by issuing shares.

That capitalism would no longer exit was actually recognized by Marx in the mid-nineteenth century, although strangely he did not realize that he realized it.

> *The stock-company business*, which *represents the abolition of capitalist private industry* on the basis of the capitalist system itself *and destroys private industry* as it expands and invades new spheres of production... Since property here exists in the form of stock, its movement and transfer become purely a result of gambling on the stock exchange, where the little fish are swallowed by the sharks and the lambs by the stock-exchange wolves. There is antagonism against the old form in the stock companies, in which social means of production appear as private property; but the conversion to the form of stock still remains ensnared in the trammels of capitalism; hence, instead of overcoming the antithesis between the character of wealth as social and as private wealth, *the stock companies merely develop it in a new form*.
>
> (*Capital*, Vol. III, p. 317, emphasis added)

In spite of acknowledging that, "The capitalist mode of production has brought matters to a point where the work of supervision, *entirely divorced from the ownership of capital*" (*Capital*, Vol. II, p. 263, emphasis added) and, "this function in the person of the manager is *divorced from ownership of capital*" (*Capital*, Vol. II, p. 315, emphasis added), the epiphany eluded him. While there can be a capital mode of production, there can be no capitalist mode of production when capital is divorced from ownership of capital by *bourgeois* capitalists. Marx failed to realize that the "new form" is not capitalism since the "new form" made *bourgeois* capitalists extinct. He was blinded to the fact that what he vehemently argued for—the end of capitalism, i.e., the abolition of the private ownership of the means of production by *bourgeois* capitalists—had already begun, replaced by corporations whose shares are traded in the public as the owners of the means of production.

Both critics and defenders of capitalism share the same irrationality. They both serve no purpose other than to continue in a state of denial. Warnings that capitalism failed or is in crisis are nothing more than sounding brass or tinkling cymbals. The warnings that capitalism is in crisis are an attempt to regress onto the present an economic system that no longer exists. Likewise, it is impossible to defend an economic system that does not exist. One may just as well defend the continued success of feudalism. Capitalism did not fail and cannot fail. It is not in crisis because it does not exist. The rhetoric that capitalism may be in crisis but still viable delays the inevitable admission that it is extinct.

Capitalism is extinct as the result of corporate law, accounting, and securities laws. Together, they dissolved the very essence of capitalism and the structure upon which capitalism is based.

Notes

1 Corporate charters were also granted for other purposes, but charters for international trade were the most prominent.
2 New York Stock Exchange, https://www.britannica.com/topic/New-York-Stock-Exchange.
3 15 U.S.C. §77.
4 15 U.S.C. §78(b).
5 *States are Leading the Charge to Corporate Boards: Diversify!*. https://corpgov.law.harvard.edu/2020/05/12/states-are-leading-the-charge-to-corporate-boards-diversify/.

Bibliography

Marx, K. (1990). *Capital, a critique of political economy* (Vol. 3). Penguin Classics.
Scott, J. T. (1979). *Corporations, classes, and capitalism*. Hutchinson.

9 Capitalists, Capitalism, Social Systems, Classes, and Power

Introduction

No discussion of capitalism and its extinction would be complete without at least briefly acknowledging social structures and the classes produced by capitalism. As Radice (1999) thoughtfully observes, "Economic behaviour cannot be separated from social relations centred on the distribution of resources and power, and the social construction of beliefs and institutions" (p. 721).

Classes have existed throughout human history. There are, of course, many ways to categorize classes, e.g., peasants and nobility; lords and vassals; or classes based on heredity as in a caste system. Classes are not necessarily diametrically opposed as are *bourgeois* capitalists and the proletariat, but can exist on a kind of continuum such as the Indian caste system known as *jati* which, while inflexible, is a hierarchical stratification of society.

Capitalism introduced two new social classes not previously seen—*bourgeois* capitalists and the proletariat who are the free wage-labor. Capitalism transformed labor which has existed throughout history into free wage-labor by separating labor from the ownership of the means of production. It is thus imperative to understand how the economic system influences and determines our society and our perceptions of it since economic behavior is centered on the distribution of resources and power and the social construction of beliefs and institutions which necessarily translates into classes.

This chapter, therefore, considers the social structure and social classes created by capitalism. Capitalism as presented in previous chapters are in this chapter reframed into classes, social structures, and power.

Structuring society into classes is more than just an academic exercise, more than just definitions and semantics. Classes are inseparably linked to political, economic, and religious factors and power.

Capitalists, Capitalism, and Social Systems

All economies, past and present, are embedded and enmeshed in social relations and the institutions of society (Gemici, 2008; Polanyi, 2001). The

DOI: 10.4324/9781003240969-13

working of the economic system not only influences society, but determines how society is perceived and structured as the sides of a triangle determine its angles (Polanyi, 1947). Every economic phenomenon is at the same time a social phenomenon, and a particular kind of economy presupposes a certain kind of society (Giddens, 1971).

Every economic institution is at the same time a social construction. Languages and culture are important factors in social construction since language and meaning structures contribute significantly to the social construction of economic institutions and *homo economicus* is essentially a cultural phenomenon (Bourdieu, 2005) which determines how we live and act and the decisions we make.

Capitalism "determines the character of the social, political, and intellectual life" (Marx, *Capital*, Vol. I, p. 58). Asserting, whether correctly or incorrectly, that "capitalism is the backbone of contemporary economics," Greif (2005) states, "Comprehending economic and social outcomes in the contemporary world thus requires understanding capitalism" (p. ix). Fully comprehending the economic and social outcomes of the contemporary world requires understanding capitalism as "a specific social structure, or equivalently, a social system, a [sic] historically unique configuration of social relations" (Melios, 2018, p. 4). The historically unique configuration of social relations of capitalism is that capitalism is "a social order characterized by a '*bourgeoisie*' culture" (Heilbroner, 1974, emphasis in original).

Social structures influence the economic actions of individuals, economic actions have an element of power, and economic power is the ability to control of resources (Granovetter & Swedberg, 2001). The ability to control resources is of course the ability to control not only land, but also capital and labor.[1] At the time capitalism was ascending the ability to control capital and labor was held by *bourgeois* capitalists. Now the ability to control capital and labor is wielded by corporations, i.e., by fictitious persons.

Therefore, understanding the social structures and cultural phenomena associated with the rise of capitalism is important in order to understand the extinction of capitalism and its vestiges.

Capitalism is not just a system as a means of production using capital resources. Capitalism is a concept that "*refer[s] to a certain perceived way of thinking in an economic system*...It is not a concept that originated in the world of business, as accounting did" (Chiapello, 2007, p. 276, emphasis added). Economic historian T. S. Ashton reminds us that the changes from a feudal system to a capitalist system were not industrial only, but also social and intellectual (Ashton, 1968).

Weber uses the expression spirit of capitalism to describe the attitude which seeks profit rationally and systematically (Giddens, 1971). "... *attitude* of mind has on the one hand found its most suitable expression in capitalistic enterprise" (Weber, 1992, p. 28, emphasis added). "Any and every 'economic' phenomenon is at the same time always a social phenomenon, and existence of a particular kind of 'economy' presupposes a definite kind of society" (Giddens, 1971, pp. 120–121), which is, of course the social construct of capitalism erected on the capitalist mode of production. The "capitalist spirit" or "spirit of capitalism," which Weber calls an "attitude," is nothing more than a social construct. It is a psychological condition. The American Psychological Association defines attitude as "a relatively enduring and general evaluation of an object, person, group, issue, or concept on a dimension ranging from negative to positive."[2] The attitude generated by capitalism has endured to the present in spite of its extinction.

Capitalism is based on an institutionalized social order (Streek, 2011). But how do we understand the institutionalized social order resulting from capitalism?

> Institutions further imply historicity and control...Institutions always have a history, of which they are the product. It is impossible to understand an institution adequately without an understanding of the historical process in which it was produced. Institutions also, by the very fact of their existence, control human conduct...
>
> (Berger & Luckmann, 1966, pp. 54–55)

But capitalism as an institution was never controlled as was Marxism, nor does (or did) capitalism control anything. It was the *bourgeois* capitalists who controlled the capital and the labor, and the wage-labor that were controlled.

Wallerstein (1974) takes "the defining characteristic of a social system to be the existence within it of a division of labor, such that the various sectors or areas within are dependent upon economic exchange..." (p. 390). In so doing, Wallerstein equates an economic system with a social system. That is, if an economic system exists, so does a social system.

Wallerstein regards capitalism not just as an economic system, not just as *a* world system, but as the *only* world system. "...in the nineteenth and twentieth centuries there has been only one world-system in existence, the capitalist world-economy" (p. 390).

Capitalists, Capitalism, and Classes

As noted, structuring society into classes, castes, or estates is more than just an academic exercise, more than just definitions and semantics. Classes are inseparably linked to political, economic, and religious factors, but with the rise of *bourgeois* capitalists and free wage-labor, capitalism abolished estates and restructured society along new class lines (Lukács, 1971).[3]

> Bourgeoisie and proletariat are the only pure classes in bourgeois society. They are the only classes whose existence and development are entirely dependent on the course taken by the modern evolution of production and only from the vantage point of these classes can a plan

> for the total organisation of society even be imagined. The outlook of the other classes (petty bourgeois or peasants) is ambiguous or sterile because their existence is not based exclusively on their role in the capitalist system of production but is indissolubly linked with the vestiges of feudal society.
>
> (Lukács, 1971, p. 59)

Marx obviously had much to say about classes, in particular *bourgeois* capitalists and proletariat; Sombart and Weber not as much. This chapter, however, does not center on Marx's, Sombart's, and Weber's views of classes, but on insightful observations about classes and power made by others that must be considered as part of the discourse on capitalism.

As previously noted, the development of capitalism as an economic system was accompanied by the replacement of the agrarian feudal economic system and its social of classes with two new social classes—*bourgeois* capitalists and the proletariat who are free wage-labor. Labor has always existed, but capitalism transformed labor into free wage-labor by separating labor from the ownership of capital. The rise of manufacturing under capitalism created for the first time the urban proletariat (Wallerstein, 1974).

There were social classes prior to capitalism that were constructed on commodity-production and exchange, such as "petty commodity production," where the ruling class lived off of the surplus labor of the workers producing commodities; e.g., systems built on slavery and serfdom (Dobb, 1958). Marx himself wrote of "petty *bourgeois*" who were small shop owners (*Manifesto*, 1848). Similarly, Bourdieu (2005) refers to "petit-bourgeois suffering" with respect not to capitalism, but to the housing market.

The petty (also referred to as the petite, or petit) *bourgeoisie* were considered as *bourgeoisie* hopefuls, aspiring to move up and become part of the *bourgeoisie* class. Capitalist growth and development is attributed to the petty *bourgeoisie* as they transitioned into the capitalist class thus fueling the growth of capitalism.[4] Crossick and Haupt (1997) provide an overview of the petite *bourgeoisie* and the role of the small enterprise. Melios (2018) discusses an intermediate social class that he refers to as the "petty *bourgeoisie*" who are neither *bourgeois* capitalists nor wage-labor. However, petty, or petite, *bourgeoisie* did not create free wage-labor and thus cannot be a legitimate class of capitalism.

But just as service companies and financial intermediaries cannot be capitalistic enterprises, whether privately owned or public owned, because service companies cannot appropriate and accumulate capital and surplus value, the petty *bourgeoisie* and mercantilists cannot be capitalistic enterprises because they, too, cannot appropriate and accumulate capital and surplus value.

Notably, regardless of class labels or characteristics, classes are occupied by real persons. Corporations cannot be a class because they are fictitious persons.

Capitalists, Capitalism, Social Systems, and Power

Consider that since the history of profit is a history of power (Levy, 2014) and capitalism refers to the organization of production in terms of a search for the realization of profit for privately owned productive capital (Giddens, 1971; Scott, 1979), then the history of capital is also a history of power. If the private owners of capital, i.e., *bourgeois* capitalists, seek profit, they seek power.[5] As the owners of capital, *bourgeois* capitalists controlled both capital and labor.

It is evident that "the dominant bourgeois *ideology*...favors the perpetuation and reproduction of the capitalist social order and in general the long-term interests of the capitalist class" (Melios, 2018, p. 17, italics in original; see also Bourdieu & Passeron, 1990).

A question that comes to mind then is, why is there a continuing belief that capitalism still exists when the most important component of capitalism—ownership of capital by *bourgeois* capitalists—is removed from the equation? The answer to that question may be found in the answer to another question.

Since the dominant ideology favors the perpetuation and reproduction of the capitalist social order and in general the long-term interests of the capitalist class, another question that comes to mind is, who benefits from perpetuating the capitalist ideology when *bourgeois* capitalists and the capitalist class do not exist?

The capitalist ideology cannot favor the long-term interests of the capitalist class because the capitalist class no longer exists. Thus, *bourgeois* capitalists do not benefit from capitalist ideology because they do not exist. Wage-labor does not benefit from capitalist ideology because they are still separated from ownership of the capital they use and the commodities they produce. Shareowners, although they may receive part of the profit of the corporation as dividends, do not benefit from maintaining the capitalist ideology because they own neither the capital nor the profit.

The conclusion must be that it is first the corporations that benefit from maintaining the capitalist ideology since it is they who own the capital and the profit and who control the capital and the labor. Yet, corporations are fictitious persons. Corporations are managed by real persons and it is they, the directors who are agents of the corporation and who manage the corporation who ultimately benefit from maintaining the capitalist ideology along with those whom they appoint—the officers and executives.

While the church wields power, the church cannot be a class. The government wields power but cannot be a class. Corporations wield power, but corporations cannot be a class.

All of the foregoing discussion regarding social systems, social construction, classes, and power share a common thread in that they all revolve around capitalism which I have proven (and I use the term "proven" unreservedly and unapologetically) does not exist. A legitimate question may thus be posed, why discuss the social systems, social construction, classes, and power created by capitalism when capitalism does not exist? The answer is quite simple.

It is important to discuss the social systems, social construction, classes, and power created by capitalism when capitalism does not exist because the social system, social construction, classes, and power that exist today were constructed on a system that no longer exists, but is treated as if it does exist. There is an irreconcilable incongruence between what exists and the reason it exists. This incongruence must end now if any meaningful advances are to be made in area studies ranging from economics and economic policy, to sociology and social organizations, social psychology, political science, and industrial relations, to name a few.

Chapter Summary

Classes have existed throughout history and across cultures. There are many ways to interpret social systems and classes. This chapter reviewed in an extremely brief manner the concepts of social systems, social classes, and power as they relate to capitalists and capitalism.

The new classes and social system produced by capitalism were the *bourgeois* capitalists and the proletariat who are the free wage-labor. *Bourgeois* capitalists owned the capital and controlled the resources of production—capital and labor.

Capitalism requires the presence of both *bourgeois* capitalists and free wage-labor such that capitalism cannot exist without the presence of both *bourgeois* capitalists and free wage-labor. Although free wage-labor still exists, it has been shown repeatedly throughout this book, *bourgeois* capitalists have been rendered extinct by corporate law, accounting, and securities laws thus destroying the foundation of capitalism.

Yet, notwithstanding the fact that both *bourgeois* capitalists and capitalism are extinct, the belief that capitalism continues to exist is enabled by the domination of the *bourgeois* capitalist ideology, which is the embodiment of what Marx called a "false consciousness" and what Bourdieu and Passeron (1990) referred to as "misrecognition." While *bourgeois* capitalists, one of the necessary conditions for capitalism, have ceased to exist wage-labor has not. But now it is controlled by corporations, fictitious persons. That is, the power previously exercised by *bourgeois* capitalists through the ownership of capital and the ability to control the resources of production is now exercised by corporations. It is the corporations and the directors of the corporations, therefore, that benefit from the assumption of this power.

Notes

1 Land is also a resource subject to control whether by the laws of private property or the state. However, land is a fixed resource and is ignored here.

2 APA Dictionary of Psychology. https://dictionary.apa.org/.
3 While "Capitalism is the dominant mode of production in the Indian economy" (Sau, 1984), the caste system is still firmly embedded in Indian society. See, e.g., "India's caste system remains entrenched, 75 years after independence," The Economist, Sept. 11, 2021, https://www.economist.com/asia/2021/09/11/indias-caste-system-remains-entrenched-75-years-after-independence. The proletariat are not a separate caste.
4 See *Marxists Internet Archive Encyclopedia*, https://www.marxists.org/glossary/terms/p/e.htm#petit-bourgeoisie.
5 In *The Social Structures of the Economy*, Bourdieu (2005) identifies several types of capital, including social capital, symbolic capital, and cultural capital. However, he also includes "commercial capital" that he defines as sales power related to the distribution network thus equating "capital" with power. Unfortunately, *The Social Structures of the Economy* is dedicated to the housing market, which is a good resource for policy making and implementation, but lacking in actual analysis of the social structures of the economy.

Bibliography

Ashton, T. S. (1968). *The Industrial Revolution: 1760–1830*. Oxford University Press.

Berger, P. L., & Luckmann, T. (1966). *The social construction of reality: A treatise on the sociology of knowledge*. Random House.

Bourdieu, P. (2005). *The social structures of the economy*. Polity Press.

Bourdieu, P., & Passeron, J.-C. (1990). *Reproduction in education, society and culture* (2nd ed.) (R. Nice, Trans.). Sage Publications.

Chiapello, E. (2007). Accounting and the birth of the notion of capitalism. *Critical Perspectives on Accounting, 18*(3), 263–296. https://doi.org/10.1016/j.cpa.2005.11.012.

Crossick, G., & Haupt, H.-G. (1997). *The petite bourgeoisie in Europe 1780–1914: Enterprise, family and independence*. Routledge.

Dobb, M. (1958). *Capitalism yesterday and today*. Lawrence and Wishart.

Gemici, K. (2008). Karl Polanyi and the antinomies of embeddedness. *Socio-Economic Review, 6*, 5–33. https://doi.org/10.1093/ser/mwl034

Giddens, A. (1971). *Capitalism and modern social theory: An analysis of the writings of Marx, Durkheim, and Max Weber*. Cambridge, UK: Cambridge University Press.

Granovetter, M., & Swedberg, R. (2021). *The sociology of economic life*. (3rd ed.). Routledge.

Granovetter, V., & Swedberg, R. (2001). *The sociology of economic life* (2nd ed.). Westview Press.

Greif, A. (2005). Institutions, markets, and games. In V. Nee & R. Swedberg (Eds.), *The economic sociology of capitalism* (pp. ix–xxxi). Princeton University Press.

Heilbroner, R. (1974). *An inquiry into the human prospect*. W. W. Norton.

Levy, J. (2014). Accounting for profit and the history of capital. *Critical Historical Studies, 1*(2), 171–214. Retrieved from http://www.jstor.org/stable/10.1086/677977

Lukács, G. (1971). *History and class consciousness: Studies in Marxist dialectics* (R. Livingstone, Trans.). The MIT Press.

Marx, K. (1990). *Capital, A critique of political economy (3 volumes)*. Penguin Classics.

Marx, K., & Engels, F. (1848). *Manifesto of the Communist Party.* Retrieved from https://activistmanifesto.org/assets/original-communist-manifesto.pdf

Melios, J. (2018). *The origins of capitalism as a social system: The prevalence of an aleatory encounter.* Routledge.

Polanyi, K. (1947). Our obsolete market economy: Civilization must find a new thought pattern. *Commentary, 3,* 109–117. Retrieved from https://www.ocf.berkeley.edu/~immer/polanyiobsolete.pdf

Polanyi, K. (2001). *The great transformation: The political and economic origins of our time.* Beacon Press.

Radice, H. (2000). Globalization and national capitalisms: Theorizing convergence and differentiation. *Review of International Political Economy, 7*(4), 719–42. Retrieved from https://www.jstor.org/stable/4177368

Sau, R. (1984). Development of capitalism in India. *Economic and Political Weekly, 19*(30), 73–80. Retrieved from https://www.jstor.org/stable/4373468

Scott, J. T. (1979). *Corporations, classes, and capitalism.* Hutchinson.

Streek, W. (2011). E plurbus unum? Varieties and commodities of capitalism. In M. Granovetter & R. Swedberg (Eds.), *The sociology of economic life* (3rd ed., pp. 419–455). Routledge.

Wallerstein, I. (1974). The rise and future demise of the world capitalist system: Concepts for comparative analysis. *Comparative Studies in Society and History, 16*(4), 387–415. Retrieved from https://www.jstor.org/stable/178015

Weber, M. (1992). *The protestant ethic and the spirit of capitalism* (T. Parsons, Trans.). Routledge.

Epilogue

Capitalism has been proclaimed not just to exist, but to be a global economic system. Yet, no one has presented any argument, proof, or evidence that capitalism actually still exists, let alone that it is a global system. That capitalism exists is taken for granted, accepted as a valid premise. Everyone knows capitalism exists. It is an axiom that needs no proof.

One reason why it is universally accepted that capitalism still exists may be due to the fact that capital and capitalism have only been studied in relative isolation. That is, capital and capitalism have been studied from sociological perspectives and from historical perspectives. Capital and capitalism have been studied from economic perspectives. Capital and capitalism have been studied from accounting and finance perspectives. Capital and capitalism have been studied from securities laws perspectives. Capital and capitalism have been studied in relation to corporations. But when capital and capitalism are linked with history, sociology, economics, property law, corporations, corporate law, accounting and finance, and securities laws, we encounter irreconcilable inconsistencies and contradictions. There can be no meaningful discourse on capitalism when that discourse is based on inconsistencies and contradictions in definitions. For discourse to take place, meanings must remain consistent across domains and disciplines.

The purpose of this book was to examine the factors that converged to contribute to the extinction of *bourgeois* capitalists, and thus of capitalism as an economic system. In furtherance of the purposes of the book, I have summarized the relationships between capital, capitalists, and capitalism. I have highlighted the basic concepts of corporations as well as property law and corporate law. I have reviewed generally accepted accounting principles and securities laws with a focus on U.S. securities laws. The inevitable and incontrovertible conclusion is that *bourgeois* capitalists and capitalism are extinct.

A summary of the previous chapters follows.

Summary of Chapters

In Chapter 1, I examined capital and the different ways the term has been used and distorted. Capital is one of the three resources of production,

DOI: 10.4324/9781003240969-14

along with land and labor. Capital, also referred to as productive capital, is that which is made by labor (humans) to be used by labor to produce commodities and is the only capital that is related to *bourgeois* capitalists, capitalism, and the means of production. Financial capital is money that is used to acquire other resources of production, in particular productive capital.

Chapter 2 reviewed *bourgeois* capitalists. *Bourgeois* capitalists are individuals (or partners, or small corporations) who own the means of production, i.e., the productive capital. *Bourgeois* capitalists hire free wage-labor. Labor does not own the capital it uses to produce commodities.

Chapter 3 was a study of capitalism in an historical context. Capitalism is both an economic system and a social system with its origins in the Industrial Revolution. Capitalism, what Marx called the mode of production, is the use of capital in greater proportion than labor to produce commodities (assuming all other factors that are necessary for the existence of capitalism such as free-trade, banking, private property, etc., are present). Like capital, the term "capitalism" has been distorted to mean things other than the use of capital as the means of production to produce commodities. However, no other "type" of capitalism has anything to do with labor using capital owned by *bourgeois* capitalists to produce commodities.

Chapter 4 considered the history and purpose of corporations, also called joint stock companies. Corporations are centuries old. The purpose of corporations is to be able to undertake ventures that present too much risk for one individual and that require more productive capital and more financial capital than one individual is capable of providing; to reduce the risk of loss for those who contribute to the venture. For centuries, corporations have been known to be fictitious persons.

Chapter 5 discussed corporate law along with property law with an emphasis on Anglo-American law, particularly U.S. corporate law. Corporations issue stock to shareowners. Shareowners are prohibited by corporate statutory law from managing corporations. Corporate statutory law confers on the board of directors the sole right to manage corporations. Corporate statutory law, along with property law, makes corporations the sole owner of all their property, referred to as assets, including financial capital and physical capital. Shareowners do not own the corporation. They only own the shares.

Chapter 6 reviewed accounting and Generally Accepted Accounting Principles. GAAP dictates what information corporations must report to the public and how it is reported. The basic financial statements are the balance sheet, income statement, and statement of cash flows. The balance sheet reports the financial position of the corporations as corporate assets minus corporate liabilities equals net assets, i.e., the corporate equity, erroneously referred to as "stockholders' equity." However, the shareowners do not own the equity of the corporation. The statement of cash flows reports, among other things, the financial capital obtained by the corporation (financing activities) by issuing shares to the public, and how it used the financial capital to acquire productive capital (investment activities). The profit reported on the income statement is a definition only. It is not money, financial capital, or productive capital.

In Chapter 7, securities laws were reviewed with a focus on U.S. securities laws. Securities laws govern how corporations are allowed to raise financial capital by issuing shares to the public. The Securities and Exchange Commission has the sole authority to dictate accounting principles, which it entrusted to other bodies, currently the Financial Accounting Standards Board. Securities laws also govern trading of securities in the market, but trading of securities in the market is not directly related to capital or capitalism, and certainly not related to *bourgeois* capitalists, since trading securities in the market does not involve the corporation and does not provide financial capital or productive capital to the corporation.

Chapter 8 summarized how corporations, corporate law and property law, generally accepted accounting principles, and securities laws coalesced to cause the extinction of *bourgeois* capitalists and capitalism. Chapter 8 presented a logical argument to prove that *bourgeois* capitalists and capitalism are extinct.

Chapter 9 discussed the relationship between the ideology of capitalism and capitalism as a social construct, corporations, classes, and power. The social system instituted by the ideology of capitalism as an economic system persists in spite of the fact that capitalism does not exist because it is the corporations that now, or more specifically, the directors of the corporations, wield the power that emanates from the ownership of capital resources of production and that benefit from the capitalist ideology.

Concluding Remarks

A global system has been constructed on false concepts of capitalism that are not legally, historically, economically, or sociologically valid. Capitalism is a function of the laws of the private ownership of capital as the means of production. Yet, economists, sociologists, and lawyers steadfastly refuse to interpret capital, capitalist, and capitalism within the parameters of corporate law and property law which preclude individuals from owning the means of production thus perpetuating the myth that capitalism still exists. The meaning of capitalist and capitalism has thus been completely corrupted.

The capitalism of which they speak is unrelated to productive capital, the ownership of productive capital by *bourgeois* capitalists, or free wage-labor. Therefore, it is not capitalism. If the definition of capitalism is changed to suit a predetermined narrative, then it is really not discussing capitalism. Indeed, there is no discussion at all. There can be no capitalism without the capitalist mode of production which requires the hiring of free wage-labor and ownership of capital by *bourgeois* capitalists.

"Companification is the substitution of an impersonal corporate legal entity for the sole proprietorship or partnership [which] has long been seen by economic analysts and commentators as *the* defining element of modern capitalism" (Johnson, 2010, p. 106, emphasis in original). While it is true that impersonal corporate legal entities have been substituted for the sole proprietorship or partnership capitalist entrepreneur, that substitution actually destroyed *bourgeois* capitalists and capitalism as explained in Chapter 8. All who subscribe to the notion of corporate capitalism have in common is their substitution of *bourgeois* capitalist entrepreneurs with corporations. But if we attempt to substitute the meaning of *bourgeois* capitalist entrepreneurs with corporations, we are confronted with the Humpty Dumpty problem.

If one accepts the theory that corporations are capitalists, that they "step into the shoes" of the capitalists and therefore are themselves capitalists, then there is simply no escaping the conclusions that since corporations are fictitious persons and corporations own the means of production, then corporations are fictitious capitalists, which means labor is working for fictitious capitalists, and the system that controls the world is fictitious.

If one accepts the proposition that shareowners of corporations whose shares are traded in the public are the owners of the corporations and that shareowners are therefore capitalists, then there is simply no escaping the conclusions that pension funds that own stock of corporations whose shares are traded in the public are capitalists; that insurance companies that own stock of corporations are capitalists; that universities, whether public or private, that own stock of corporations whose shares are traded in the public as part of their endowment portfolio are capitalists; that the retired octogenarians who live off the dividends of the stock they own of corporations whose shares are traded in the public are capitalists; that churches and other not-for-profit institutions that own share of stock of corporations whose shares are traded in the public are capitalists; and when the United States government took shares of General Motors as part of the bailout following the crash of 2008 and subsequent recession, the United States became a capitalist. And if shareowners are *bourgeois* capitalists, what does that say about day-traders who own shares for less than a day, or flash-traders or own shares for a few minutes? What does that say about trusts where the trustee is the legal owner of shares for a beneficiary? Who is the *bourgeois* capitalist? The trustee as the legal owner, or the beneficiary as the beneficial owner?

Compounding the problem is that many wage-laborers own shares of the corporations they work for as part of their retirement portfolio. If shareowners owned the corporation or the productive capital of corporations, if shareowners were in fact capitalists, the proletariat are now transformed into capitalists, something only Grindlewald or Voldemort could accomplish!

Capitalism did *not* prevail. It is not a global system. It is not a system that controls the world. One searches in vain for any explanation, any justification, any logical, economic, or legal argument, that capitalism still exists.

One may just as well say that feudalism still exists, or mercantilism still exists. But they don't. There are no signs that either still exists. So it is with capitalism. There are no signs that capitalism still exists.

What can conclusively be said is that the capital is there, but both the capitalist and capitalism are missing. The system previously known as capitalism is today merely an artifact of history. *Bourgeois* capitalists and capitalism are extinct.

Capitalism served its purpose, for good or for ill. It's time for history to move on.

Notes

1 Capital and capitalism have also been studied from religious perspectives such as Weber's *The Protestant Ethic and the Spirit of Capitalism*, and Novak's *Catholic Ethic and the Spirit of Capitalism.*

2 Corporations may of course purchase their own shares in the market and resell them. Such shares are called treasury stock.

3 If one insists that corporations have replaced the *bourgeois* capitalist entrepreneur, then it must be conceded that shareowners do not own corporations or the means of production, which renders void the theories of the separation of ownership and control of corporations and directors as agents of shareowners, a pillar of the theory of the firm.

4 Ignoring the conundrum presented by churches or other religious corporations being capitalists because they own stock, not-for-profit corporations owning stock completely nullifies any argument that shareowners are capitalists since by definition capitalists pursue profit and not-for-profit corporations are prohibited by law from pursuing profit.

5 As of August 20, 2012, the U.S. government still owned 500 million shares (32%) of GM's outstanding stock. See Automakers' Report Card: Who Still Owes Taxpayers Money? The Answer Might Surprise You, https://www.forbes.com/sites/joannmuller/2012/08/29/automakers-report-card-who-still-owes-taxpayers-money-the-answer-might-surprise-you/?sh=27893a1e6735. See also The Auto Bailout and the Rule of Law, https://www.nationalaffairs.com/publications/detail/the-auto-bailout-and-the-rule-of-law.

Bibliography

Johnson, P. (2010). *Making the market: Victorian origins of corporate capitalism.* Cambridge University Press.

Novak, M. (1993). *Catholic ethic and the spirit of capitalism.* Free Press.

Weber, M. (1992). *The protestant ethic and the spirit of capitalism* (T. Parsons, Trans.). Routledge.

Index

For Product Safety Concerns and Information please contact our EU
representative GPSR@taylorandfrancis.com
Taylor & Francis Verlag GmbH, Kaufingerstraße 24, 80331 München, Germany

www.ingramcontent.com/pod-product-compliance
Ingram Content Group UK Ltd.
Pitfield, Milton Keynes, MK11 3LW, UK
UKHW020003200926
475702UK00015B/2456
* 9 7 8 1 0 3 2 1 4 7 6 2 8 *